THE NEW OPTIONS MARKET

The New

Options Market

REVISED EDITION

Max G. Ansbacher

WALKER AND COMPANY   NEW YORK

First published in the United States of America
in 1979 by the Walker Publishing Company, Inc.

Library of Congress Cataloging-in-Publication Data

Ansbacher, Max G.
   The new options market.

   "Bibliography of free material, periodicals,
and option services": p.
   Includes index.
   1. Put and call transactions. I. Title.
[HG6042.A57 1987] 332.64'52   87-18892
ISBN 0-8027-7308-7 (pbk.)
Library of Congress Catalog Card Number: 78-58600

Printed in the United States of America
10 9 8 7 6 5 4 3 2

This book
is dedicated to
my parents,
Heinz and Rowena

CONTENTS

PREFACE TO THE PAPERBACK EDITION

A great deal has changed in the world of options since this book was first written in 1975, and there have been many changes since the second edition was published in 1979. But in rereading the second edition now, I am struck by the fact that all the fundamental principles are exactly the same as they were.

The basic idea of an option is still the same, and the basic strategies are still the same. In a few cases where prices of individual stocks were given, it is amusing to note the large changes in price which have taken place, but as examples of the principles of option trading they are as valid today as they were when first written. One of the biggest changes is that the premiums which option buyers are willing to pay for options has shrunk since the early days. Thus, some of the estimates given for the amount of money which could be made by covered call writing are significantly lower today. But the lower margins required for selling uncovered (naked) options have offset the decline in premiums to some extent for the naked option seller.

The most important additions to the option scene since 1979 are the new index options, which have become extremely popular. But here again, the same principles which are presented in this book apply to options on the Standard & Poor's 100 Index (commonly referred to as the OEX), the Major Market Index, the Institutional Index, and all the others. If one just thinks of the index as a stock with the same price as the index, every thing written in this book about options on individual stocks will be applicable.

The only difference of any significance is that the index options have a cash settlement instead of an actual delivery, as is the case with options on individual stocks. This means that if one is long a call on an index at the expiration, he can exercise just as in the case of a call on an individual stock, but what he receives will not be a part of an index, but rather that amount of money by which his call was in the money. For example, if one is long a 290 call at the expiration, and the index closes at 293, and one decides to exercise his call, he will receive the difference, here $3, in cash. Thus, for each call which is exercised, the holder of the call will receive $300. The person who was short that call at the expiration will simply be charged $300 for each call he was short. From the practical point of view, this is frequently advantageous to options traders, because it means that they no longer have to be worried about becoming involved with large blocks of stocks and the relatively high commission costs of buying and selling them.

Expiration months have changed recently. The index options were the first to have expirations every month, typically with the next three months available. Then a number of the major stocks began to have the next two months available, plus the regular expirations, which were every three months for the next three periods. Right now there is no one rule which governs each, so the best thing to do is to check the newspaper or ask your broker or the option exchange.

Margins

A great improvement in naked-option writing was made a few years ago when the margin requirements were reduced. The basic formula for determining the requirements is the same as it was, but the percentage used has been reduced. In the case of options on individual stocks, the percentage is 25%, and in the case of index options it is 5%. When the percentages were reduced, the requirements were also changed to require that the current price of the option be included in the formula as a final step. To illustrate, let us assume that an index is at 270. You wish to sell the 280 call which has a current price of 2. To figure the requirements you follow these 3 steps: 1. Take 5% of the index. Here that is 5% of 270 which gives us 13.5. 2. Subtract the amount by which the call's strike price is above the price of the index, or in other words the amount by which the call is out of the money. Here that is 10, which when subtracted from 13.5, gives us 3.5. 3. To this amount we add the current price of the option which is 2, giving us a total margin requirement of 5.5, or $550 per call. In addition to this three-step formula, there is a further minimum requirement for options on both individual stocks and stock indexes, and this is that the margin requirement must not be less than 2% of the stock or index. In this case, 2% of 270 is 5.4 or $540. Since we had previously determined that the margin was $550, the minimum does not apply. But, if the previous determination had been $490, then the minimum would have overridden the normal requirement, and the requirement would have been $540.

Taxes

There have been major changes in taxation since the last revision of this book. Today the taxation is much simpler than it was. Starting with 1987, the distinction between long-term and short-term capital gains rates was eliminated, and they were both taxed at the same rate as ordinary income.

For 1987 only, an exception was made, and the maximum rate on long-term gains was 28%, even though the maximum rate for other income was 38.5%. Now all gains and losses from transactions in options on stocks and on indexes are capital gains or losses, and are taxed accordingly. The elimination of the distinction between short- and long-term means that the option trader has complete freedom to take action at the time he wants, without regard to the tax consequences.

All options transactions will result in portfolio income or losses and as such, only portfolio losses may be used to reduce option income, and losses from options may only be used to reduce other portfolio income.

Other Changes

The restricted options referred to in the book have been eliminated so that now one can freely trade options of any price, even $\frac{1}{16}$ if he desires.

The prospectus published by the Options Clearing Corporation, which is referred to in the book, still exists, but it is no longer given to options traders. Instead, the five exchanges which trade options, and the Options Clearing Corporation and NASDAQ publish a booklet titled *"Characteristics and Risks of Standardized Options"*. This is now the official publication that is given to each new options trader by his brokerage firm to familiarize him with the risks involved in options. It is an excellent booklet, which does a wonderful job of imparting a lot of information in a few words and is recommended reading to all.

One of the changes for the good is the welcome availability of quotations on current stock and index prices. For example, everyone who has access to a cable TV system which carries FNN (Financial News Network) can now get minute by minute real-time quotes on the OEX, plus prices on individual stocks, which are delayed 15 minutes. Two companies produce pocket quote terminals that operate from FM radio signals and will provide real-time quotes on any stock or option. For those who have computer terminals in their home or office, there are a number of vendors who will provide systems which give real-time prices on all the stocks and options. The result is that in this day and age, anyone can be his own broker right in his own home, and experience all the minute-by-minute action formerly reserved for those who were professionals or who did enough business with their broker that they could talk to him every few minutes. Whether this close attention to short-term moves will improve a person's investment results, is, however, an open question.

PREFACE TO THE SECOND EDITION

When the first edition of *The New Options Market* was written, in 1974, option premiums were sky high compared to what they are today; trading in puts was still years into the future; the tax treatment of options income was completely different from what it is now; spreads were just beginning to develop, and few people had even considered writing options against convertible bonds. This second edition now covers each of these topics plus many more that were either not known when the first edition was written or have changed substantially since then.

But perhaps the biggest difference that has occurred since the first edition was written and now is that in the intervening years a great body of experience has developed, not just in deciding what situations make attractive opportunities for profit, but in learning how to monitor and modify those positions as time goes on. As a vice president at a leading brokerage firm, I have been the broker for many options investors and traders and have taken part in many thousands of options trades. From this experience I attempt not only to show you how to make money, but also to explain what to do in the more difficult situations where a position is turning out to be a money loser. It is in those situations that help is the most surely needed, and it is exactly there that other books and pamphlets are so often silent.

Thus, this book might be thought of as the opposite of the type that is advertised as "Now; a proven method of making a fortune in one year starting from only $1,000 through the magic of options!" The only positive accomplishment of such efforts is to reaffirm that in the United States there really is freedom of the press. If anyone wonders whether such a method is really possible, he need only ask why everyone who bought the book is not now a millionaire, or why anyone knowledgeable in options is probably still buying U.S. Treasury Bills, which pay about 6% a year, as part of his investment program.

My philosophy is rather that options have unique benefits for traders and investors, and that with careful planning and follow-through it is possible to implement a wide variety of investment objectives through the use of options. The chapters that follow tell you how to do it and how to get the most profit out of each situation. But, because I am writing for adults, I point out the risks involved in each strategy so that the reader can evaluate for himself the profit potential versus the risk. It is my belief that a thorough understanding of this equation is the heart of every successful options program. And the purpose of this book is to make you successful with options.

INTRODUCTION

On April 26, 1973, the directors of the Chicago Board Option Exchange held their breaths and crossed their fingers. For, on that date, when they opened the first exchange in the world's history to deal in stock options, they took on a large risk. If they could have foreseen that in the next seventeen months the stock market would fall into one of the deepest and longest declines in its history, and that because of declining stock exchange volume, many brokerage firms would be driven out of business, it is questionable whether they would have dared to open the new exchange.

Even without this foreknowledge, however, there were plenty of reasons for doubt. The traditional market in puts and calls had been part of the American investment scene since almost the turn of the century, but it had never caught on with the investing public. Many professional Wall Streeters therefor predicted flatly that the new exchange, limited at first to options on just 16 stocks, would be a disastrous flop.

But in less than a year the outcome was clear. The CBOE became the biggest success in the shortest time of any financial exchange that has ever existed in the United States! In the first days of the CBOE its directors were overjoyed when it traded 1,600 calls a day. The volume quickly grew to 5,000—to 10,000—to 20,000 calls a day. At this point the baby CBOE, then trading calls in 32 stocks, was actually trading options on more shares per day than the venerable American Stock Exchange was trading with on all its 1,000+ listed stocks.

By now the press was beginning to sit up and take notice. In a front-page story *The Wall Street Journal* hailed the CBOE as "a glittering success, attracting flocks of individual investors." *New York Magazine* wrote, "Options are well on their way to becoming the next financial bandwagon." Even as the stock market declined further and drove more of the public away, *Fortune* noted that the new options could lead the individual investor back to Wall Street.

ASTOUNDING VOLUME GROWTH

Volume on the CBOE continued to rise ever higher, to 30,000 options a day, and by October 1974 the CBOE began to have 40,000 options days. The increasing volume forced the CBOE to move to larger quarters, where it would have five times more trading floor space. Then the American Stock Exchange announced that it too would be offering options on 20 additional stocks; later the Philadelphia, Pacific, and Midwest stock exchanges began trading options also. Today these five exchanges routinely trade 200,000 options or more a day, options based on approximately 240 underlying stocks.

What made this astounding growth even more amazing was that the institutional investors, who had come to dominate the stock markets in the 1970s, where by and large conspicuous for their absence from the options exchanges. This meant that at a time when the public was fleeing the stock market it was moving into the new options markets in unprecedented numbers.

What explains this sudden explosive growth? What had happened is that by simply making some basic changes in calls, the new options exchanges had made buying and selling options as easy as buying and selling stocks. The prices for both were now listed in the major newspapers every day, and both had the liquidity that investors require so that they can get into and out of investments quickly.

With the obstacles of the traditional puts and calls now overcome, the public was able to realize the advantages that options offer to sophisticated investors. These unique advantages are:

Leverage. When an investor buys 100 shares of a stock for $100 each and it goest up $10, he has made a profit of $1,000. But when he invests the same amount of money in calls of that stock and the stock goes up $10, he can make a profit of $10,000. If the stock goes up more, the disparity becomes even greater. Chapter 2, Buying Calls, thoroughly explores the exciting potential of buying calls but concludes that the disadvantages often outweigh the advantages. Buying puts creates similar opportunities to make money when a stock declines, and Chapter 5 explores the many possibilities presented by puts.

Income. By selling calls on stocks that he owns, an investor can expect to generate an income of 10% to 20% a year on his investment. And the additional options income comes without any more risk of loss than if the investor continued to own the stock without selling any calls. Chapter 3, Selling Covered Calls, explains just what the drawbacks to selling calls are and how to wring out the highest possible annual income by selecting options offering the most profitable strike prices and durations.

High Return. For those who don't mind taking unusually high risks, selling options on stock that one does not own can lead to returns of up to 40% of one's investment a year. The risk of loss, however, is high. Chapter 4, Selling Naked Calls, weighs the potential high income against the risks and tells how you can limit you potential loss in advance.

Sophisticated Strategies. Since the options exchanges usually offer several options on the same underlying stock, shrewd investors can have a field day selling the short-term and buying the long-term options on the same stock, selling the high strike price call and buying the low one, or doing just the reverse, selling the stock short and buying a call as perfect insurance policy. The objective of these spreads and straddles is to make money for the investor within a broad range of stock prices; because of the large variety of options available, it is now possible to custom-tailor a hedge program to fit almost any investor's objectives. Even spreads and hedges have their drawbacks, however, and Chapter 6, on spreads, points them out—as well as the profit one may expect to earn.

These are the basic benefits that investors can derive from the informed use of stock options. By being aware of the margin requirements for options, the brokers' commissions, and the necessary record-keeping procedures, all of which are described in detail in Chapters 8, 9, and 11, the investor should be able to benefit greatly from the new options markets.

In short, I have written this book to give the intelligent investor everything he needs to know to start a profitable investment program in America's newest and most exciting form of investing.

Listed Options Quotations

Closing prices of all options. Sales unit usually is 100 shares. Security description includes exercise price. Stock close is New York Stock Exchange final price. p-Put option.

Chicago Board

Option &	price	– Oct – Vol.	– Oct – Last	– Jan – Vol.	– Jan – Last	– April – Vol.	– April – Last	N.Y. Close
Alcoa	45	6	2	12	3	a	a	46
Alcoa	50	27	¼	24	1	101	15-16	46
Am Exp	35	a	a	5	5½	a	a	40⅛
Am Exp	40	7	¾	a	a	11	2½	40⅛
Am Tel	60	38	2½	49	2⅞	29	3⅛	62⅜
Am Tel	65	21	⅛	75	½	46	13-16	62⅜
Atl R	50	123	2⅝	56	4⅜	60	5½	51⅜
Atl R	60	88	1-16	154	¾	430	1¼	51⅜
Avon	45	378	2½	136	2⅞	71	3⅝	46¼
Avon p	45	370	13-16	83	1⅝	6	2 5-16	46¼
Avon	50	544	3-16	294	13-16	170	1½	46¼

● ● ●

Option &	price	– Oct – Vol.	– Oct – Last	– Jan – Vol.	– Jan – Last	– April – Vol.	– April – Last	N.Y. Close
Homstk	30	b	b	96	3¾	22	4½	32¾
Homstk	35	265	5-16	175	1¼	167	2	32¾
Homstk	40	99	1-16	349	⅜	61	¾	32¾
Homstk	45	a	a	1	⅛	5	3-16	32¾
Hou OM	20	b	b	863	2¾	490	3½	20¾
Hou OM	25	1309	¼	1048	1	675	11-16	20¾
Hou OM	30	200	1-16	345	⅜	309	11-16	20¾
Hou OM	35	27	1-16	51	⅛	18	¼	20¾
I N A	35	105	4¾	38	5⅛	15	5	39⅜
I N A	40	118	11-16	116	1⅜	169	1⅞	39⅜
I N A	45	17	1-16	a	a	b	b	39⅜
I B M	240	3567	5⅛	425	10¼	131	13⅜	240¾
I B M p	240	4111	4	747	7⅞	179	9⅞	240¾
I B M	260	2075	5-16	1016	3	241	5¾	240¾
I B M p	260	731	19¼	166	19¾	11	21¼	240¾
I B M	280	254	1-16	302	11-16	487	1 11-16	240¾
I B M p	280	29	39	5	36¼	a	a	240¾
IN Har	25	10	2⅜	31	2⅞	6	3¼	27¼
In Har	30	33	⅛	106	⅝	35	1	27¼
In Min	35	23	3	10	3¼	6	3½	38⅛
In Min	40	110	3-16	79	⅝	12	1⅛	38¼

● ● ●

Option &	price	– Oct – Vol.	– Oct – Last	– Jan – Vol.	– Jan – Last	– April – Vol.	– April – Last	N.Y. Close
U Tech	40	45	5-16	100	15-16	18	1⅜	36⅛
J Walt	25	a	a	a	a	12	3⅞	27⅜
J Walt	30	26	⅜	55	15-16	34	1⅜	27⅜
J Walt	35	2	1-16	a	a	b	b	27⅜
Willms	20	6	15-16	19	1½	16	2	20
Willms	25	21	1-16	40	¼	48	7-16	20

Total volume   82,755   Open interest   1,864,519

a—Not traded.   b—No option offered.   p—Put.

THE FUNDAMENTALS OF
STOCK OPTIONS

Facts you need to know

There are two basic types of stock options, puts and calls. Since calls are the more popular, we will discuss them first.

ELEMENTS OF A CALL

A *call* is the right to buy 100 shares of a certain stock or stock index at a stated price within a given period of time. For example, a call might be the right to buy 100 shares of Stock A for the price of $60 per share at any time between now and the third Saturday in January. The price per share at which the call buyer has the right to purchase the stock or index is called the *strike price,* or *exercise price.* Thus, if a call is the right to acquire a share for $60, that call would have a strike price of $60. The time limit on an option is called the *expiration date.* The expiration date is always the Saturday following the third Friday of the named month. Traditionally, options on a stock were available in cycles which started either in January, February, or March, and then included the month falling three months after the first month, and the month falling six months after the first month. For example, if a stock option were in the January cycle, and it were now December, the options expiring in January, April, and July would be available. When the expiration date for the January options passed, the options exchange would immediately begin trading the October options, and so forth, so that there were always three different months available. Those stocks which had options in the February cycle would be trading the three nearest months of February, May, August, and November, while those in the March cycle used March, June, September, and December. This cycle is still used for many options. Under this system, the nearest available option will vary from just a few hours (on the expiration day) to three months (when the new options are put on). On the other extreme, the longest duration option will vary from just over six months (on expiration day) to nine months (when the new options have just been added).

A new system was introduced for the stock index options. This is simply to trade the three nearest months, and in the case of the OEX, the nearest four months. Thus, if it were now August 3rd, the index would be trading the August, September, and October options. Once the August options expired, the exchange would bring out the November options, and so forth. Under this system, the longest duration option is only three months, four for the OEX, and the advantage is that there is always a near-term option which has a month or less before expiration.

Some stocks now use a hybrid system, in which they have the nearest two months, and then the regular cycle. For example, IBM uses this system, and in early April the IBM expirations that are traded are April, May, July, and October.

All options expire at 5:00 P.M. Eastern Time on the Saturday immediately following the third Friday of the named month, and this Saturday is the date you will see in the description of your option in the confirmation slip you receive from your brokerage firm and in its monthly statements. But this date is a technical one and of no importance to you. More important for you is the date by which your broker requires that he receive your instructions for exercising your option. This will vary from firm to firm, but it cannot be later than 5:30 P.M. Eastern Time on the business day preceding that technical expiration date, normally the preceding Friday. And even more important than the cutoff date for exercising an option is the last time it can be traded. Normally options on individual stocks trade until 4:10 P.M. Eastern Time, which is ten minutes after the stock exchange closes, while options on stock indexes trade until 4:15. On the final day of an option, the expiring options on individual stocks stop trading at 4:00, and options on stock indexes stop trading at 4:10. Many brokerage firms require that orders for expiring options be entered at least 30 minutes before the final trading time due to the large influx of orders that often develops at the close.

Thus any call can be fully described by stating all of the following critical aspects, always given in the same order: first the name of the common stock or stock index, then the expiration month, and finally the strike price. A call termed "Ford January 75" is the right to acquire 100 shares of Ford Motor Company common stock for the price of $75 per share at any time between now and the Saturday following the third Friday in January.

Reading the Newspaper Reports

Now that you understand the elements that define each call, it is an easy matter to read the prices in the daily newspaper reports. (See example.)

The first item is the name of the stock with the strike price. This is followed by three columns listing the price for the call of that strike price for each of the three expiration months that are currently being traded. The next three columns contain the same information for the put of that strike price. The number below the name of the stock is the closing price of the stock on the New York Stock Exchange. This may or may not be the same price you will see for the close of the stock on the stock market pages of the paper, since that price is the consolidated close, and may have taken place at a stock exchange other than the New York Stock Exchange.

Let's take a look at the illustration. The first stock is American Greeting, which we see closed on the New York Stock Exchange at 27⅛. Moving to the right of the stock name, the first column we come to should give us the price of the February call for the 25 strike price. Instead we find the letter "r" which means that this option was not traded on that day. This means that there is such an option, i.e., a February 25 call, but simply that during the day there was no one who wanted to buy it badly enough to pay the offering price, and there was no one who wanted to sell it badly enough to be willing to accept the bid price, and no one else was willing to make a trade in the middle. So there was no trade. But it is significant to note that you could trade that option if you wanted. You would first ask your broker what the bid and asked prices of the option were. Perhaps it would be bid ¾, which means that is what you would receive if you wanted to sell it; and offered at 1, which means that is what you would have to pay if you wanted to buy it. Of course, you are free to say that you want to buy it for ¾ or ⅞ and put in your order and wait to see if anyone takes you up on it.

The next item is another "r" for the March calls. The April 25 calls have a price of 2⅜. This means that the last sale of the day for the American Greeting April 25 calls took place at 2⅜. Continuing to move across the line, we now come to the prices for the puts. Under Feb. we find another "r" and under Mar. we find an "s." This means that there is no such put. How can that be? Simply that new options are brought out at the discretion of the options exchange, and if in its opinion there would not be enough volume to justify bringing out a certain option, they do not have to do so. Apparently that was the case here.

At the end of each section you will find the total volume of puts and calls. This must be multiplied by 100 to get the equivalent number of shares of stock involved. You will also find an "open interest" figure, which tells you the number of options that are outstanding on that date.

THE FUNDAMENTALS OF STOCK OPTIONS

The open interest figure is the cumulative total of all the calls that have been sold (or "written) to create new positions. When a call writer writes a call contract, the open interest figure goes up by one and will continue to reflect that contract until the contract expires, is exercised, or until the writer closes out his position by purchasing an identical call.

Certain Sunday newpapers and *Barron's* publish more complete reports of the week's activities, including the high and low prices of each call for the week. But all the important information is contained in the daily reports, even though some newspapers do not report the volume figures for the individual calls in order to save space.

One note of caution is in order. One cannot rely upon the figures to be a guide as to what you may do on the following day, because all the figures are closing figures; that is, they describe the final transaction of the day. Since some options have very little volume, the final transaction might have occurred at 2:00 P.M., when the stock was at 87, and by the time the stock market closed the stock might have sunk to 85. But of course the figure you will read for the option is the price when the stock was 87. Obviously, if the stock opens the next morning at 85, the price of the call will be less, to reflect the decline in the stock. If you ask your broker after the market close but on the same day, he should be able to tell you when the final trade for any call took place and what the closing bid and asked prices were for the option, which are accurate price indications for the closing stock price.

The value of options

The right to acquire a stock for a given price between now and some future date is almost always worth a certain amount of money. This is true whether the stock is currently priced at more or less than the strike price. The reason is that, even if the current price of the stock is below the strike price, there is a possibility that by the time the expiration date comes around, the price of the stock will have risen above the strike price. The owner of the call will then be able to purchase the stock at a bargain price. This is called exercising the call. If the call owner wishes, he can sell the stock immediately after exercising the call and make a cash profit of the difference between the strike price and the then market value of the stock.

For example, if on the third Friday in January the Ford stock used in our initial example was selling at $65 on the New York Stock Exchange, the owner of the call with a strike price of $60 would be able to acquire the stock by paying $60. He would then own stock worth $65. His profit on purchasing the call would be $5, less what he paid for the call and his commissions. Thus, on

its expiration date a call is worth the price of the stock minus t
with an adjustment for commissions.

On the other hand, if the price of the Ford Motor Company stock was $60
or less on the expiration date of the call, then the owner of the call would have
nothing of value. His right to purchase the stock for $60 is worth nothing if
anyone can do the same thing without owning a call. So he would not acquire
the stock through his call; whatever he had paid for the call would be a
complete loss.

The amount that a person pays to acquire a call is called the *premium*. In
effect, this is the price of the call, but it is called a premium to distinguish it
from the underlying common stock, which has a "price." Premiums of calls are
quoted for individual shares, but the actual price of a call is the quoted
premium multiplied by 100. Thus, when one reads that a Ford Motor
Company call is selling for 2¼, this means that the premium to acquire a call
on one share of Ford stock is $2.25, so the cost of purchasing one call is $225.

Buying options—the advantages

Perhaps these definitons have left you slightly less than trembling with
excitement. Your reaction might well be, so what? What's so exciting about
the right to buy or sell a stock for a given price within a given amount of time?

The answer is that nothing known to man in the securities sphere offers as
great an opportunity to make or lose a fortune in as short a period of time as
stock options. You've heard the old adage that when the elephant sneezes, the
mouse is knocked down by a hurricane. The option is the mouse and the
underlying common stock is the elephant. When the common stock moves up
by 5%, the call can move up by 100% . And that, in its simplest form, is what
calls are all about.

Leverage

Options give a person the chance to make a large gain on his money with
a relatively small investment. They give the investor tremendous leverage. For
a small investment, usually 10% or less than the price of the underlying
common stock, the option purchaser gains the right to participate in the price
increase or decrease of the underlying stock for a period of time, just as if he
actually were an owner of the stock. The call owner differs from the stock
owner in that he has to pay for the cost of the call but he has his right only for a
limited time and he does not receive dividends. But, thanks to the liquidity of
the options exchanges, a call buyer can always overcome the time limitation by
buying another call when his first one expires.

Let us illustrate this leverage with an example, using our Ford call option with a strike price of $60 expiring in January. Let us assume that the current price of Ford stock on the New York Stock Exchange is, more or less by coincidence, also $60. If the expiration date in January is three months away from the date when the call is purchased, the premium (price) of the call might be $3. Now let us assume that you are considering purchasing 100 shares of Ford stock for a total price of $6,000.

You firmly believe, on the basis of everything which you have read, that Ford is underpriced and that within the next three months it is pretty certain to go up to $70 a share. You intend to purchase the stock as a short-term investment only, and will sell the shares at the end of January. Let us compare how much money could be made by buying the stock as compared to buying the call. If you buy 100 shares of the stock for $6,000, and the price of the stock does go up to $70 a share by the end of January, it would be worth an additional $10 a share and you would have a profit of $1,000.

On the other hand, if you invest the same amount ($6,000) in calls at a premium of $3 each, you will be able to purchase calls on 2,000 shares. Now, if the price of the underlying common stock goes up to $70 a share, the right to acquire the stock for only $60 will be worth $10 a share. In other words, your calls will have gone up in value from $3 a share to $10 a share. The calls that you bought for $300 each are now worth $1,000, and your original investment of $6,000 is worth a full $20,000. You have just made a 233% profit on your $6,000 investment in only three months.

If you want to figure out what this would come to in annual terms—since three months are a quarter of a year, you multiply by four and find that you are making a profit at the rate of 932% a year! Pretty good. And this all from a stock that had a rise of only ten points. By comparing the $1,000 profit you would have made on buying and selling the stock with the profit of $14,000 you would make by buying a call, you can understand what the excitement is all about.

And of course, had the stock gone up more, the difference in profit would have been even more sensational. If the stock had gone up 20 points to $80 a share, the profit on the common stock itself would be $20 a share for a total profit of $2,000, while the purchaser of the call would have made a profit of $17 a share, giving him a total profit of $34,000. That would be his net profit on a $6,000 investment in just three months.

But, you might wonder, aren't there any liabilities to be incurred in buying a call? What if you should be proven wrong and the price of the stock falls, or just stays where it is? Will you then have to come up with more money? This is a natural question for anyone who has tried to get a little more leverage from common stocks by buying them on margin, only to see the price of the stock fall and receive a call from his broker asking for more money immediately to protect his investment. With respect to a call, the answer to the liability question is a clear and emphatic "no." The buyer of an option can never be required to put up more money. The only liability he has is to pay for the cost of the option when he buys it. The only risk he faces is that it will expire when the price of the stock is at or below the strike price and the call will then become worthless. Then the call purchaser will have lost the entire premium he paid for the call, but that is all that he will have lost.

Stock price declines. And while we're on the subject of liabilities, this is a good time to look at the purchase of calls from another point of view, namely that of restricting your losses in case of a decline in the price of the stock. Suppose in our original Ford Motor Company example, you think that the stock is probably going to go up, but you know that if certain developments occur, the price is likely to go down. Now, you could purchase the 100 shares for $6,000 as we mentioned before and pray hard that the price will go up and that your fears of a decline will not materialize.

Or in the alternative, you could decide to invest in calls that would give you a profit potential similar to the 100 shares. More specifically, you could decide to buy a single call contract for $300. If the strike price is $60, you would make $100 for every dollar the stock rises above its cost (less the premium of $300 which you paid). What this means is that you are obtaining the same leverage as a $6,000 purchase with an outlay of cash of only $300. In addition to conserving your capital, the big advantage comes if the price of the stock should go down.

Let us suppose that the price of the stock falls by $10, to $50 a share, during the period of the option. If you had purchased the stock for $6,000 it would now be worth only $5,000, for a loss of a full $1,000. On the other hand, by purchasing a call for $300 you limit your loss to just that $300. Thus, the call buyer is ahead by $700. And remember, no matter how fast the stock falls in price and no matter how far it finally plummets, the $300 you paid for the call is the most that you can possibly lose. So the farther the stock falls, the better the call purchaser does in relation to a person who bought the stock.

Since buying a call seems like such a wonderful way to make quick money in an upswing and such a great way to cut losses in a downturn, you might wonder who is stupid enough to sell you a call. After all, if you are going to buy one, it means that someone has to sell you one. And if you are going to make a 100% profit on your purchase, doesn't that mean that the person who sells you the call is going to lose an equal amount? If buying a call is such a wonderful investment, why should anyone in their right mind ever sell one? Well, we will explore just how wonderful an investment buying a call is in more detail in

Chapter 2. But right now, we'll explain that the seller of a call doesn't necessarily lose any money at all when the underlying stock goes up above the strike price.

In all probability the seller of your call is also the owner of the underlying stock. Thus, when the stock goes up and you make money on your call, he is losing money on the call he has sold you, but at the same time he is also making money on the rise in the price of the stock he owns. In fact, the two equal each other and the gain in one completely cancels out the loss in the other so that he is not losing anything on the rise in the price. But he is making money to the extent that he sold the call originally for more than its actual cash value. For example, if a stock were $42 a share, the option with a $40 strike price would have a cash value of $2, and if he sold it for $4, he would have a profit of $2. He would, however, have made more money if he owned the underlying common stock and had not sold his call. He is therefore losing potential profit which he could have made. But he doesn't mind this because no matter what happens to the price of the stock, he gets to keep the entire premium as his profit. The seller of a call figures that this pays him to give up some potential profit when the stock goes up. And remember, even when the stock goes up, he still has the profit of his premium, to the extent it exceeded its cash value.

Exercising the call. When the expiration date for the option arrives and the price of the stock is above the call's strike price, the owner of the call can exercise the call, meaning that he directs his broker to buy in the stock at the exercise price. This, however, involves paying a commission. He must pay a commission on the purchase of the stock, and if he sells the stock immediately to realize his profit, he must pay another commission on that sale. But, the call owner has an alternative. Instead of exercising his option he can sell it. Even on the last trading date for that option, there will be a buyer for it who will be willing to pay the approximate difference between the price of the stock and the strike price.

You might wonder who in the world would want to pay $7 for a call that is going to expire in one day. The answer is that for every person who owns an option—is long an option—there is a person who is short an option—who has sold an option that he didn't have in the first place. Unlike common stocks, which start out their existence by being issued by a corporation, an option is a creation of the options exchange itself. It is created simply by selling it short.

So, on the last few days of trading, if you own a call that is worth some money, that means someone sitting on the other side of the fence is short a call, which is going to cost him either money or stock to redeem. When a call expires "in the money"—that is, when the stock is above the strike price—the seller of a call must either deliver the stock or close out his position by buying a call to offset the one he is short. If the call writer owns the shares, then he has no problem. But if the call writer must go out and buy the shares he may not have the money to obtain them. He therefore must buy a call instead, to close out his position. This is why in the last few days of an exchange option period there is often a frantic amount of trading in those calls that are in the money.

The person who buys a call must always pay cash for the full premium. There is no margin possible on a call, because there is a probability that the call will soon be worth nothing, so that a brokerage house putting up the margin would have no collateral for its margin.

Selling a call. How much must a person pay if he decides to sell a call short? After all, there has been no expense incurred by the options exchange in issuing the call, and the call buyer has paid the full amount of the premium. What is there for the seller to pay? Yet it stands to reason that selling calls cannot be free to everyone who wishes to do so because if the underlying stock goes up, the person who sells short may be called upon to deliver a large amount of money.

The answer is that the seller of a call must put up money, which is held in escrow by the exchange as the guarantee that he will fulfill his obligations upon expiration. The amount of margin that the exchanges require is computed under formulas that are discussed in Chapter 8. Normally the required margin is much greater than the amount of the premium received for the call. In addition, the margin must usually be "marked to the market" every day, which means that if the stock underlying a call you are short goes up today, you must deliver an additional amount for each call you are short to your broker. Because of this requirement for daily computations, most brokerage houses require that you maintain greater margin balances than are actually required. This also discourages rampant speculation and provides a degree of safety to the broker should the price of the call suddenly escalate. Instead of having a cash margin, you can deposit the required number of shares of the stock.

So far, we have concentrated on calls. And yet calls are only half of the stock option picture. Puts make up the other half. Although puts are not now traded on all the stocks which have call options, it is intended that they eventually will be.

ELEMENTS OF PUTS

A *put* is the right to sell 100 shares of particular stock at a certain price within a given time. It differs from a call only in that a call is the right to purchase a stock for a set price whereas a put is the right to sell a stock for a set price. A person buys a call when he expects the price of a stock to go up and he buys a put when he expects the price of the stock to go down. An easy way to remember which is which is that you call *up* your broker (calls if a stock is going up) and then you *put* down the phone (puts if the stock is going down).

For example, a put might be the right to sell a share of Sears, Roebuck & Company stock at 35 at any time between now and the January expiration date. This would be denominated a "Sears January 35" put. If the price of the stock on the day before expiration was 30, the holder of the put would have the right to require the put writer to purchase a share of Sears stock from him for 35. He would "put" the stock to the put writer. Since he could acquire the share for only $30 just before exercising his put, the value of the put would be $5.

The owner of a put is under no obligation to exercise the put, and if the price of the stock goes up (against the expectations of the put buyer) the only liability which he faces is the loss of the premium that he paid. Thus, puts are very much like calls in that the purchaser has no liabilities and no potential losses other than the premium paid for the option. Because most investors usually expect that the market will go up, there is not usually as great a demand for puts as there is for calls, and accordingly the premiums for puts are generally less than for comparable calls.

As with a call, the buyer of a put traded on an exchange would not need to actually purchase the shares of stock and deliver them to the put seller in order to make a profit. The put owner will probably prefer to simply close out his put transaction by selling a put during the final period of its existence. Since he is the owner of a put, when he sells it he is out of the market, and the difference between his cost for the put and his selling price is his profit. This profit will normally be just about what he would have realized if he had actually purchased the share on the open market and delivered it to the put writer. By selling a put he eliminates the need to have enough cash to finance the purchase of the stock and saves the commissions on the purchase and sale of the stock.

ADJUSTED STRIKE PRICES

In addition to the regular strike prices of 20, 35, 60, etc., you may have noticed that some stocks have odd strikes, such as 46⅝, 37⅜, and so forth. These odd strike prices are the results of stock dividends paid on the shares of stock, or of stock splits. One of the innovations of listed options is that there is no adjustment made in the exercise price when the common stock pays a regular or special cash dividend. In a way, it could be said that this is unfair to the purchaser of a call option because the payment of a dividend will normally reduce the price of the stock by the amount of the dividend. The reason is simply that if a company is going to pay a 50¢ dividend, the day before the dividend it has cash of 50¢ per share in its treasury, and the value of the stock reflects the value of this cash. After the dividend is paid out to the share-holders, the company's treasury is reduced by 50¢ per share, and therefore the shares, which represent the value of owning a part of the company, are worth 50¢ less than they were before the dividend was paid out. So the stock will generally fall by 50¢. This means that the value of any call options that are in the money will fall by a related amount. But, while this may be unfair theoretically, it was felt that administrative convenience and the need to standardize options made this inequity unavoidable. And, in practice, the inequity is reduced by the fact that options tend to have unusually low premiums just before a stock goes ex-dividend.

But what happens when a stock declares a stock dividend of, let's say 20% of the value of the stock? Now we have a more drastic situation. Let's assume that a shareholder owned 100 shares of stock before the stock dividend, each with a value of $100. Thus the value of his holdings was $10,000. Once there is a 20% stock dividend, he will own 120 shares, but his total holdings will not have changed in value by one bit. He still owns the same percentage of the company, and the company has not become worth any more or any less by issuing some additional shares. His holdings are still worth $10,000, but since he now owns 120 shares, a little simple division will reveal that each share of stock is now worth only $83.33. So, if the stock closed at $100 before the ex-dividend date of the stock dividend, it will open the next morning at $83.33. That's fine for people trading in the stock, but what about the guy who owns the $100 strike price option?

Obviously, unless something was done, his option would suddenly have lost almost all of its value when in fact there was no real decline in the price of the stock. So there had to be an adjustment of strike prices to reflect stock dividends, and that is what the odd strike prices are. When a stock goes ex-dividend after a stock dividend, the strike prices of all existing options are reduced proportionally, and in this example, a $100 strike price option would become an $83⅜ strike price option. But that is not all. Remember, in addition to lowering the price of each share, more shares were created. To reflect this fact, the number of shares in each option is also increased. Instead of one of these odd strike price options being the right to buy 100 shares of stock, it becomes the right to buy 120 shares or some other number. So be careful when you buy or sell these options. If you are a buyer, and your broker quotes you a price of $2, your cost of one option is going to be not $200, but $240, since the price per share is multiplied by the figure of 120 shares per option.

While this could be awkward, it is not as dangerous as the hazard faced by the option seller. Let's say you are a covered option seller. After a stock split you buy 1,000 shares of the stock. You proceed to sell 10 options with the $83⅜ strike price and sit back to reap your profits. You are happy to see the price of the stock go up smartly, and you wait to have the stock called away so you can go on to greener pastures. The stock moves up to 100, and sure enough your stock is called away. All 1,000 shares! Plus 200 shares you don't own! To your horror you find that you were naked on 200 shares, which you must now buy in at the current price of $100 and deliver at $83⅜. The moral is simple: If you see an odd strike price, or any option with the symbol "o" after it in your newspaper, be sure to ask how many shares are included in each option. This also is crucial in spreads where you may wish to combine some regular strike price options with some odd priced ones. Be sure that you get the right ratio of options.

As soon as there is a stock dividend, the options exchange will introduce new options with regular strike prices. Thus, in this case there would be that 83⅜ strike price option, and right below it would be the new 80 strike price option. There often are some interesting spreads between the two, but please remember that you need 12 of the 80 options to offset 10 of the 83⅜.

RESTRICTED OPTIONS

To understand the strange phenomenon of restricted options it is necessary to take oneself back to the first few months of the Chicago Board Options Exchange. When the Securities and Exchange Commission first gave approval to the exchange to trade listed options, it did so on a pilot basis only. But once the CBOE became a success, other exchanges worried that they would lose business to options, and pressure began to build up on the SEC to ban options trading altogether. Of course, as options became more and more popular with investors and speculators, it was obvious that options trading was serving a very real purpose, and the pressure to permit it to continue and expand prevailed.

But the SEC, in its efforts to supervise the marketplace, decided that it could permit option trading to continue, and at the same time mollify some of the criticism of this new form of "gambling," if it prohibited new uncovered positions in what it determined to be the most speculative options. And that is why it is now illegal to buy an option or sell an uncovered option if the price of the option at yesterday's close was less than ½ and the stock was more than 5 points under the option's exercise price. Both these conditions must have been present at yesterday's close for an option to become restricted. But once it becomes restricted, it will be restricted for the entire next day, regardless of what happens to the stock price or the option price.

The rule against trading restricted options leads to a paradox. As long as an option is priced at ½ or more, you can buy all of them you want, subject only to a limit of no more than 1,000 options on any one stock.

Thus, if an option is priced at $3, you can buy $300,000 worth of that option.

But, if a stock is more than five points above the strike price, should you decide that you want to buy one option for ⅜ point, in which case you risk losing up to $37, *that* would be reckless speculation beyond the bounds of even our free capitalist society. There the SEC in its wisdom has drawn the line and made your intended purchase strictly illegal. Not only is it against the rules of the Options Prospectus for you to buy such an option, but both you and the brokerage firm which permitted this outrage to take place can be seriously disciplined, and upon its discovery the trade would be immediately annulled, like a former hero in Soviet history whose memory has become so disgusting that he is simply erased from the history books, never to have existed at all.

Were it not for the SEC pointing out the error of our thought, we could go through life mistakenly believing that it was more speculative to buy options for $300,000 than for $37.

Now that we've had the editorial, let's get back to the facts. As noted above, the rule is based upon the previous day's closing prices. If the stock closed at 35, and the option at ⅜, and was previously not restricted, the $40 strike price option will not be restricted the next day. The rule is that both (1) the option must be less than 50¢ and (2) the price of the stock must be more than $5 below the strike price. Here it is not more than $5 away. On the day you want to buy or sell the option, it can go below 50¢ and the price of the stock can be more than $5 below the strike price, but this is immaterial. What it does mean is that this may be your last chance to do what you want to do, before it becomes restricted tomorrow.

Once an option becomes restricted, it will remain restricted until either the price of the stock closes at less than $5 below the option's strike price, or the price of the option is more than 50¢.

Fortunately, as is so often the case with absurd rules of any kind, this one is literally riddled with exceptions. In fact, there are so many exceptions that it becomes almost a matter of finding an exception, rather than being stopped by the rule.

The most important exception is that you can always close out a position. If you own an option, you can sell it regardless of whether it is restricted, and if you are short an option you can buy it in at any price under any circumstances. The second most important exception is that you can always use a restricted option in a covered transaction. For example, you can sell a restricted option if you are doing a covered write and are long the stock. But you don't have to own the stock, it is sufficient that you are covered by owning or buying an option, which is a valid covered situation from the margin point of view. You can even buy a restricted option as long as you sell or are short an option on the same stock of equal or greater value than the one you are buying. The basis for this exception is that once you are covered with another option, then you are no longer engaging in such reckless speculation that it must be prohibited.

How to buy a "restricted" option

Now, here is a tip, which in many instances will enable you to outwit the SEC and its silly rule. Let's say that you are interested in buying a short-term option on a certain stock, which is now selling at $9/16$. The stock is a high-priced stock, and you want to buy the 90 strike price option, and the stock is at 83. You want to buy the option all right, but not at this price. Instead, you are willing to wait a week or two, and if the option ever gets down to ¼, while the stock is still above 82, you would like to buy that option. But at that price it will be restricted and you will not be permitted to buy the option. What to do?

Due to a quirk in the rules, there is a perfectly legitimate, although little known, method you can use. The rule prohibits buying an option which is restricted at the time you put in your order. You cannot place an order to buy or sell an option which is already restricted. But what you can do instead is to place a "good till cancelled" order to buy an option at any price you want, provided only that the option is not restricted when you place the order. Thus you can place your order to buy the option at ¼ when the option is not restricted. Two weeks later, after the option has been restricted perhaps over a week, you will buy your restricted option at the restricted price and be completely within the rules. This method works beautifully for buying options at restricted prices, but since there is no such thing at the present time as a stop-loss order on options, there is no way in which this method can be used to sell uncovered options at a lower price.

In addition to being a nuisance, the restricted rule operates in a more serious way to disrupt the market. This occurs when there might be a very active market in an option, and then when it becomes restricted, it is not available to over 90% of the potential buyers and sellers. Suddenly an option that has been trading 300 contracts a day will be trading 30 a day. This means that if you are either short or long a large number of options that you want to close out, the restricted rule has robbed you of most of your market. Ironic, since a large part of the SEC's efforts in relation to options is to ensure that there is liquidity. Maybe some day wiser minds will prevail, and we will see the abolition of the entire restricted option rule.

SPECULATIVE NATURE OF OPTIONS

There is one final point that belongs in this chapter on the basics of dealing in puts and calls. That is, that with the exception of selling calls when you own the underlying shares, this is a highly speculative business. That sounds like a pretty tame statement, especially for anyone who has read a number of prospectuses for newly issued shares. The SEC makes stock issuers write "highly speculative" all over the prospectus, sometimes even in red, in capital letters. Well, if a new issue is speculative, then dealing in calls is about five times more so. If you think that certain stocks are speculative, let me tell you that they loom as solid as the Rock of Gibraltar in comparison to puts and calls.

When you buy a call with the price of the stock near the strike price, the chances are 50% that when the call expires it will be worth absolutely nothing—that's right, not one single penny. Whether you paid $200 for it or $1,000, the money you paid will have simply disappeared into thin air. And unlike the stock market, where that only happens occasionally when a company goes into bankruptcy or receivership, this is the norm for calls. Remember, *most* of them become worthless!

So unless you are completely willing to kiss your money good-bye the minute you buy a call, you had better not invest in puts and calls. Or do it in the only safe way, which, as described in Chapter 3, is to be on the selling side when you own the underlying stock. Of course you won't get rich overnight by this method, but as that chapter explains, you might be surprised at just how fast you will earn money.

On the other hand, the person who sells calls without owning the underlying stock—"naked options"—can face an almost unlimited risk. He not only must be prepared to lose the money that he puts up as margin when he sells his call, but he must also face the possibility that every day the price of that underlying stock may jump and he will get an urgent call from his broker demanding more money to cover the margin requirements. In Chapter 4, I explain how to reduce the risk so that it is no longer unlimited, but the risk is still there.

With the exception of covered call writing, this is not a game for the person who is trying to accumulate enough money to send three children to college in another five years. This is not the investment for the person who is concerned with building up a substantial nest egg to retire on in ten or fifteen years. This is not for the person who wants to get out of the job he is in and needs to accumulate some capital in order to go into a business of his own. If you need to accumulate some money for a particular purpose that is important to you, then this is not the method for you. The one exception would be to sell calls on stock that you already own. And that method is one I do recommend in such a situation.

Selling and buying calls, with the exception noted above, is for the person who has some extra money that he does not need. It is for the person who has made some money in the stock market and is now looking for a quicker, more exciting way to increase it. For the professional man who had a good year and now has more money in his savings account than he really needs. For the businessman who has already made his payments into his retirement plan, paid for his disability insurance, made the mortgage payments, put away something for a rainy day, and still has money left over. For the single person who works for a corporation that pays for his retirement, his Blue Cross, and his disability insurance, and who figures that anything he has left over after paying his current expenses is money that he can easily afford to lose. For these people trading in calls can be extremely rewarding, as this book will demonstrate.

But one cannot warn the reader often enough that trading in options is only for the speculative person who isn't going to miss his entire investment if it is lost. At this point it is worth reprinting the third paragraph of the Options Clearing Corporation Prospectus, which appears in boldface type on the first page:

> Both the purchase and writing of Options involve a high degree of risk and are not suitable for many investors. Such transactions should be entered into only by investors who have read and understand this prospectus and, in particular, who understand the nature and extent of their rights and obligations and are aware of the risks involved. An investor should not purchase an Option unless he is able to sustain a total loss of the premium and transaction costs of purchasing the Option, and should not write an Option unless he is able to sustain substantial financial losses, or in the case of a Call, unless he owns the underlying security.

Anyone contemplating trading in options is urged to read the entire prospectus.

Having said that much, let me point out that if you can afford to lose your investment, there is no method I know of that can be more rewarding in as short a period of time than trading in options. While it is risky, experience shows that trading in carefully selected calls can produce an extremely high income on the amount of the investment.

BUYING CALLS

2

Low cost and potentially large profits

Friday, July 6, 1973, was a poor day for the New York Stock Exchange. The averages had been taking solid losses for months, and while the Dow Jones Industrial Average had fallen by 181 points from its January high of 1051, many of the individual stocks had plummeted by a much greater percentage. July 6 was particularly bad for Texas Instruments. The darling of many institutional investors, it boasted a price earnings ratio of 32 and earlier that year had traded as high as 100½.

By July 6, institutional investors were disgusted, after having watched their positions being eroded away month after month. Individual investors were even more depressed, after seeing some of their stocks cut down by a third or even a half. Thousands had been forced out of the market altogether by margin calls from their brokers that they were unable to meet. The brokers themselves were having one of their worst years in a decade as the volume of shares traded shriveled up to less than one half of what it had been a year earlier, and many of them were operating in the red. So it was not too surprising that on Friday, July 6, the price of Texas Instruments stock fell on the New York Stock Exchange from its closing price of 85⅝ the day before to 83.

A SUCCESS STORY

The only call being traded on the CBOE at that time in Texas Instruments was the 90 strike price. There were only about three weeks left for the July call and the distance from the current price of 83 to the 90 strike price seemed like an awfully long one, especially in view of the market's decline and Texas Instruments' loss of 2⅝ points the day before. If this down trend continued just a few days more it would be impossible for Texas Instruments to get even near the strike price by the option's expiration. The atmosphere on Wall Street was

17

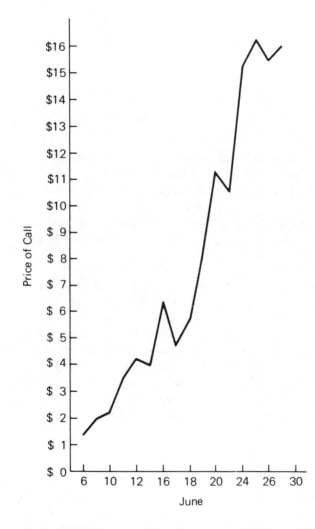

*Figure 1. Price increase of Texas Instruments call
in three weeks*

(Closing prices of July 90 calls)

gloomy and the drop of 2⅝ the day before did nothing to console the downhearted investors who were trading in the call.

Considering all this, the premium of 1⅜ at the close of trading on July 6 seemed quite generous indeed for the July 90 call option. After all, in order for the call ever to be worth anything, the price of the stock would have to go from 83 up to the strike price of 90, then up an additional 1⅜ to cover the premium to 91⅜, then up some more to cover the commission in and out, making a final price of almost 92 to which the stock would have to climb in order to merely let the call buyer get back the money he had put in.

Just to have the call buyer break even, the stock would have to climb a full 9⅞ points, an increase of 12%! And it would have had to do this in just three weeks, because as sure as your tax return is due April 15, that option would become worthless on the expiration date with no extensions possible. Anyone who contemplated buying a July option on Texas Instruments presumably was aware of all this and firmly expected that it would climb to well over 92 so that he could make a profit to compensate for the enormous odds against him.

In fact it was only the tremendous faith that some investors had in Texas Instruments and its tremendous performance as a growth stock that kept the premium as high as 1⅜. Just think for one minute. For a stock to climb over 12% in three weeks, it would have to increase by 4% a week, which means that if one annualized that rate it would turn out that anyone purchasing that call was expecting Texas Instruments for the next three weeks to increase by the annual rate of more than 208%! In my opinion no sane person should have touched that call with a ten-foot pole—or even an eleven-foot one for that matter. And yet investors purchased 38 calls.

The next trading day was Monday, July 9. Texas Instruments stock made a nice recovery, going up to 85⅜, and on the basis of this favorable development the July call went up to 2. At this point anyone who had bought at the closing price the day before could have gotten out by selling his call for a profit of ⅝, or 45%. Not bad for an over-the-weekend investment. On Tuesday, Texas Instruments took another remarkable jump up of 2½ points to 87⅞. Now it suddenly seemed as if an upward trend had developed and the strike price of 90 seemed tantalizingly close. So the premium for the July call went up to 2¼.

On Wednesday, Texas Instruments made the big jump; it "crossed the Rubicon" as the stock closed above the strike price, at 91⅜. Now, within a period of one week, the July call had been transformed from a highly speculative, extremely risky possibility of gain, into something that had actual cash value, and accordingly the call went up a full 1¼ points, to close at 3½. This may not seem like much, but let us remember that a person who had bought an option for $137.50 the previous Friday, now found the following Wednesday that it was worth $350. A profit of $212.50, or 155%, in just five days!

But more is yet to come. On Thursday the price of the common stock stabilized at 91¼, and option traders, suspecting that the stock had not peaked out the previous day, bid the price of a call up to 4¼. The price of the stock declined slightly on Friday (yes of course, it was Friday the 13th) but then on Monday shot up an amazing 4½ points, to 96. In one day, the call went from 4¼ to 6⅜. In just a week and one trading day a purchaser of a call on Texas Instruments would have seen the value of his option go from $137.50 to $637.50.

Subsequently the price of the stock fluctuated, hitting 97¾ on Thursday, July 19. At this point the call went to 8⅛. The next day the stock went up farther, by an almost unbelievable 4⅜, to close at 102⅜. The call went up 3¼ points to 11¼. The stock continued to rise until by the last trading in July, which was July 27, the stock was selling at 108¾.

The call closed at an even 16. So, the investor who just three weeks earlier had bought one for $137.50, now owned an option $1,600. That's not bad, as they say in Vermont. Obviously the serious investor who had bought ten for $1,375 suddenly found himself with options worth $16,000. Some people don't earn that much in a whole month of hard work! In case anyone is interested, that amounts to a gain of 1,063% in just three weeks. And I won't bother to tell you what that comes to in terms of annual return; suffice to say that it is over 18,000%, a difficult concept to grasp. But the basic fact that on a very small investment in calls one can very quickly make a great deal of money is one that everyone can easily comprehend.

Well, you might ask, what are the drawbacks? If you are an experienced hand at the stock market, you might ask whether the call purchaser would have had to put up some margin in case the underlying stock had gone down. No, the purchaser had to pay only the cost of the call, nothing more, and no matter what happened to the stock, this was the most that he could lose. Or, perhaps again if you are a stock market veteran, you are saying to yourself, well, that was a nice paper profit, but how many of the people who owned the Texas Instruments call on July 27 were lucky enough to sell at that very point in time? Didn't the stock fall subsequently, taking with it much of the profit? The answer is that this was no paper profit. Since the calls expired on their face that day, every single owner got out just at the right time.

No, there was no hitch. Everyone who bought a July call on Texas Instruments on July 6 and held it made an enormous profit without assuming any risk other than the possibility of losing the modest cost of 1⅜ per share.

And while this Texas Instruments example is spectacular, it is by no means unique. Literally thousands of calls have doubled at various times, and many options have tripled and quadrupled. Three specific cases out of many are: The Boeing August 45 options, which went from $1^5/_{16}$ on April 11, 1977, when the stock was 42⅛, up to 13¼ on June 16, when the stock was 58. Asarco April 15 calls were 1⅛ on December 8, 1976, when the stock was 15, but just four months later, on April 1, 1977, the options were worth 7¼ with the stock at 22⅜. Babcock and Wilcox October 45 options were 2⅞ on June 1, 1977, and after a take-over of the company was made they were worth an even 15 just three months later.

The sudden run-up of 80 points in the Dow Jones Industrial Average in the two weeks of April 1978 just preceeding expiration of the April options produced a number of even more dramatic examples. To take a well known stock, the IBM April 240 calls were $1^{15}/_{16}$ on April 7, and closed at 15¼ two weeks later. Merck April 50 calls were $^7/_{16}$ three weeks before expiration and closed at 3⅞. The Merrill Lynch April 15 call was ⅜ on April 7 and closed at 3¼ just two weeks later for an increase of almost 800%. Or to put it another way, $1,000 used to purchased Merrill April 15 calls would have grown to $8,904 in two weeks!

And now that I have shown you how easy it can be to make your fortune buying calls, I am going to summarize in one sentence the entire lesson of this chapter, and by far the principal teaching of this entire book: Never, n-e-v-e-r, NEVER, N E V E R buy a call until you have carefully considered these three points: (1) there is a very good chance that you will lose all or most of your money; (2) there is a very good chance that you will lose all or most of your money; and (3) there is a very good chance that you will lose all or most of your money. Only after you have carefully and *thoughtfully* enunciated these three points to yourself should you ever buy an option, at any price. It doesn't matter how cheap the option is, or how long it has to run, or how deep in the money it is.

Whenever you buy an option you are engaging in an extreme form of speculation, which is to say you are gambling. If you want to gamble you are welcome to do so, but when you lose your money, remember that you should have known beforehand that it could happen.

And if this still isn't enough to cool your ardor for buying options, just take a look at the actual results of option buyers in the past. If a picture is worth a thousand words, the chart shown in Figure 2 should be worth at least three books like this one. That chart is an objective analysis of what actually would have happened to $100 which was used for buying options on April 29, 1975, compiled as accuarately as possible by Value Line. By August 1977 the amount had fallen so far that it literally went through the bottom of the chart and a new set of graphs had to be supplied. By December 1, 1977, that $100 had shrunk to $1. Interesting, isn't it?

Figure 2. The Value Line Option Indices

The dotted line of this chart shows that buying most options between April 29, 1975, and July 1978 was a disaster. One can see that after August 1977 the index literally dropped off the chart. (Buying options before that date was even worse.) Note, however, that while option buyers on the average lost virtually their entire investment, option writers of covered calls, as shown by the solid line at the top of the chart, could have made a respectable profit. (Chart copyright by Arnold Bernhard & Co., Inc. and reprinted with permission.)

Of course this doesn't mean that history will repeat itself. Maybe option buyers in the next few years will go on to reap untold riches. But it does kind of make you pause and think, doesn't it?

THE GAMBLE OF BUYING CALLS

Why should you be very reluctant to buy a call? First let me state the obvious, which is that, like the purchasers of the July Texas Instruments call described above, a certain number of call purchasers are going to have their stocks rise smartly, just as they expected that they would. They will make money and a few will make a lot of money. But this does not mean that most people will win by buying calls, any more than the fact that some people win at every race means that the way to make money is to bet consistently at the track.

To understand why the consistent buyer of calls could be a loser in the long run, let's analyze just what buying a call means. It means that you are paying a premium for the right to participate in the rise of a stock within a specific period of time. This sentence contains many elements. Perhaps the most damaging is the final one, which limits a call to a specific period of time. Let's discuss just why this can be so adversely important.

Time limits

You may be convinced that a stock is drastically undervalued, that its position is fundamentally sound, that technically it is ready for a big recovery, that its industry is in for tremendous growth, and that the market in general is about to experience a major upward thrust. You may be right. But before committing yourself to buying a call, ask yourself this question. If you are right, then why isn't the stock selling at a higher price today?

All the factors you mention for its increase in price are known to you today and are influencing you today. Surely, other potential buyers of the stock are also aware of them. And yet the stock is no higher than it is. So, why do you think that these same factors, which are public knowledge today and are not pushing the price of the stock up, are suddenly going to have a magical effect after you have purchased a call?

You might argue that others don't know how to properly evaluate the information that you have, and once they do, the price of the stock will surely rise. Now you are bringing in another factor, which is that it will take other investors time to appreciate the value of the stock at its present price. Once you concede that it may take some time, how can you possibly be sure that enough people will come to this realization within the life span of the option you are buying? Believe me, there is nothing sadder than to see the price of a stock rise dramatically above the strike price—one week after the option has expired!

So the first reason for not buying an option is that neither you nor anyone else can know that a stock will go up within a relatively short period of time. As a matter of fact, a number of studies have been made as to how well professional securities analysts can forecast the rise of stock prices. American Telephone and Telegraph Company conducted a particularly comprehensive survey because it invests billions for its pension funds, and if one analyst or one bank pension management team could do even a quarter of a percent better than another, it would mean millions of extra dollars for the fund. Many other surveys of less depth have been conducted over the years by economics professors and others. All have reached one unanimous conclusion: No one and no group of people, over the long term, has done any better than a purely random selection of stocks.

Unpredictability

Put in graphic terms, this unanimous conclusion of all the studies made means that, in the long run, all the Phi Beta Kappas, MBAs, and PhDs in Economics wearing their expensive pinstripe suits in their elegant offices, with all the information that is available to them from every source including personal interviews with company presidents and reams of computer printouts, do not do one jot better at picking stocks than anyone could do by simply throwing darts at the stock market page of the newspaper.

Therefore, when you believe truly and surely that a certain stock is going to go up, and that it will definitely go up within the next three months, remember that either you are the first person in the history of Wall Street who really could tell when a stock would go up (in which case you should be writing a book of your own instead of reading this one) or your feeling of certitude is simply misfounded. Chances are that it is the latter. Therefore, the first thing you must do is face up to your own limitations, and the most obvious one is that you do not know whether a stock will go up or not, and you certainly do not know whether or not it will go up within the next three months.

Having disposed of your divine power of prophecy, we can proceed to the next argument made in favor of buying calls, which is that even if you can't pick a particular winner, the odds in favor of a call buyer are so great that given enough tries he will come out a winner. The reasoning is that most calls are so cheap, and the potential reward so great, that you can easily afford a number of losses, because you will more than make up for them on the big winners like Texas Instruments.

STATISTICAL SUPPORT FOR OPTIONS BUYERS

There is some statistical support for this position, see Figure 3. A simulation of returns obtained from various strategies was recently conducted for the period July 1963 to December 1975 by Robert C. Merton of the Massachusetts Institute of Technology, Myron S. Scholes of the University of Chicago, and Mathew L. Gladstein of Donaldson, Lufkin & Jenrette Securities Corp. During that period $1,000 invested in the Dow Jones average would have grown to $2,226, and $1,000 invested in the 136 stocks which had exchange-listed options on December 1975 would have grown to $5,043, including reinvestment of all dividends. A strategy of investing 90% of the portfolio in commercial paper and the remaining 10% in the purchase of options produced significantly better results. By buying on-the-money options with this strategy, $1,000 using the Dow Jones stocks would have grown to $3,138 and using the original 136 optionable stocks would have grown to $6,372. What was surprising about the study was that as the exercise price of the options purchased was increased, so that only out-of-the money options were purchased, the results were even better. When options 10% out of the money were purchased, the result on the 136 stocks was $11,178, and when options 20% out of the money were purchased, the result was a phenomenal $25,670!

The reason for these results is that a profit is not made on most of the options, and in fact a very large percentage of them are losers. Rather, the profit comes from the relatively few options which are extremely profitable, due to abnormally large increases in the price of the stock. This study indicated that by purchasing out-of-the money options one could take advantage of these aberrational moves in stock prices and capture a large percentage profit on the option.

A number of qualifications must be made. First, 90% of the money was kept in safe, short-term, interest-earning notes. Second, the period started with a long bull market. Third, it would be difficult for most investors to obtain the diversification necessary to get these results. Finally, it may take many years for the bull market situation to be duplicated. Certainly, if there is an unusually flat market, the results of this study would not be duplicated, because while stocks would remain stable and the portfolio would increase from the interest yield, most of the options that had been purchased would expire worthless, resulting in a constant decline. Nevertheless, it is good to know that option buying, if done under the proper circumstances, has statistical support. But before anyone runs out and buys options on the results of this simulation, he is asked to look again at Figure 2, which shows the results of actual option prices, and shows that for the period 1975 though early 1978 any strategy would have worked better than that of buying options.

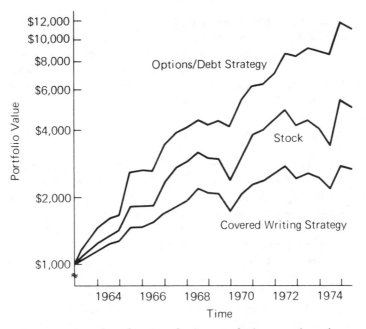

Figure 3. Results of a simulation study into various investment strategies

The Stock strategy was an equal dollar allocation to each of the 136 optioned stocks at that time with all dividends reinvested. Covered Writing Strategy consisted of continuously writing six-month calls which were 10% out of the money and rewriting upon expiration. Options/Debt Strategy consisted of investing 90% of the money in high-quality certificates of deposit and the remaining 10% used to purchase calls which were 10% out of the money. No taxes or transaction costs were deducted.

SOURCE: "A Simulation of the Returns and Risk of Alternative Option Portfolio Investment Strategies," R. C. Mertens et al. in the *Journal of Business* (April 1978). Reprinted by permission of The University of Chicago Press.

Breaking even

It may be true that each call is not expensive, but one still must ask what must happen for a call buyer to make money. If we take a simplified example in which the price of the stock happens to be exactly at the strike price, what must happen is that the price of the stock must move up enough to cover the premium plus the cost of the commission paid buying the call, plus the commission incurred in selling the call.

If a stock is selling at 25 with a strike price of 25, an option with a six-month duration might typically be selling at 2½. In other words, for the buyer of the call to just break even, the price of the underlying stock must move up to about 27¾: it must move up to 27½ just to cover the cost of the call, and up another ¼ point to cover the commissions on buying and selling, which will total approximately ⅛ point each way if you bought three calls. Well, you might think, that doesn't seem so hard. After all, stocks frequently move up a point in one day in a good market, so why shouldn't this stock move up more than three points, which is only one point a month. Surely, that can't be very difficult.

Let's analyze that. In the first place, the trend of the stock market over about 50 years has been dissected, analyzed, and described about as much as anything else in the world. The conclusion is that over the long haul, which has included some pretty wild bull markets, the average annual increase in stock value, including dividends that were constantly reinvested, has been just over 8%. Now, note that this includes the reinvestment of dividends. If we assume that dividends have averaged only about 3% per year, this leaves us with an annual appreciation in the price of the stock of 5% a year.

If you want to take the trend of stock prices over the last ten years, however, you will see that by just about any measure you choose, whether it be the Dow Jones average, the Value Line Survey, or Standard & Poors 500, there has been almost no increase in value at all, or the prices have actually gone down.

But in trying to demonstrate the falsity of the call buyer's thinking, let us take the facts most favorable to his case, as lawyers do when they are requesting a judge to grant them a summary judgment. So we will accept 8% as the average increase of all stocks over all the years. Although the past cannot predict the future, it is the only guide we have, so in the following discussion I will assume that the past growth rate will continue over a long period of time.

Returning now to our call buyer, his stock must rise from 25 to 27¾ in order to break even. This works out to an increase of exactly 11%. But the average increase of 5% is less than half that. So from the start, the odds are stacked against the call buyer. Remember that with this required 11% increase the call buyer still wouldn't make a single dime. He has risked his money, his stock has gone up far more in six months than the average stock does in an entire year, and he still hasn't made a thing.

Doubling investment

Let us say that the call buyer expects to double his money. To do this, the call buyer in our example must net 2½, so that he must sell his call for 5¼ to regain his original investment of 2½ plus his profit plus the commissions of approximately ¼ point. Thus, the stock must rise to 30¼, an increase of 21%. Does anyone really expect that a stock is going to shoot up by this amount? By a percentage three to four times as much as the average stock has actually gone up throughout recent history in an entire year?

By now you may be inclined to believe that buying a call is not such a sure thing. And remember the downside risk. Should the buyer be wrong and the stock stay right at 25, he will lose his entire investment! And if it goes down, he will, of course, also lose his entire investment, but it will happen more quickly. In any event, from a purely mathematical viewpoint, the odds are approximately 50% that the stock will either stay where it is or go down, and the call buyer will lose everything. And that is a pretty substantial loss to suffer in just six months. By way of comparison, it's pretty hard to think of many stocks that have done that in six months.

How to end up broke

One thing is pretty certain. If you continue to buy options with all your money, you are eventually going to end up broke. This is true regardless of any survey showing that option buyers end up making more money than others. The reason for this is simply a result of the highly volatile nature of options.

Let's assume that a solid, long-term bull market comes along, and you are buying three-month options. You triple your money in the first three months. You reinvest this in more options, and that also triples, so that now you have nine times your original investment. You reinvest this in more options, and this time they double. Now you have eighteen times your original amount. You reinvest and the bull market goes on.

But this time, there is a brief lull in the upward rise in prices, as there is in every bull market. The stocks in which you have bought options fall back, but only slightly. Just enough to be below the striking prices of all your options on their expiration dates.

How much money do you have now? Back to only nine times what you started with? Just three times? Or just the small amount you originally had? No. You have absolutely nothing. And this is the insidious aspect of buying options. Because no matter how much money you speculate with in buying options, 100% of the money is at total risk, able to be totally wiped out in a single option expiration period. And furthermore, it can be said with almost absolute assurance that if you play the options game long enough in this manner, you will lose every penny you have invested in call options at that time.

This is the reason why all studies of option buying limit the amount of exposure so carefully to a given percentage of a person's total assets. By so limiting your exposure, you will lose only that small percentage of your assets when the nearly inevitable shake-out in options takes place.

CALLS VS. STOCKS

One argument often cited in favor of buying calls is that it limits your risk in case of a downward slide by the stock. The argument is that by purchasing a call on 100 shares for, let us say, $5, you are capturing the same upward potential as the person who buys the shares for $50 each. Since your total outlay is $500, whereas his is $5,000, the conclusion is that you are smart, because your total risk is only $500 while he is risking ten times as much. Although this argument is true, it is also a deceptive method of comparing a stock purchase with a call purchase.

It is deceptive because you have not bought the same potential capital gains with your $500 worth of calls as the other person did with his $5,000 of stocks. If this were really the case, why would anyone buy stock at all? Can it be that everyone who buys stock is really a sucker paying ten times as much as he could if he only knew the "secret" of calls?

There are some pretty savvy people making their living on Wall Street, and they have more money invested in common stocks than in calls. Many of these men know more about puts and calls than you will ever know. Sure, they could all be wrong, but it does kind of plant the seed of doubt in your mind, doesn't it?

Why do I say you don't get the same profit from calls as stocks? For two very good reasons. The first is the premium. It's easy to overlook the premium because it's not very large in relation to the price of the stock, but it usually is very large in comparison to the actual gains made by the stock. If you are paying a 10% premium for your call, and during its term the price of the stock goes up 10%, you have made nothing, while the owner of the stock has made a nice 10% gain. Not bad for him, especially if he does it in only three months. But not good for you.

Furthermore, if the stock is purchased on margin of 50%, then a gain of 10% in the price of the stock is a gain of 20% on the investment, which looks good compared to the 0% on the call. But what if the price of the stock only goes up by 5%? The person who bought the stock has made a 5% gain. You, on the other hand, have suffered an enormous loss, equal to 50% of your investment! Now what were you saying about having the same right to participate in gains as if you had bought the stock?

The second reason why the purchase of a call is not equal to the purchase of stock is that the call buyer has only a limited time in which to make his gains. Let us take three months for example. If the stock doesn't go up in three months, the call buyer has lost his entire investment.

He now has a choice. He can shrug his shoulders and walk away, having lost all the money he put up, or he can try to recoup it by buying another three-month call on the same stock. The temptation is very strong to try to recoup. Let us assume that he does purchase another call. Now his investment in premiums is 20% of the value of the stock.

Mathematically, there is no more chance that the stock will rise during the second period than there was that it would go up in the previous period. There certainly is no more chance than before that it will go up more than before, and yet unless it leaps up by 20% the investor will be losing money. If the call purchaser did this for a whole year he would have paid a premium of 40% by the final quarter and still would only have a call that was good for three months. Is there much chance that any stock will go up 40% in three months?

The purchaser of the stock, in contrast, has the perpetual right to enjoy its possible appreciation, without putting up a single extra penny. It costs him nothing to wait two, three, or more years for a stock to go up. And while he is waiting, instead of paying ruinously high premiums of up to 40% a year, he may be collecting handsome dividends that compensate him for his cash investment in the stock.

For the two reasons stated above, it is clear that buying a call on a stock does not give the same chance to benefit from a stock's appreciation as does buying the stock itself. Rather, the two are investments of different kinds— they both involve the same stock, but they are still completely different investments. Just as renting a house for five years is quite different from owning it for five years, even though in both cases you can live in it for five years.

A practical comparison

To be meaningful, a comparison of one investment to another should compare investments of equal amounts. Thus, to determine whether a call is really a better risk against a downward stock price movement than is the stock, one should compare an investment of $1,000 in the stock with an investment of $1,000 in calls on the stock. Now, comparing the two investments on an equal basis, it is obvious that buying a call is no protection against downside risk at all. In fact, it is exactly the opposite, because the owner of the call will lose 100% of his money if the stock goes down and will even lose everything if the stock stays right where it is! The owner of the stock, on the other hand, will still have his original purchase and is sitting pretty waiting for the stock to move up in the next quarter.

Figure 4. The advantage of buying calls instead of stock

Results of investing $1,000 in calls compared to an equal investment in stock. (Price of stock when purchased: $100; premium of $100 strike price calls: $10)

Chart shows the remarkable leverage calls provide, so that every $1 increase in the price of the stock above the strike price provides an additional $100 profit, as opposed to only $10 for the stock. But see text discussion pointing out that if the stock is anywhere between $0 and $111, which is *the most likely area,* the *stock* buyer comes out ahead.

So, when someone says that buying a call instead of a stock is a good way to hedge against a downward movement of the stock, I reply that buying a call is only a good way of protecting yourself from a price decline if you consider losing 100% of your investment a good protection. As for me, I would rather protect my investment by retaining a good portion of it as the owner of the stock—or retain a bigger portion of it by keeping the stock and the premium that I receive by selling calls on it.

Liquidity and risk

Another argument that is made in favor of buying calls is that with the liquidity provided by the options exchanges, the risk is not as great as it was. This is a new era and now you can have the excitement of making a fortune from a small premium, while protecting yourself on the downside by selling out if the call should go down. Yes, you could cover yourself by selling out your position, but in my opinion this really doesn't help the buyer of a call very much. Here's why.

Let's say you pay $10 for a three-month call with a $100 strike price when the stock is at $100. Three weeks after you buy the call, the stock drops to 92 and your option is worth $5. Of course you *can* now sell your option and receive $5, thus limiting your loss to only $5. But you would be giving up the chance to make a large profit if the stock goes up over 100 in the next two months.

If you thought that the stock was worth more when it was selling for $100, presumably you think that it is worth a lot more now that it is only $92. It seems to me that you might as well hold on and hope that the price will go back up. You paid for a three-month call and you might as well get its benefit for the full duration.

Furthermore, when you bought the call for $10 you thought it was a reasonable price, one which merited your buying it, rather than selling it. Now that it has declined by half to only $5, it certainly doesn't seem like a good price at which to sell it. It has been my experience as a broker handling many option trades that, for these reasons, almost no one ever sells an option when it has gone down in price, and I'm not sure that one should try to break such a strong pattern. But if you have the discipline it is a good idea.

RULES OF STRATEGY

But no matter what is written here, there will be some investors who will continue to buy calls as the easy way to get rich. Lured on by the apparent low cost and the potential ease with which their money could double, they will bravely ignore any odds against them. If you are one of these people, then at least give yourself as good a chance as possible. There are methods by which you can make certain you get the best odds possible. And you may very well end up making money. If there is a sustained strong bull market and you adhere to the following strategies, you probably will. One study of calls found that if you had purchased six-month calls on U.S. Steel during the period 1946 to 1955, you would have made a substantial amount of money. And it could happen again. Follow these rules of strategy and you will maximize your chances of making money by buying calls.

Strategy Rule Number 1: Never buy a call when the underlying stock is more than slightly below the strike price. It is the consensus that only about 40% of old over-the-counter calls were ever exercised. Their strike price was usually identical with or very close to the price of the stock. Now, if you add the hurdle of requiring the stock to go up substantially before it can even get beyond the point of complete worthlessness (that is, beyond the strike price), you have just decreased your probability of ever making money on the call.

The savings in the premium of the call are often not proportional to the increasing difficulty of the feat that your stock must perform during the limited life of the call. We can measure this by analyzing the premiums and chances of making money on a stock that has calls outstanding with three strike prices.

Let's take an actual example of a volatile stock that in late 1977 had four regular strike prices available. The price of the stock was 49½ and the intermediate-duration options had just four months to go and were selling at the following prices:

Strike Price	Option
50	4⅝
55	2⁹⁄₁₆
60	1¼
70	⅜

To the novice the calls with the highest strike price might seem like the real bargains. Imagine being able to buy calls on 1,000 shares of a really volatile stock for only $337 (ignoring the restricted option problem for the moment). Or for a little fun, just buy one option for $37. If the stock goes up to 71 you will more than double your money. And if it goes up to 74 you will have multiplied your cost by ten! This could become another Texas Instruments bonanza just like the one described in the beginning of this chapter.

Let's examine all the possiblilities if the stock goes to various prices in increments of 5 on the call's expiration. Assume that a person spends $4,630 on options, which means that he could purchase 10 of the 50 calls, 18 of the 55s, 37 of the 60s, or 123 of the 70 calls. Here's what happens.

Price of stock at expiration	Profit or (Loss) from $4,630 worth of calls			
	Strike Price 50	Strike Price 55	Strike Price 60	Strike Price 70
$ 50 or under	($4,630)	($4,630)	($4,630)	($4,630)
55	370	(4,630)	(4,630)	(4,630)
60	5,370	4,420	(4,630)	(4,630)
65	10,370	13,470	13,870	(4,630)
70	15,370	22,520	32,370	(4,630)
75	20,370	31,570	50,870	56,870
80	25,370	40,620	69,370	118,379

Now let's analyze these figures. Yes, they do show that if the stock goes up to 80 or higher, the purchaser of the 70 option is the biggest winner. But what are the chances of this happening? To start with, there is a 50% chance that the stock will go down rather than up.

Then the largest probability is that after four months the stock will be just about where it was when the options were purchased, that is, just around 50. How many times does a stock move up 50% in price in four months? Even though it happens more often to stock prices than the statistical model of a random distribution would suggest, it is still very infrequently. If you would like to know just how infrequent this is, just try to remember the last time you owned a stock that went up 50% in four months. Or better still, look through a chart book and write down the number of stocks that have done this. Unless there has just been a rousing bull market, you will find very few such stocks.

In the 50% of the cases in which the stock ends up at 50 or lower, the purchasers of all the calls will lose all their money. But the purchaser of the 50 call will lose $1,000 less for every point rise in the price of the stock above 50, and when the stock reaches 55 he will actually have a modest profit of $370. But at 55 all the other call purchasers will still have a 100% loss.

If the stock really does well and gets up to 60, we have a different situation. Now the purchaser of the 50 option has a very nice profit of $5,370 for well over a 100% profit on his cost, the buyer of the 55 option has a profit of $4,420 for almost a 100% profit, but the other two option buyers still have a complete loss. Even though the stock is up a solid 20% in four months, the stock might as well have gone down to 35 as far as they are concerned.

If the stock should really do well and get up to 65, we would find that the purchaser of the 50 option was making a profit of $10,370, the purchaser of the 55 option was making a profit of $13,470, and for the first time even the purchaser of the 60 option was making a good gain of $13,870. But whoever purchased the 70 option still had a complete loss.

Right stock, wrong option

Sad but true. Even though he was right in thinking that the stock would have an outstanding rise in four months, he still loses every dime he invested. Just imagine the dismay, disappointment, and perhaps disgust and bitterness when he realizes that as smart as he was in correctly predicting a very rapid upswing for the stock, as far as the effect on his dollar-and-cents return on his investment, it might just as well have gone down 15 points. In short, he picked the right stock but destroyed himself by picking the wrong striking price.

If the stock should really do well and get all the way up to 70, then the purchasers of the 50, 55, and 60 options will really be in the chips. The 50 option will be producing a profit of $15,370, the 55 will produce a profit of $22,520, and the 60 option will produce a whopping profit of $32,370 on that initial cost of $4,630. Everyone will be cheering. Everyone, that is, except for the buyer of the 70 option.

With the stock at 70, he has correctly picked out what would be one of the outstanding winners in the stock market. Stocks that go up by 41% in four months don't come along very often. So the call purchaser can pat himself on the back as having picked the stock that probably is on everyone's lips as an outstanding perfomer. He can look at himself in the mirror when he gets up in the morning and say that he sees the face of a pretty savvy guy, and he can tell all his friends at the club when the conversation turns to stocks that he not only thought four months ago that the stock was in for a good rise, but that he had the guts to put his money where his mouth was and that he actually bought calls on it. Yes, he'll be the envy of them all, and he can be pretty proud of himself.

The only thing he can't do is spend the profits he made from being right. Because, you see, he lost 100% of his cost. So how smart was he after all?

I can hear people now saying that my example isn't really relevant, because everyone knows that a call with a strike price 40% out of the money is a way-out investment, and that the smart investor puts only a little money into that kind of a call. It's sort of a lark: You put up some money that you can easily afford to lose and you forget about it until just before the expiration period. If the stock doesn't really go up, you lose your money. But so what, you knew in advance that you probably would, and that's why you invested only a small amount.

A little of a bad thing

On the other hand, if the stock should surprise everyone and go over the strike price, wow! You get a free paid vacation or whatever else you want with your unexpected but very welcome bonanza. This no doubt describes the human psychology of a person who buys such a call. But it in no way changes the odds or makes it a better investment. What such a person is really saying is that he knows it's a risky investment and that's why he invested only a little in it. Here's my tip on how to improve that investment strategy: If you know that you are so unlikely to make a profit, then why not invest *very* little in it—specifically nothing. A little of a bad thing is not necessarily a good thing.

Especially now, when option premiums are so much less than they were, there seems to be no need to reach for the far-out-of-the-money options, when anyone can afford to buy just slightly out-of-the-money options that will make a profit even if the stock goes up just a little bit.

This may seem to contradict the conclusion of the Merton, Scholes, Gladstein study mentioned earlier. These are, however, two important differences between the study and the typical investor. First, the study assumes an almost infinite diversification, that is, buying options on every one of the optionable stocks, so if any one goes up by 50% you own it. Obviously this is not the case for most investors, and so, to make for this lack of diversification, it is my conclusion that it is necessary to own options that will make money for smaller price increases. And second, the study was based upon a period that had great bull markets and times of tremendous volatility, two conditions that have been absent from the market in recent years.

To summarize, it is hard enough to make money on a call, even when you buy a call with a strike price just about where the stock is. Historically there is almost a 50% chance that the stock you select will go down rather than up, and another 10% chance, that it will remain so close to the strike price that you will barely cover the expenses of buying an on-the-money option. Thus, even when the stock starts out at the strike price the odds are 60 to 40 against you that you will make a profit on your cost. For every point that you require the stock to climb before you can begin to recoup part of your investment, you are making the odds against you just that much worse. The only advantage of a higher strike price is that the calls are cheaper, but as the example in this section showed, that is a tricky economy indeed. Since they are cheaper, you can make a higher percentage profit if the stock exceeds that strike price than someone who bought the lower strike price calls. But, in my opinion, the profit on a successful call with a low strike price is high enough, without making it any more risky. Thus, *Strategy Rule 1* is *don't buy a call when the stock is significantly below the strike price.*

Strategy Rule Number 2: Never buy a call when the stock is substantially above the strike price. When you do buy a deep-in-the-money call you are giving a free insurance policy to the seller of the call, which can cost you heavily but will help you only very little.

To illustrate this rule and the reasoning behind it, let's take another actual example.

A stock was 24¾ and had options at 15, 20, and 25. They were all for the October call, which had about seven weeks left to run. The premiums were 10⅜ for the 15 strike price call, 5¾ for the 20, and 1 15-16 for the 25. If you purchased calls worth $1,037, you would get 100 of the 15 strike price, 180 of 20, and 534 of the 25.

Let's see what happens to the purchaser of these calls on their expiration date when the stock is various prices, again ignoring commissions for the sake of simplification.

Price stock reaches on call expiration date	Profit or (Loss) on calls purchased for $1,037		
	Strike Price 15	Strike Price 20	Strike Price 25
$15 or under	$(1,037)	$(1,037)	$(1,037)
20	(537)	(1,037)	(1,037)
25	(37)	(137)	(1,037)
27	163	223	31
28	263	403	565
29	363	540	1,099
31	563	900	2,167
33	769	1,260	3,235

If we were to carry the table out farther, the 25 would continue to outgain the other two calls by an increasingly wide margin.

What this table shows is that if the stock moves up two points or more from its present level, the purchaser of the call with the strike price nearest the current level of the stock is going to be the winner, and the more the stock moves up over two points, the more he is going to be ahead of the other calls.

Note that only in the under 27 and over 20 range is the 25 call really far behind the other calls. Once the stock price falls below 20, all the calls, including the 15 strike price, are heavy losers. My conclusion would be to buy the 25 call because if you don't expect the stock to move up at least two points, then you should not be buying the call in the first place.

The reason for the large difference in potential profit is clear. The purchaser of the call at the 25 strike price is paying his money strictly for the future time value of the option itself. You might say that he is buying a pure call.

The purchasers of the calls at the other strike prices are buying an

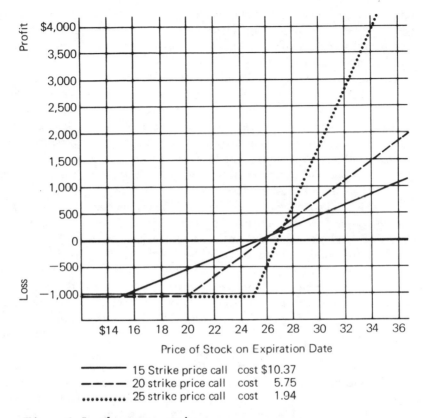

Figure 5. In-the-money options

Profit or loss on buying calls with different strike prices, (price of stock when calls were purchased 24¾)

This chart illustrates that calls with strike prices substantially below the current price of the stock will not provide as good a profit to the call buyer as those with higher strike prices. See Strategy Rule #2.

option—the right to gain if the price of the stock goes up—but they are paying a large portion of their money for the purchase of an interest in the current value of the stock, i.e., current cash value or intrinsic value. And this is what makes their calls so expensive and gives them so little upside profit potential.

Let me explain. Since the price of the stock is already at 24¾, a call with a 20 strike price is worth 4¾ if it is exercised today. And of course it could be exercised today, because a call can be exercised at any time until the expiration date. Therefore, the premium includes not only an option to profit by future gain on the price of the stock, but 4¾ to pay for the present value of the option due to the current price of the stock.

The premium for the 20 strike price call is 5¾, and of this 4¾ represents the stock's present value. Therefore, only $1 actually goes to buy the "pure option" part of the call. What benefit is the purchaser receiving from the other 4¾? The answer is clear. Absolutely nothing in terms of options. In effect he is paying out money to buy that portion of the stock that is above the strike price. This greatly reduces his leverage, which of course is at cross-purposes with the very reason for purchasing calls at all. The only advantage is that the call with the lower strike price has a lower cost for the "option part" of the premium. That is, the 25 call costs $1^{15}/_{16}$, but the "option part" of the 20 call costs 5¾ (premium) minus 4¾ (present value of option), or just 1, which is about half as much at the 25 call. But should the price of the stock go down, that lower cost is quickly transformed into a much larger loss per share.

These factors can be seen in even more extreme form in the case of the 15 strike call. With the stock at 24¾ and the strike price at 15, the difference between them is 9¾, which is the value of the option. Since the total premium is 10⅜, the "pure option" part of the premium is 10⅜ minus 9¾, or ⅝, versus 1 for the 20 strike price call and $1^{15}/_{16}$ for the 25. This lower cost for the "pure option" is the only reason for buying the 15 strike price call.

If the stock goes up, that portion of the premium that pays for the present stock value will not increase. There is absolutely no leverage in the portion of the option representing the existing value of a stock. On the other hand, if the stock goes down, the call buyer loses a large portion or even all of the money that he had to pay for the present value of the stock.

Thus, his gain is sharply limited by the fact that the calls are so expensive. For a given amount of money he can buy only a relatively small number of calls, thus greatly reducing his chance to make a large amount of money on the upside. Also, since he has paid so much to offset the fact that the stock was already above the strike price when he bought it, he stands to lose a great deal.

This disadvantage of the lower strike price call can be better illustrated by a table showing the effects of varying prices of the stock upon 100 calls of the 15 strike price, costing $1,037, versus 300 of the 25, costing $581. I am doing this to show that even the one supposed advantage of buying a call with a low strike price, namely that you will lose less if the price stays where it is or goes down, is largely unfounded.

The better way to accomplish this objective of minimizing loss is simply to buy fewer calls at a strike price closer to the current price of the stock as this table clearly shows.

Price stock reaches on call expiration date	Profit or (Loss) on calls	
	100 Calls at 15 Strike Price	300 Calls at 25 Strike Price
$15 or under	$(1,037)	$(581)
20	(537)	(581)
25	(37)	(581)
27	163	19
28	263	300
29	363	600
30	463	900

For every additional dollar that the stock climbs in price, the purchaser of the 15 call makes an additional $100, while the purchaser of the 25 call makes an additional $300.

I hope this makes clear that the purchaser of the call with the low strike price is a real loser. Looking at the table, we can see that if the stock falls below 20, the buyer of the 15 call loses more money than the 25, until at 15 or under he has lost twice as much. Furthermore, on the upside, the purchaser of the 15 call doesn't do as well once the stock gets up to 28, which isn't an impossible gain from its current 24¾. And over 28 the difference is quite marked, with the 25 call outgaining the other by three to one.

Only when the stock is between 20 and about 28 does the 15 strike price call come out ahead and even in this range the difference is not usually very much. At 21, for example, the 15 call loses $437 versus $581 for the 25. And the fact that the purchaser of the 25 call in this example is only risking a total of $581 as opposed to the $1,037 risked by the purchaser of the 15 call is another important factor favoring the 25.

In summary, the reason for Strategy Rule #2 of never buying a call when the strike price is far below the price of the strike is that you really get stuck when the price of the stock goes down, and when the price of the stock goes up, you have paid so much for each call that your leverage and profit potential are severely limited. Considering the risk that you will lose all or a large part of your investment, there just isn't enough upward leverage to make it an attractive speculation.

Strategy Rule Number 3: Before buying a call, carefully compare all three durations for the most favorable one. This seems like an easy thing to do, and indeed an obvious one, but oddly enough it is one to which very few call buyers seem to pay any attention.

If you will compare the trading volume of the various expiration dates of a call, you will invariably find that the highest volume is in the current call.

This is usually true right up to the end of the current call's duration. The reason for this is, I believe, that the short-term call is faster and more exciting. Also it is a great deal cheaper, and thus has much more leverage. If the call has only a very short term left, and the stock is above the strike price, then its entire premium reflects the current value of the option, so that a change of ¼ point upward in the price of the stock will result in a full ¼ point upward rise in the price of the call. If the stock is selling below the strike price, the premium will be very cheap, so that a rise in the stock's price of just a few points would have an enormous percentage increase in the price of the call.

Yes, there is a lot of action in short-term calls, but the purpose of this book is not to advise the reader how to get a lot of action, or how to gain thrills and excitement from puts and calls. We assume that that is not the purpose for which a person invests in stock options. If anyone wants excitement, there are many commercial gambling games that provide more action than stock options, not to mention other legitimate investments such as commodities, for example. We are assuming that the reader is interested in making money. And making money is often not synonymous with excitement.

In addition to the fast pace, one might be tempted to buy a short-term call because one is pretty certain the stock will move up a few points within the next few days or weeks, but he is not at all certain what it is going to do over the next few months.

There may be many reasons for this belief. Perhaps his reading of certain technical indicators has shown him that the stock is ready to break out of a resistance level. Perhaps he believes that a certain industry is about to experience higher profits than had been anticipated. Perhaps he senses a trend in the market that will soon transfer itself to this stock.

In any event, it is quite common for a person to feel certain that a stock will move up perhaps five points within the next few weeks, and he is therefore interested only in a call which will cover the next few weeks. Why pay more money for a longer-term call than he needs?

The answer is one that unfortunately is apt to be demoralizing and ego shattering and therefore not listened to. But I present it anyway, for those who have the detachment to profit by it. The reason for not looking solely at the short-term option is that neither you nor anyone else can be certain of correctly predicting what a stock will do within the next few weeks.

The reason is that the short-term trend of a stock depends upon almost everything except the fundamentals. The fundamentals of a company, an industry, or the market as a whole don't normally change very much, if at all, within a period of weeks. There might be a company interim earnings report, but it would be the height of foolishness to think that you can be more accurate in predicting what it will report than the many Wall Street professionals who follow the stock.

You may in fact turn out to be more accurate than they were, but this, I submit, is due not to your really being any better able to predict the earnings than others, but simply to your good luck. If you don't believe me, just keep track of how accurate you are over a period of time with various stocks.

Rather than fundamentals, the short-term fluctuations of stocks are caused by the feelings of the investor community, and these feelings are a mixture of thousands or millions of different inputs, ranging from the price of wheat on the Chicago Board of Trade to the current interbank interest rate in Zurich, to the spot price of crude oil in Libya, to the health of the United States President, to the latest figures on the number of new housing construction starts, to the value of the West German mark in the world market, to the number of automobiles produced in Detroit last week, to this morning's statement on taxes by the House Ways and Means Committee Chairman, and so forth indefinitely.

If you will consider it, I think you will agree that no one can correctly predict what the investment community will be thinking in four weeks because no one can predict what all these inputs will be in four weeks. And even if you could do this in a general way, how in the world could you focus this general mood into what the investment community will be thinking about a particular stock?

If the investment community believes that a stock is worth $55 today on the basis of everything that is known about the stock today, this price evaluation includes the community's assessment of what is likely to happen within the next few weeks to change that evaluation. So, if you believe you can predict the future price of a stock, you must believe that you have greater knowledge than the investment community or that you have superior methods for evaluating that knowledge. But the probability is that you, like everyone else, have neither. If you had either one, you would not be reading this book. Instead you would be quite wealthy from all the money you would have made in the past from your short-term trading of common stocks. Look back over your past transactions. Were you always right in the past? If not, then what makes you think that you are going to be right this time? My point here is not that anyone is always going to be wrong, but that you cannot be sure that this time you are going to be correct about the short-term movements of any one stock.

Now that we have concluded that you will not necessarily be correct in predicting the short-term movement of a stock, we can go to the next step. There are two ways in which you could be wrong in your belief that the price of a given stock will go up within the next few weeks. The first is that it might not go up at all. The second is that it might indeed go up just as you had expected, but that it does so not within the time you had anticipated but only after your option has expired.

Let's see what you can do to select calls to reduce your risk of los... If you are wrong in the first way mentioned above, and the stock goes down, then there is no method of buying a call that is going to elimate a loss. If, however, you are wrong in the second way, so that the price of the stock goes up later than you thought, you can protect yourself by buying an option for a term longer than you believe you need.

Now let us look at the rights that a call confers in a different light— namely, that a call has value because for a certain amount of time you can profit by any increase in the price of a stock. Therefore, one of the most important factors in determining the value of a call from your viewpoint is: How much is it costing me to have this privilege for a given length of time? In other words, what does it cost me per week to have the privilege of making money from this stock?

Therefore, before buying any call you should compute the cost of the different expiration date options available on a cost-per-week basis. You will find that the most popular call, which is usually the shortest-term call, is also usually the most expensive on a per-week basis.

Let's take an actual example. The prices given here were closing prices on a Friday five weeks before the expiration of the October calls. RCA is a good illustration because it closed at 25¼ with a strike price of 25, so that the premium represents almost the pure option value of the call. The October call was 1¾, the January call was 3⅛ and the April call was 3¾. This comes out to a per-week cost of $.35 for the October call, $.17 for the January call, and $.12 for the April call. In other words, the person who bought the shortest-term call was paying twice as much per week as the purchaser of the January call, and three times a much per week as the purchaser of the April call, for the privilege of making money on a rise in the price of RCA stock. To put the figures another way, the market evaluated a call for the first five weeks of option at $1.75, but the final entire quarter consisting of thirteen weeks cost only $.62½. Yet, statistically, the chances of a price rise in the final quarter are just as great as the chances of a price rise in the first. Thus this exercise should lead one to purchase the longest-term RCA option in order to get the lowest cost per week.

The shortest term is not always the most expensive. Sometimes the investment community apparently thinks that the chances for a near-term rise in a stock are small, while the probability of a rise over a period of a few months is greater. This is particulary common for far-out-of-the-money options. In this case it might be prudent to buy the shortest call.

As a general rule, the various options are most nearly equal in cost per week during the beginning of a quarter. At this time the current option has about half as long a term as the following one, and premiums usually have a ratio close to 1 to 2. As the current option period comes to an end, its future life rapidly decreases, whereas the next option period still has a full thirteen weeks, plus whatever is left in the current period.

When there is just one week left in the current option, the next period calls have a life span fourteen times as long as the current calls but it is very rare to find such a disparity in the premiums. The result is that as the current period draws to its close, the current calls are greatly overpriced on a per-day basis. You'll be wise to pass them by and invest in the better per-day bargain.

Rule #3 for buying a call is to carefully compute the cost of the call per week or day, and compare it with all the other calls available in that stock at the strike price you select. Then carefully evaluate the results in making your final selection. Generally it will pay you to pick the longer-term option.

Strategy Rule Number 4: Annualize the premium in order to appreciate the cost you are paying for the call. By annualizing the premium I mean simply to multiply it by the proper amount so that you can determine the premium you would be paying if you were to buy a one-year call at the same rate per day or week.

For example, if there are seven weeks left in the life of a call and you are paying $2^1/_{16}$ for it, then the annualized cost of the call would be determined as follows: Divide the number of weeks in the year by the number of weeks left in the life of the option—52 divided by 7 is 7.4. Multiplying the premium of $2^1/_{16}$ by 7.4 we obtain an annualized premium of 15.26. This is the amount your premium would be if you were to buy a 12-month option at the same rate per week as you are now paying.

To utilize this figure more fully, compute it as a percentage of the underlying stock. The figure, $2^1/_{16}$ used in the example actually came from the premium for a Digital Equipment 50 call when the stock was selling at 48¾. Doing the arithmetic, we find that the annualized premium of 15.26 comes out to be 31% of the price of the stock. What is the significance of this to a person who is planning to pay only $2.06 for a call? The answer is that if we accept the premise stated earlier in this chapter that it is impossible to know just when a stock will go up, then we face the possibility that it might be necessary to buy another call if the first expires without being profitable. This could be repeated. It then becomes important to know the amount we are paying per unit of time—the *rate*.

The most meaningful rate is the annual one, because investors are accustomed to determining stock gains on an annual basis. If you don't think that the stock will go up by the amount of the annualized premium in the course of the next year, then think twice before buying the call.

Of course it is true that the stock only has to go up $3^5/_{16}$ (the $2^1/_{16}$ you paid for the call plus 1¼ to the strike price) points for you to get back the entire amount of your investment, and that seems like a relatively minor amount of gain. But, you must realize that you are expecting this to happen in just seven weeks. While the chances of this happening are greater than the chances that the stock will go up 15.26 points during the year, just keep in mind that on a per-day basis this is exactly what you are expecting.

Mathematically, if the stock went up $3^5/_{16}$ every seven weeks, it would go up 24.6 points in a year. So, you are betting that at least for the next seven weeks, it will go up at the rate of 50% a year. And that is a pretty damn high rate, although it is certainly possible keeping in mind Digital's past performance.

Another way of using the annualizing concept is to consider whether there might be better methods of achieving your goal. For instance, if you buy the call now and the stock does not go up, do you intend to purchase the call again during the next quarter? And if so, at the same rate for the premium? If you don't purchase the second call, then you have thrown away 100% of your investment.

If you do buy another call, then you make it just twice as hard to come out a winner, because the profit from your second call must now pay not only for its own premium but also for the premium that you lost on the first call. Of course, if you follow this reasoning out to the third quarter, it becomes almost absurd. Remember that unlike the money that one pays for a stock itself, the money spent for an option is not an investment in anything tangible unless the stock is above the strike price by the expiration date.

The moral of this story is that if the annualized premium is as high as 50%, an investor might do far better to buy the underlying stock on margin. To buy on margin under current regulations, the purchaser need only put up cash equal to 50% of the price. Thus, for approximately the same cost as the annualized premium of a call, a person could actually obtain the same leverage power by buying the stock itself. And he could be much better off. For the money would actually have bought an asset with lasting value. He would also get any dividends on the stock.

Whether the stock goes up, stands still, or goes down, the purchaser of the stock will own something at the end of the year. It may be worth more than he paid for it, or it may be worth less. In extreme cases, where the stock declines drastically in value, the purchaser might have to put up more money for margin or lose some of the stock. But under normal circumstances, the purchaser of the stock on margin will continue to own the stock.

The purchaser of the call, on the other hand, if he repurchases a similar call each quarter and the price of the stock remains unchanged or goes down, has paid out $24.60 per share, for which he has obtained absolutely nothing. And even if the price of the stock were to go up a very dramatic 24.6 points, or

50%, during the year, the purchaser of the calls has probably only recovered his cost. He has not made a single dime!

The purchaser of the stock would have the 50% profit on the stock, and if he had bought on margin, the gain on his cash investment would be 100%! (his interest costs but plus any dividends). So, there would be no question that a one-year call at the rate of the seven-week option would be completely absurd. If this is the case over a one-year period, why is the call any more of a bargain over a period of only seven weeks? Thus, Strategy Rule #4 is to annualize the call's premium and consider the value of the call accordingly.

Strategy Rule Number 5: Sell one half your calls when they have doubled in price. Most people buy calls when they expect that a stock has the potential to move up by a really substantial amount. When the stock does start moving up, this serves to confirm their view that it is going to go much higher. The natural tendency is to hang onto your options, or even to roll them up, rather than get out of half your position. And certainly, if the stock continues to go up, you might be sorry that you did sell half your position. And yet, in suggesting this rule to my clients, I do not know of a single one who is sorry that he applied this rule. Although it is the arch example of an arbitrary rule that can easily be ridiculed by mathematicians and stock traders, who will say that if you like a stock you hold onto a call, and if you don't you sell it. And I am also certain that I will get many comments from people who will say that they never could have made the money they did in options if they had ever followed this rule. It has nevertheless served me well, and here is why.

We start with the principle that buying options is extremely risky. As pointed out often in this book, your entire cost is constantly at risk of going to zero in a matter of weeks. Let's assume that you originally decided to buy 10 calls at 1½ on your favorite stock. This means that you wanted to have $1,500 at risk in options on that stock. Now the option goes up to 3, and your investment becomes worth $3,000. That's wonderful, but let's not lose sight of the fact that you now have at risk exactly twice as much as you originally intended. You have $3,000 on paper, and that is how much you stand to lose. This rule of strategy says that you should now sell out half your position so that you will bring the amount of money at risk back to your original commitment. In other words, why should you let the action of the marketplace force you to have twice as much at risk as you originally planned?

Another major benefit of this rule is that once you have sold half your position at twice the original cost, you have recovered your entire original investment, less commissions. Incidentally, commissions can easily be covered by selling for twice your *net* cost of the options. The beauty of recovering your entire original investment is that the entire cost of your remaining position has been paid for by the market increase. You have gotten back your cost, and now the entire psychology of owning the calls is different, because now no matter what happens, you can never lose anything. So you can decide to hold onto them until the last day and be completely free of worry, because no matter what happens you can only be a winner.

A final reason for this rule is that in a trading market that is characterized by short stock price moves up and down, it is surprising how often an option will double in price and then drop down again to where it was. With hindsight it would have been better to sell out your entire position, but the big advantage of this rule is that it lets you get back your entire cost and permits you to continue being in the position of making more money if the stock continues its rise.

Strategy Rule Number 6: Know and understand the Beta of the stock underlying your call. The Beta of a stock is the propensity of the stock to move with the market. The market as a whole is assigned a Beta of one. The most wildly moving stock would be assigned a theoretical Beta of two, and a stock that never moved would in theory have a Beta of zero. In actuality, of course, there are no such extremes, so a stock that has a Beta of 1.8 is extremely volatile, while one with a Beta of 0.2 is extremely stable. Appendix A contains a Beta and volatility factor for each optionable stock.

The philosophy of this book is that it is impossible, at least for the short duration of a stock option, for anyone to accurately predict the price movement of the stock. But it is very possible to state whether a particular stock is likely to have large price movements based upon its historical performance. With respect to volatility of movement, as distinct from direction of movement, I believe that historical performance has a great deal of validity in predicting the future action of a stock.

Note that I do not say that past history can predict whether a stock is likely to go up or down, only that it can accurately tell us to what extent it is likely to move if the market as a whole moves. Certain stocks, throughout many years, have always moved up sharply when the market as a whole moved up, and these stocks are very likely to do so again.

Typical stocks that have large swings are airline stocks; automobile companies; anything connected with housing, building, or real estate; travel and resort businesses; and stocks that have a high price/earnings ratio. On the other end of the scale, stocks that are apt to move only slightly include utilities; companies supplying basic commodities for which demand remains fairly constant, such as tires, canned foods, soaps; supermarket chains; and life insurance companies.

The importance of the Beta and volatility of a stock to successful stock option trading cannot be overemphasized. It is the sine qua non of successful option buying. The reason is quite simple, as the following comparison with purchase of a stock shows.

The purchaser of a stock typically buys the stock for many reasons. He hopes that the price of the stock will go up in the next three or six months, but this is far from the only reason why an investor buys a common stock. He may be perfectly willing to have no price increase in the next few months, feeling confident that the next few years will amply reward him with a slow but steady growth. He may not be looking for any increase in price at all, having bought the stock because it pays a good dividend, and he is quite content to realize a high rate of return on his investment exclusively via dividends. Or he may have selected a certain stock because he believes that it represents a secure, safe investment, which may eventually go up, which pays some dividends, and which he feels quite certain will not decline in value very much if at all.

Stock purchaser vs option buyer. Thus, to the stock purchaser, the short-range price movement is only one of many factors that may have influenced his decision and that will eventually determine whether he made a successful investment.

The contrast with the call buyer is startling. The call buyer is interested in one thing and one thing only. That is, how much the stock is going to go up within the highly limited duration of the option. This is all that matters to him. He will not share in the dividend, so he couldn't care less about its rate. He will not be around next year to realize the gains from an increase of price then (at least not unless, at great cost to himself, he constantly buys one call after another). If the price of the stock stays the same or goes down just a little bit, this is of little solace to the option buyer who usually can then say good-bye to 100% of his investment. Every other consideration that enters into the decision of the stock buyer is obviated for the call buyer. For him there is only one question of any interest, only one point that makes any difference to him at all. That is, whether this stock will go up during the period of his call, and if it does, by how much.

In determining the answer to this question, the behavior of the stock price movement in the past is invaluable. And the stock with the greatest movement has the highest volatility. Therefore, the call buyer should seek a stock with as high a volatility as possible. A high Beta and high volatility do not indicate that the stock will necessarily go up. Alas, it could go down, but presumably our call buyer has satisfied himself that the stock should go up within the duration of the call or he would not be considering the call in the first place. Having made that judgment, he then must determine how high it is likely to go.

In order to be successful, the call buyer needs to find stocks that have the potential of going up at least enough so that he can double his money. And if the typical premium for a three-month call with a strike price close to the price of the stock is 3% to 8%, this means that the stock must be capable of going up

6% to 16% within the three-month period, plus an amount to compensate for commissions. This requires a stock with high volatility.

On the other side of the equation, it is no coincidence that the calls on stocks with the highest Betas are the ones that command the highest premiums, and that stocks with low Betas have low premiums. For example, when AT&T closed at 50¾ and the 50 call was selling for a premium of 1⅝, Ford closed at 60⅛ and its premium for the 60 call was 2⅜.

Thus, because AT&T is known as a slow mover, its premium was substantially less than Ford's, although it was selling ⅝ of a point higher above its strike price than Ford. Call buyers knew that AT&T would probably not go up much higher but they believed that Ford did have the potential.

In the final analysis it comes down to a matter of judgment. Is the higher premium made worthwhile by the greater probability that the stock with a higher Beta is going to go up faster and farther than one with a low Beta? My answer is that in almost all cases it is worthwhile.

Take the example above. AT&T is famous for moving only a fraction at a time. It has been hovering around the same level for just about a decade. Ford, on the other hand, is a fast mover. Its high in 1973 was 82, so there was a long way that it could go upward. For only 75¢ more in the price of the premium per share, the buyer gets a much better chance of receiving a really good return on his money. Remember, the call buyer is not looking for a nice little increase. By the very nature of his investment, he must be seeking a big increase in a relatively short time.

If you have to pay a little more in the cost of the premium, or even substantially more, it is usually money well spent. Don't forget that a low Beta is no assurance of safety either. In the above example AT&T could easily slip down ¾ to 50 and the call buyer would then lose his entire investment regardless of how safe the AT&T common stock is.

How does one find out the Beta of a stock? (Appendix A gives them as of January 1978, but they do change with time.) There are a number of services that compute Beta factors. This is not a cut-and-dried statistic, such as the price/earnings ratio, which can be precisely calculated by a computer. The Beta must be derived very carefully from many sets of figures, and the results will vary depending upon the period of time that is chosen, the average that is used to measure the overall market performance, and the number of stocks that are included in the analysis. Perhaps the most readily available sources are the *Value Line Survey* and *Options Alert*, which compute the Beta for every listed stock. Your stock broker should be able to tell you the Beta for any stock.

Rule 6 may be summarized by saying that the buyer of a call wants to be certain that the stock he is buying is one that has a good probability of going up enough so that the premium for his call will at least double. This means that it must be a stock that can move fast, and the measurement of that movement is the Beta and volatility of the stock. Although stocks with higher Betas have calls with higher premiums, their extra performance potential is usually well worth the extra cost. In short, buy calls on stocks with high Betas and volatility.

Strategy rule Number 7: *Never buy a call unless you have checked the stock's chart for at least ten years.* Before you buy a call you will naturally ask yourself how high the stock must go in order to realize your investment goal. Assuming that your investment goal is to at least double your money, you will calculate how high the stock must go by the call's expiration date in order for you to double your money and cover two commissions. Once you have that answer, check it against a ten-year or longer chart of your stock to find out how many times the stock has gone up by that much in the period of time left in the option.

For example, if you find that your stock must go up six points, and there are three months left in the option period, look at the chart to find out how many times in the past the stock has gone up by six points or more in any three-month period.

A fairly easy way to check the chart for this is by means of a simple indicator that you can make by measuring off on the lower right-hand corner of a piece of paper the distance representing the number of points it must rise on the vertical scale along the right edge. Then make a horizontal measurement for the period of time that the option is in effect along the bottom edge. When you have this right angle you can cut it into a triangle. Move the indicator along the chart, keeping the bottom line horizontal. See Figure 6. Note how many times the upper right-hand corner meets the price line on the chart. If the stock did not go up a full six points in any three months during the entire ten-year period, this would clearly be an indication that it is not very likely to do so during the next three months. Obviously, even if in the ten years it had often gone up the required points in three months, that is no guarantee that it will do so in the future, but it shows you have a fighting chance.

It is possible that the next three months will see a rise in the price of the stock that exceeds any in its past ten-year history—but the odds against it are overwhelming, and you're not getting those odds when you buy a call. The odds you are getting may be the chance to double, triple, or quadruple your investment.

But what are the odds that the market is taking from you? If a stock didn't go up the amount you wish in any three-month period in the past ten years, that means that it failed to do so a single time out of 117 chances. And now you are betting your money that it will go up that much on the 118th chance. I don't know what the odds are against you, but my guess is that 118 to

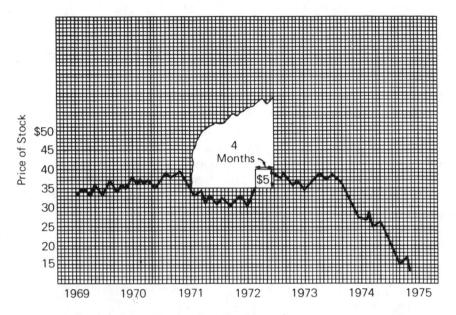

Figure 6. Using the indicator described in rule 7

On a 5-year chart of the underlying stock's performance

1 is an understatement. Just compare that to the odds that the market is giving you. Yes, I'm sure we'll both agree that there must be better ways to invest your money.

Suppose you discover that in the past ten years there have been 33 three-month periods during which the stock has gone up by an amount that would be enough to let you double your cost. What does this indicate for you? As every brokerage report states, past performance is no guarantee of future performance. But when you are trying to forecast the possibility of certain short-term movements, it does give an indication of the range of future conduct.

If your stock went up the right amount in 33 three-month periods out of a total of 117 three-month periods, it did this 28.2% of the time. Subject to all the qualifications given above, the odds of it going up the required amount in the next three months are just about 28.2%. And that is probably too low for a bet that will get you only 2 to 1. You might find, however, that in most of those 33 three-month periods, the stock had gone up much more than the amount needed for you to double your investment. It may be that in 30 of those times it went up enough for you to quadruple your investment. Now you are talking about something that gives you fair odds, namely, a 30 out of 117, or 25.6%, chance to quadruple your money. This is worth considering.

Rule #7 is therefore to check a long-term chart for the stock whose call you are considering buying and make certain that in the past it has gone up by the amount needed to achieve your investment goal enough times to give you odds equal to what you expect to get from your call.

Strategy Rule Number 8: Never put all your eggs in one basket. The experienced call buyer expects to lose on half his calls, and perhaps more. He does not expect to lose money on his calls as a whole because he expects to win far more than 100% on the calls that are successful. Nevertheless, this type of strategy requires as wide a diversification as possible. And even the small investor can easily scatter his purchases over at least five different calls.

But you must first overcome the temptation to concentrate on one or two stocks. You may think that a certain call is far more likely to be profitable than any other. The stock may be selling at the strike price, the premium may be modest, the Beta may be fabulous, and the charts may show that it has made the gain you need to double your investment at least 40 times in the last ten years.

The temptation will be almost overpowering to put all your eggs in this one basket. And in addition to the statistical indicators, you may have an inner feeling that the stock is poised on the brink of a tremendous price break-through. My advice is simple: resist the temptation.

Anyone experienced in buying calls will tell you that you can never tell in advance which calls are going to work out and which are not. All you know is that, based on past performance, half of them are not going to work out. So don't risk your entire investment on one call, when that may turn out to be the one that goes down.

Always keep in mind that when you buy a call, there is no tomorrow. The stock buyer who sees his stock go down can decide to hang onto it anyhow because he is convinced that eventually it will get back up to where it belongs. But for a call buyer who sees the stock go down, or even just stay still—when the final gong sounds on the trading floor the day the option expires, that's the end of the ball game. And mighty Casey has struck out. Finally and permanently. Your call is worthless, absolutely, and irrevocably, and for infinity.

There is no reason why you shouldn't diversify. In the stock market anyone buying less than 100 shares pays slightly more for his stock than the 100 lot purchaser. This is not true for options. The price per option (on 100 shares of stock) is the same whether you buy 1 or 1,000. Only the commission cost per option is less as volume goes up.

The only point to watch for is that the minimum commission at most brokerage firms for any option of over $1 is $25. Therefore, if you are buying one option and your actual commission should be less than $25, you will be paying excess commissions. But two will get you up over the minimum. The actual number of different calls to buy is a matter of judgment, but since you want to purchase only those that are the very best for you, I would suggest restricting yourself to between five and ten stocks.

Rule #8 may be summarized very easily. Since most calls turn out to be a loss to the purchaser, you must be willing to lose your investment on some calls because you expect to more than make it up on the ones that are winners. But since you cannot predict with any degree of accuracy which calls will be the winners, it is necessary to give yourself protection by diversifying your purchases among a number of different calls. Far better to win some and lose some than to have one great big loser.

SUMMARY

Now you know the eight rules of strategy for buying calls to make you as successful a call buyer as the experts. This chapter on buying calls may be summarized by stating that the purchasers of calls will lose their money much of the time. The general purpose of these rules is to reduce those losses to a minimum while making certain that you actually get to keep as much of the profits as possible.

Rule 1. Never buy a call when the stock is more than slightly below the strike price. The premium of the call may be low and it may look like a bargain, but it's not nearly enough of a bargain. The odds are against any call buyer, and when you expect the price of the stock to go up before it can even begin to cut into your loss, you're really stacking the deck against yourself. Get a fair deal, buy a call where the stock is in the area of the strike price.

Rule 2. Don't buy a call where the stock is more than slightly above the strike price. This is simply making you underwrite an insurance policy for the owner of the stock. You are paying so much for the present value of the stock that is above the strike price, that you won't have enough money to buy many options. Because of the huge cost of these calls, your upside leverage is small, too small. And the downside risk is still there. It may be small, but it is there, and the fact that it is small is no consolation if you are one of the unlucky ones who has to watch that stock fall and fall. True, this may be a more conservative investment than others, but if you want conservative investments you don't want to buy calls in the first place. Calls are for swingers. If you want a safe investment, ask your stock broker for his recommendation. It won't be calls.

Rule 3. Check all three option durations on a cost-per-week basis. If there is a large discrepancy, it would be well worth your while to buy the more economical one, even if it costs more because it is for the longer term.

Rule 4. To fully comprehend the cost of your call, annualize the premium. Although your stock doesn't have to go up nearly as much as if the call actually were for a year, this exercise will give you a clearer understanding of the rate at which the stock will have to climb before you can make any money. And if it turns out that the annual rate of gain is staggering, ask yourself why the stock should climb at such a high rate in the next three months, if you will concede that it wouldn't do so for an entire year.

Rule 5. Stocks go up, and stocks go down. A statement so obvious that one sometimes forgets its everlasting truth. But if you have bought an option and watched it double in price, only to have the stock fall back down again leaving you holding a worthless option, you will not forget this statement so quickly. The solution is to sell out half your position when the option price doubles. Other advantages are that you are maintaining the amount of money at risk at your original level, and you are now free of any psychological worries because no matter what happens, you will no longer be able to lose any money from this position.

Rule 6. Before you buy a call, know the Beta for the underlying stock. This is a number which tells you whether a stock is likely to make price swings which are larger, smaller, or about equal to the price movements of the market as a whole. Since you are not going to make any money on your call unless the price of the stock goes up substantially in a relatively short period of time, it is important to select a stock with a high enough Beta to do the job.

Rule 7. Check the ten-year record of the stock before you buy a call. While the future is never going to repeat the past exactly, it is also true that the past is prologue to the future. To gain the most from the past record of your stock, compute how much the stock would have to increase in order to double your investment in the call. Then go over a ten-year chart of the stock to learn how many times in the past the stock has gone up that much in the period of time left on the option you are considering. If the stock has risen that amount only a few times, the odds are sadly against you and another call would be indicated.

Rule 8. Diversify your investment by buying at least five different calls, and perhaps as many as ten. The experienced call buyer expects to lose money on many of his call purchases. Therefore, it makes good sense to be sure that you don't invest all your money in one of those that turns out to be worthless. Play the percentages and you'll do better.

These are the eight rules for sensible call buying. They have been developed from experience, and will stand you in good stead.

SELLING COVERED CALLS

3

A conservative method for increasing the return on stocks

Option trading is generally recommended only for investors who have money they can spare for speculative investment. If an investor would suffer financial hardship from losing his entire investment, then he should neither buy nor sell naked options or engage in option spreads. There is, however, one method of taking advantage of options that is recommended for investors who are not willing to assume the high risks associated with the methods described elsewhere in this book, and this is to sell covered calls. A call is covered when its seller owns the underlying stock. For example, if a person sold a call option on RCA when he owned 100 shares of RCA common stock, he would have sold a "covered RCA call."

Covered call writing has now become so established as a prudent, conservative method of investing that it has received official recognition by almost every regulatory body that has the control over investments. The Comptroller of the Currency, who regulates the national banks, has ruled that covered option writing is appropriate for use by bank trust departments in investing their trust funds. The insurance commissioners of most of the states have now ruled that insurance companies may use covered option writing on a portion of their own investments, and various officials charged with seeing that pension plans are properly administered have given their blessings to the use of covered option writing for pension plans. In addition, an enormous number of conversative, professionally managed investment groups have begun to use covered option writing, including church, university, and college endowment funds and union welfare plans. Clearly, the time has now come when the speculative stigma of options should be completely and irrevocably removed from the concept of writing covered options.

Perhaps nothing can explain so well why covered option writing is appropriate for the conservative investor as to note that it is more conservative than simply owning stock. By its very definition, the word "conservative" means to be more concerned with protecting what one has than with increasing it through possible changes in market prices. Covered option writing by definition protects the investor from declines in the price of the stock up to the amount of the premium received from the sale of the option. Thus, covered call writing is conservative in that one of its basic effects is to protect against a downside move in the price of the stock. Its other purpose is to make money on the future time value of the option price. As we shall see in this chapter, these benefits are bought with the cost of giving up some or all of the chance to make a greater profit from an upward movement in the price of the stock. Thus, covered option writing perfectly matches the concept of the conservative investor, i.e., one who is interested in protecting his capital first and, second, in making a modest return on his investment while foregoing potentially large profits from changes in the price of the stock.

There are two other reasons for the rapidly increasing popularity of covered option writing. The first is that covered option writing from the viewpoint of economic participation is about 90% owning common stock, and since investors already have a very good concept of what owning stock is all about, it is a relatively easy matter for them to learn about writing options against stock that they will continue to own. It is not like asking an investor to write two-on-one option spreads, where he is starting out with a totally foreign concept. Here the concept is to continue owning common stock, but to give oneself some downside protection and to take in some profit if the stock stays still or moves up.

The second reason that covered writing has become so popular is that it is one of the few forms of investing where one can compute exactly what the return on investment will be if the position is successful. When one buys a stock one can compute the dividend, but the result of that investment a year from the date of purchase is going to be determined mostly by what has happened to the price of the stock, and only to a minor degree by the amount of the dividend. Similarly, when one buys an option, there is no way to calculate in advance how much profit one can expect to make. And many serious investors like to go into a situation where they can calculate in advance that they should be able to make an annualized profit of, let's say, 27% on their investment. It gives a degree of certainty to the investment which is very comforting. As we will see, there is no guarantee that the investor will actually make his expected profit, but at least there is a wide parameter of stock prices at which he will be able to make that expected profit, and in a world of unknowns, it is worth something to have a precise figure that one can lean on.

Disappointments

Perhaps no other concept in the investment world has been so thoroughly sold by so many brokers who sincerely believed in it as that of covered option writing. And it is also unfortunately true that many of those who have undertaken covered writing have been disappointed with the results. There are a number of reasons for this, and after you have read this chapter, hopefully you will be able to avoid some of the pitfalls that can lead to this disappointment. Perhaps the original cause of the disappointment was that some brokers oversold the idea. Some almost put it in terms of "How can you lose? If the stock stays where it is or goes up, you will make 18% in six months, and even if the stock goes down, you have the income from the option to offset the loss."

The problem arises when some of the stocks under option are more volatile than one would have expected. To use a simple example, suppose that two stocks are both 100, and both have 100 strike price options at $10. An investor buys 100 shares of each, and sells one option on each. Stock #1 goes up to 150, and the investor makes his $10 per share, which he receives from selling the option. This is fine because he has made his 10% profit in six months, just as promised. Stock #2 is not so fortunate, and declines by 50% to $50 a share. The investor has received $10 from the sale of the option, so that his loss is cut from $50 to $40 a share. Combining his loss of $40 on stock #2 with his profit of $10 on stock #1, we come up with a loss of $30. Not so good. If he had just bought the two stocks and not written options, his $50 loss on the one would have been completely offset by the $50 gain on the other. So the first cause for disappointment comes when some of the stocks in an option-writing portfolio decline steeply in value.

The second disappointment with covered option writing has been that the level of option premiums has dropped almost continuously from the time options first came out until the writing of this second edition. There are many reasons for this. Perhaps the most important is that, by and large, option buyers have not made money during this period. In fact, they have lost large amounts of money, despite the fact that there have been exceptions during brief periods of bull markets and for certain stocks which produced enormous profits. But on the whole, option buyers have lost money, and when you have lost a large amount of money buying options, you don't feel like buying them again, even if you can still afford to. Thus, the demand for options has decreased.

Second, more and more institutions are beginning to get interested in writing options on their vast stock portfolios. This has greatly increased the supply of options. Applying fundamental principles of economics to option prices, we find that when demand falls and supply rises, the price of the commodity must go down. And basically that is what has happened. So that a person who acquired a stock for the purpose of writing an on-the-money option for six months for 15% found that six months later he might be able to get 10% for a six-month option, and that next time he was able to get only 7.5%. Each time, he is giving up the same upside potential profit, and he is assuming the same downside risk on the stock.

In summary, selling covered options has become a much tougher strategy to make money on, and thus is it more important than ever that anyone who wants to embark upon such a course be fully familiar with the potential, the risk, and all the rules of strategy which can possibly help him. That is what this chapter will try to do.

Limited risk

The covered call technique does not involve any risk if the price of the stock soars upward. In that case, a covered option seller loses money on his call when the stock goes up but he offsets the loss by gaining an even greater amount on his stock. Thus, he cannot lose money by the stock's rise. In effect, he has perfectly hedged the risk incurred by being short the call, by being long the stock.

As an example let us assume you sell an RCA call with a $25 strike for a $2 premium when the stock is at $25. If the price of the stock rises to $26, let's assume that the premium on the call will go up to $3. Although you have now lost $1 on the sale of this call, you have made $1 on the increase in value of your stock. If the price of RCA now advances another $3 to $29, the price of the call may go up by $2. Thus, every step of the way, the loss on your call is either exactly offset by the gain on your common stock, or more than offset by it when the stock goes up by more than the option and the future time value of the option shrinks.

Finally, when the expiration date of the call arrives, there is no need for you to produce any money to cover. You simply sit back, and your shares of stock are called away from you.

What is the advantage to the seller of the covered call? The advantage is that he gets to keep the entire premium, and this can add up to a very hefty percentage of the value of the common stock, considering that there is no risk of loss when the stock goes up. The gains measured as percent return on investment are not usually as attractive as for a naked seller who does not have to cover, but then the risk simply isn't anywhere near as great.

The owner of 100 shares of common stock who decides to sell a call on his shares does so because he has made a decision that he would rather take a given certain gain on his stock in the next period of time than take the risk that his stock will perhaps go up much more, but perhaps will not go up at all.

To continue with the RCA example, when we started out, our investor owned RCA with a value of $25. At the end of the example he had received a premium of $2 and he had tendered his stock for $25, so that he had a total of $27 for a profit of $2. This is a gain of about 8.5%, which is nothing to sneeze at, especially if we assume that the call was for the current quarter, so that the annualized return is 34%, excluding commission, but see Chapter 9 for an explanation of how important commissions are. This profit was made without taking the big risk of losing money if the price of RCA was to go sky high. Why doesn't everyone sell calls on their stock all the time? There are reasons for not doing so.

Profit-limiting decisions

The seller of a covered call must make two decisions before he sells a call. I would not call them risk-taking decisions, but rather profit-limiting decisions, because they create two disadvantages concerning potential future profits.

The first limitation that a covered call seller must accept is that he is giving up possible large future appreciation in exchange for a premium that rarely if ever will exceed 10% for a three-month period. (An exception to this would be the case in which the price of the stock is above the strike price, but this is only because the premium for the option then represents a part of the present price of the stock.) By selling a call, the investor is giving someone else the chance to make all the appreciation over the strike price (minus the future time value of the option).

If one thinks of a stock as a vertical bar graph, one could say that selling a call is like breaking the stock up into two portions, with the buyer of the call purchasing the top part of the bar. Therefore if a person believes that his stock is grossly underpriced; that there is about to be a major market breakthrough; that his stock could easily double in value within the next six months to a year—then under these circumstances he should not sell someone else the right to skim this cream off the top of his stock. So, disadvantage number one for a potential seller of a covered call is that he must be willing to give up the chance to make any gain over the strike price on his stock except for the premium he receives.

Disadvantage number two is that regardless of how badly his stock performs during the period when the call is outstanding, he will not be able to sell the stock unless he buys back the option he sold, or is willing to accept the great risk of being a naked call seller. This means that the covered call writer is subject to the risk of loss from a decline in the value of his stock, although this is offset by the amount of the premium received.

What kind of investor can best benefit from selling covered calls? The answer is anyone who wants to make a good annual return on his stock and who is (1) willing to absorb the risks of a downside turn in the price of the stock, and (2) willing to give up the possibility of any spectacular gains if the stock suddenly takes off. But the rewards for making these two sacrifices can be meaningful, and they can come without any risks other than the two mentioned above.

Making your decision

So, if this concept appeals to you, here's how to do it. Buy 100 shares (or multiples of 100) of a good-quality stock that you are willing to own for the long haul, and for which calls are listed. It is important to select a solid stock that you are willing to stick with even if the price should go down substantially because, as pointed out above, even after you have sold a call, you continue to bear the risk of loss if the stock declines significantly in price. Then make up your mind that you are willing to part with the chance to make more than a 5% to 7% return every three months. If you think that the stock will go up more than that, then selling a call on it is not for you.

If you have made the two decisions above, however, then you are ready to sit back and make up to a 28% annual return on your investment assuming your stock does not decline below the strike price. And your rate of return can be even higher. The reason for this is that when you sell a covered call, in the eyes of your broker you are selling a call short, but instead of the usual cash margin requirement, you are depositing the stock instead. It is not necessary to put up fully paid-for stock, however. The stock used to cover the call can be owned on margin. This greatly increases the return.

Taking a typical lively stock that is selling at the strike price, the return might be 10% for a six-month period. This works out to 20% a year if you have paid in full for the stock. But if you have bought the stock on full margin, and put up only 50% of the price of the stock, your 10% premium now represents a return of 20% on your investment twice a year, or 40% annually.

Please note, however, that these are gross returns before commissions and interest expenses and that these costs have a surprisingly great impact on reducing actual returns. If you are buying 300 shares on margin of a $40 stock paying a 2% annual dividend, and you are selling a six-month on-the-money option for $4, the return to you, excluding transaction costs, is actually 25%. You buy the stock for $40, pay 50% on margin, making it $20, take in $4 from the option, leaving $16 which it costs you. The $4 received from the option is 25% of this. If we deduct all transaction costs, including interest on your margin debit at 7%, the actual net return on your six-month investment, using the commission figures in Appendixes G and H and assuming the stock is called away, would not be 25%, but rather 15%. Even more dramatically, if the return without transaction costs had been 15%, the actual return less transaction costs would be only 5%. So you can see what an enormous difference they make. Of course, if the price of the stock declines, it will not be possible to achieve the returns on your investment. See Appendix J for a worksheet showing exactly how to compute the annualized return on covered writes whether purchased for cash or on margin.

It is worth noting that the seller of a covered call continues to receive the dividend on the stock. In some covered writing situations the yield from the dividend makes up a very large proportion of the total expected profit. This is particularly true in the case of utilities, where the dividend is large and the option premiums are very low.

Premature assignments. One potential problem that all covered writers have is that their stock may be prematurely assigned, i.e., called away from them. If you made your original estimate of the return from your investment based upon receiving two dividends, and the stock is assigned the day before the stock goes ex-dividend on the second dividend, your return could be substantially lower than you had expected. There is no way that you can prevent your stock from being assigned. The Options Clearing Corporation (OCC) makes assignments to various brokerage firms on a random basis, and then each brokerage firm allocates these assignments in accordance with a method it has previously elected. Each brokerage firm can decide to make its assignments either (1) on the basis of first in, first out, that is, the first person to write the option is the first one assinged, or (2) a random assignment to everyone who is short the option, and (3) certain large option writers, primarily institutions, at some firms can elect to have all or none of their options exercised to save them from the bother of being exercised on one option a day.

Premature exercise is particularly likely to happen to an in-the-money option on the day before it goes ex-dividend when there is only a short period of time remaining on the option. The reason for this is that some of the option owners may wish to exercise the options rather than sell them. By exercising the day before the stock goes ex-dividend, they receive the stock for the same cost as if they had waited until the expiration, but in addition to the stock they pick up a free dividend. The moral is that when you are computing your expected return from a covered option situation, perhaps you should not count on the final dividend if the stock goes ex-dividend just a week or two before expiration. Obviously, the larger the dividend the greater the chance of this happening.

"Getting a cash flow". One claim that is sometimes made for covered option writing must be particularly well qualified if it is to be accurate. This is the claim that "We'll sell some options in order to get a cash flow." This presumably is being said to someone who is now getting an income from the dividends on the stock and would like to get a higher yield. The difficulty with this claim is that it will work only if the investor is willing to let the stock be called away when the option expires. If he is not, then the sale of covered calls may not produce cash, and could do just the opposite. For example, if your stock is now at 50, and you sell a 50 option for $5, you certainly have created a cash flow, and you could have your brokerage firm send you a check for $500. But the story doesn't end here.

If the stock remains at $50 at the expiration of the option all is fine and good. If, however, the stock rises to $60, and for reasons such as high capital gains tax exposure you do not want to part with that stock, you must now buy back the option for $10, for a cost of $1,000. Instead of creating $500 in cash, this maneuver has used up $500 in cash. So if someone tells you that he wants to create some cash flow on your portfolio, make sure that you realize this might not be the case unless you are willing to have the stock called away at $50 a share. It must be noted that in either case you are making a profit of $500; it is just that if the stock appreciates too much you are not doing the very thing you set out to do, namely creating a positive cash flow.

IMPLEMENTING A COVERED CALL PROGRAM

So much for the theory of selling covered calls. If you're not convinced by now that this is for you, just skip the rest of this chapter and go on to the next. If you are interested, you probably have questions about the best way to go about selling covered calls. The next few pages will try to answer them.

If you already own 100 shares or more of a stock that has a call traded on an exchange, then your decisions are already partly made for you. Your only questions concern which of the available options you should sell. Since there are always at least three durations available, your first question is probably whether you should sell the shortest-term call, the medium-term one, or the longest. The first step in answering this question is to get all the options on an equal basis so that you can compare them in a meaningful manner. The easiest way to do this is to compute what each call is paying in terms of weeks or months. Generally the shortest one should be paying the highest return on a per-week basis. Just remember that the longer-term options don't involve such frequent commissions, and this is a significant savings that should be taken into consideration.

Determining the best duration

If you want to let your theories on the market's future come into play and guide you, then you can make further refinements. If you believe there is a good chance your stock will decline in value during the current period, then, when the current call expires, you will not be able to get nearly as high a premium for the next term. In such a case you should sell the longer-term call, even if it does not pay the highest premium on a per-week basis, because over the full span of the longer call it will give a higher return per week.

To illustrate, let's assume you own a volatile stock with a current market price of 100. For the 100 strike price option, the shortest-duration call might be 6, the next one 10, and the longest one 13. Assuming that these prices are for the beginning of an option quarter, the per-month return on the calls is respectively 2, 1.67, and 1.44. Normally you would of course sell the shortest-term call, expecting that if the call is not exercised you will sell another short-term call for the same amount, continuing indefinitely until (assuming circumstances stay the same for purposes of this example, which in real life they will certainly not) you will have received a total of 3 times $6, or $18, over the nine-month period versus the $13 that you would have gotten if you had originally sold the long-term call. And thanks to the liquidity of the options exchanges you will always be able to sell a new call on your stock as soon as each old one expires.

If you are afraid that in three months the stock will be down 10 and selling at 90, you should sell the long-term call. The reason is that if you sell the short-term call for 6, and if you are correct that the stock will be selling at 90 when the call expires, the premium on the next three-month 100 strike price call may have dropped to around 2, and the same thing will be true in another three months if the stock stays at 90. Thus you will receive total premium income of $10 over a period of nine months, when you could have received $13 by selling the long-term call. And you will pay three sets of commissions instead of one.

If the price falls to 90, the directors of the options exchanges will start trading a call with a strike price of 90, and the premium at this strike price for three months could well be 5½ or 5. This is the call you could sell after your first three-month call expired. But the danger here is that if the price of your stock then goes up to 100, to buy back the option for $10 you incur a $5 loss and in effect lock in a loss.

On the other hand if you believe that your stock has a good probability of going up during the next three months, then you should sell the shortest-term call. The reason is that if your stock does indeed do as well as you expect it to, you will be free to cover the call and reinvest your money elsewhere. Perhaps you will decide to sell another call at a much higher premium. For example, if your stock has risen to $110, you could allow your stock to be called away and be left with the $100 you received for your stock (the strike price) and the $6 premium.

Using the perfect hindsight with which we are all gifted, you will realize that you made a mistake by selling a call on the stock. Remember, however, that we are playing the averages and you should expect to lose a few. Furthermore you could well argue that getting a 6% return in three months, equaling 24% a year, is hardly losing. Getting back to our example, you now have $106 and you're a free person, able to do with it what you will. Had you sold the 9-month call you would be sitting with your capital tied up in the stock and with no chance of investing it in anything else, or of ever making more than the premium you already received.

Having sold the three-month option, you might even decide to scrape up $4, add it to your proceeds and buy 100 shares again. You could of course at this point sell another call, and if there is now a call with a 110 strike price you will be receiving a premium of $6 or $7 again. At the end of six months you will have made a total profit from premiums of $12 to $13. And you can make another $6 or $7 in the third quarter. The fellow who sold the long-term call will just be sitting there waiting for the nine months to finally expire so that he can get out with his $60 and the $13 premium.

These examples show how you should plan your strategy concerning duration if you believe that the stock is going to go up, or if you believe that it is going to go down. But what if you really don't have any strong feelings? This, incidentally, is the best attitude to have in my opinion. In that case you follow the general and simple rule of selling the call that gives you the highest return on a per-week basis.

Determining best strike price

You may have to answer one other major question if you own a stock and are planning to sell a covered call, because your stock probably has calls available at two or more strike prices. This occurs because when an option first comes out and a stock is selling at 102, the strike price will be set at 100. Then if the price of the stock declines to 95, a new option will be issued with the strike price at 90. If the stock price declines further, another call will be issued and so on indefinitely. Thus, at one time Avon had no less than six different strike prices. What are the consequences to the covered call seller of choosing a high strike price rather than a low one?

Obviously a low strike price gives a higher premium but the amount of this premium, which represents future time value, will be relatively low. And it is only the future time value of the option which is the potential profit. The rest of the premium represents its current cash value and provides downside protection but does not represent an opportunity to make any money. A high strike price gives a much lower premium but the future time value of the option may be higher. In addition, if the option is out of the money, the call writer can make any profit caused by the stock rising up to the strike price.

Figure 7. Writing covered calls with different strike prices
(Price of stock when calls sold: 78)

The call with the highest strike price will be the most profitable if the stock goes up, but the call with the lowest strike price will perform the best if the stock goes down. See p. 69 for an answer to the quandry of which is preferable for the covered call writer.

To use an example (see Figure 7), when Hewlett-Packard was selling at 78 its five-month calls at one time were priced as follows:

70 strike price: 11½
80 strike price: 5¼
90 strike price: 2

If we assume for purposes of this example that the stock remains at 78 until the expiration date of the option, the seller of the 70 call will realize 70 from the exercise of the stock plus the 11½ premium, making a total of 81½. The seller of the 80 strike price call will receive 78, if he chooses to sell it, for the stock plus a premium of 5¼, making a total of 83¼. The seller of the 90 will keep his stock, which we will value at 78, and will have the premium of 2, making a total of 80.

On the other hand, if the price of the stock had gone up to 90, the seller of the 90 call would be the clear winner, because the seller of the 70 option would have the same amount as when the stock was 78, i.e., 81½ and the seller of the 80 option would receive 80 for his stock plus the 5¼ option premium, making a total of 85¼. The seller of the 90 call would have the value of his stock, $90, plus his premium of $2, giving a total of $92. Sounds as if the smart strategy is to sell the call with the highest strike price. But wait.

What if the price of the stock had gone down? Let us suppose that the price falls from 78 to 68. In that case, none of the options will be exercised, and each seller will be left with the stock and his premium. So, each call seller has stock worth $68, and the investor who sold the Hewlett-Packard 70 call has a premium of 11½ in his bank account, the one who sold the 80 strike price call has 5¼, while the big winner in our previous example ends up with a measly 2. As the great commercial asked a few years ago, "What's a poor mother to do?"

To answer this question, one has to go back to an understanding of the basic reason for selling covered calls in the first place. The reason is that the sophisticated investor is willing to give up a large potential future gain, which may never materialize, in exchange for a certain gain in hand now, which is the amount of the premium. How much is the actual premium being paid for the option in this example?

At the 80 and 90 strike prices, the answer is clear. It is the full amount of the option. To determine how much is actually being paid for the option at the 70 strike price, as opposed to how much of the premium represents a payment for the current price of the stock, one has to find the difference between the strike price and the current price of the stock. Since the stock is now selling at 78 and the strike price is 70, for a difference of 8, we subtract 8 from the premium of 11½ to learn that the actual amount of the premium paid for the future time value of the option is 3½. Thus the amounts paid for the future time value of the option are 2 for the 90 strike price call, 5¼ for the 80, and 3½ for the 70.

So that the highest price for the future time value of the option is at the strike price closest to the price of the stock. This stands to reason, because the premium for the high 90 strike price call must reflect the fact that the stock is not very apt to rise 12 points to reach the strike price, and the premium for the future time value of the option at the low strike price of 70 is small because a large amount of the total premium represents a heavy insurance premium in case the price of the stock falls. Since the call buyer can only lose from this "insurance" he demands a reduction in the call premium as compensation.

Preference for lower strike price. Now, back to our basic philosophy of selling a covered call, which is to get an assured income. The one big risk is that the price of the stock you hold will fall. Therefore, my general rule is that when selling a covered option, you should give first preference to the call with the lowest strike price. This gives you as much protection as you can get against the one Achilles heel of selling a covered option. Of course, if the price of the stock goes up, you would have been better off selling at a higher strike price, but so what? You're still making a good profit with the lower strike price. The proper mental conditioning to have when you sell a covered call is that you are translating possible future windfalls into specific present gain. The moment you sell your call, you have accomplished this conversion.

In our example, the moment you sell the 70 strike price call you have made an extra 3½ on your stock, which turns out to be 4.4%. Since this gain will be earned in five months, it means that you are earning an annual rate of 10%. This is not bad, especially when you consider that the buyer of your call is giving you free insurance for every single dollar that your stock could fall down to 70.

Obviously, if you strongly believe that your stock has a good chance of rising you may wish to sell at the highest strike price. In a way you might think of a high strike price option as selling a partial option. You get to keep the benefit of a fairly good rise in the price of the stock, and only have to turn over to the call buyer the excess increase in your stock, which wouldn't bother you a bit. But, if the price goes down, you will be left with a loss on your stock and only the tiny premium to console you.

SELECTING THE RIGHT STOCK

If you do not already own any stock and would like to sell a covered call, you face the major decision of deciding which stock to purchase. You will limit yourself to stocks whose calls are traded on the exchanges. First, you should check the quotations to find out what the premiums are for the various stocks. The amount of the premium varies greatly depending upon many factors. For details on this see Chapter 1.

It is sufficient to note here that if you are buying stock for the specific purpose of selling calls on it, you should first select a stock whose call has a reasonably high premium. The Hewlett-Packard example mentioned is a stock that carries an unusually large premium. Utilities usually have the smallest premiums. Generally the lower-priced stocks bear the higher percentage premiums. For a detailed discussion on the relationship between volatility and option premiums see Strategy Rule #3 later in this chapter. For sources of information which evaluate options in relation to the volatility of the underlying stocks and point out options which currently are overpriced, see Appendix I.

Second, you should select a stock that you personally will be happy to own and hold. For instance, if you feel that there will soon be a downturn in retail store profits and stock prices, there is no point in buying K Mart stock just because it may have a high premium or be attractive in other ways. Pick a stock that you would want to own, just as if you were not going to sell a call. Remember, if the price of the stock falls, you will be left holding the stock, and the only risk in selling calls is that the price of the stock may go down.

Third, notice what the strike prices are for the stock you are considering. As suggested earlier in this chapter, the safest call to sell is the one with the lowest strike price. So if you are seeking safety, pick a stock whose call has a strike price well below the current market price of the stock. On the other hand, if you are an optimist, you can pick a stock that has a strike price well above its current price, realizing, however, that this will reduce the amount of your premium and provide you with little downside protection.

While checking the strike prices available, it would be a good idea to check not only the current option period, but those for the next three-month period, and the one after that, because not all strike prices may be available for future periods. If the price of the stock has declined substantially, then the highest strike price is not going to be offered for the longest-duration call.

USING MARGIN

One of the interesting aspects of covered writing is that the use of margin can increase the percentage profit on your investment by a suprisingly large amount. Investors in the stock market know that if the maximum margin is 50%, a brokerage firm will lend you one half the money needed to purchase a stock, so that in order to buy a $50 stock you have to put up only $25. In regular stock trading this will double your leverage. But strangely enough, when it comes to covered writing, it is possible for margin to increase your return even more. The following example will show how. To simplify things I have excluded interest charges against the amount you are borrowing from the brokerage firm, so the results may be slightly overstated, but often the amount of dividends received from the additional stock you buy on margin can go a long way toward offsetting the interest cost.

In the first example you buy the stock for cash:

Buy stock for 12	12
Sell 10 strike price option for 3	−3
Cash required	9
Potential profit (future time value of option)	1
Profit on investment	11%

In this second example, the stock is purchased on margin:

Buy stock for 12	12
Cash required = 50% of the cost	6
Sell 10 strike price option for 3	−3
Cash required	3
Potential profit	1
Profit on investment	33%

In this example, we can see that the use of margin did not double the return, it actually tripled it. The reason that margin can increase the rate of return so dramatically is that while the investor pays for only half the stock, the entire premium is applied toward this half of the cost. Thus, a three-dollar option is paying for six dollars' worth of stock. Now that premiums are down, anyone who is legally able to purchase stock on margin (this excludes many trusts, pension funds, custodial accounts, and endowment funds) should seriously consider doing so. Much of the risk usually associated with a margin account is reduced, provided that Strategy Rule #2 of this chapter is followed.

Once you have written your call you could wait until it expires and then decide what to do next. But in most cases it will be to your advantage to carefully monitor the position to determine whether there are changes which could be made before expiration which will increase your profitability or decrease your downside risk or do perhaps both. If you are writing in-the-money options, you may wish to see all your stocks called away. In such a case, the only concern you have is if the stock should fall below the strike price. See Strategy Rule #2 for the correct procedures.

Two times to take action. In all other option-writing programs you will be watching your positions to see if you are earning the maximum amount from the future time value of the options you have sold. There are therefore two situations which should immediately alert you to the need for action. The first is if the current price of any option you have sold declines to a small fraction. The exact amount depends upon the price of the stock, but certainly if any of your outstanding options are selling for ¼ or less it is time to do something. The reason for this is twofold: (1) no matter what happens, the maximum profit you can make from that option is only 25¢ a share, and (2) your downside protection is now only 25¢ a share, which is almost meaningless. This reduction in the price of your outstanding options results either from the passing of time or a decline in the price of your underlying stock, or a combination of both.

The second situation that should alert you to immediate action is if the future time value of your outstanding in-the-money options has fallen to a small amount, such as ¼ on low-priced stocks and a relatively small amount on higher-priced stocks. As you may recall, the future time value of an in-the-money option is found by adding the price of the option onto its strike price and subtracting the price of the stock, and represents the maximum profit you will be able to make from the option. When this amount begins to approach zero, there is no point in maintaining the position. You still have the chance of loss if the stock declines, but you no longer have the possibility of a meaningful profit, so you should take action at once to change this. An in-the-money option reaches a low future time value with the passage of time and with an increase in the price of the underlying stock.

MANAGING THE COVERED WRITING PROGRAM

There are four types of action you can take in managing a covered writing program: (1) rolling out your option, which means buying in the option you previously sold and selling another at the same strike price with a longer duration; (2) rolling up, which means buying in the option you previously sold and selling one with the same expiration date but a higher strike price, typically done when the stock has gone up in price; (3) rolling down, i.e., buying in your existing option and selling one with the same expiration at a lower strike price; (4) buying in your existing option and not writing any other option. This means that you are out of the option-writing program and this is typically done when there simply are no options available which meet your criteria for writing. You then should make a decision of whether you want to hold the stock without writing any options on it, or whether you want to sell the stock. Let us now look at each of these strategies in more detail.

Rolling out

Rolling out is the simplest of the strategies, and like the others, should be entered as a spread order. That is, rather than buying your existing option at a certain price and then trying to sell the longer one, the orders should be placed simultaneously for a net credit. If you were trying to buy back your April 45 for ¼ and sell the July 45 for 1¼, you would enter the order as a spread order for a 1-point credit, since it makes little difference to you what the prices of the options are as long as you get one point more for the July option than you pay for the April.

The big question in rolling out is when to do it. If the price of the stock were to stay constant, then you would be best off waiting until your current option expires before writing the next one. But since your stock is probably going to fluctuate, you take the risk that by waiting too long the credit you might be able to get by rolling out now will be less. If your option is out of the money now, and the stock goes down, you will be able to get less for the longer-duration option later. If your option is in the money now and it goes up, you will also get less of a credit for the spread if you wait. You should roll out when the future time value of your present option has declined to the point where the future profit potential no longer justifies the risk of holding the stock.

The decision of which duration option to roll out to is made in exactly the same way as you decided which option to sell in the first place when you entered into the position.

Rolling up

Rolling up is what you do when your stock has gone up in value, and should be done as soon as the future time value of your existing option declines due to an increase in the price of the stock. By then an option will be trading at a higher strike price, and it will be offering more future time value. Another way of deciding when you should roll up is if doing so will result in your new option bearing the same relation to the stock price as the original option did to the stock price when you put it on. That is, if you originally decided to write an option one point out of the money, so that you wrote the 35 option when the stock was 34, and the stock is now 39, you would be keeping with your original plan by rolling up from the 35 to the 40 option.

Supposing that when you bought the stock for 34, the 35 option you sold was 2. Now, a few weeks later, with the stock at 39, the 35 option you sold might be selling for 4½ and there would be a 40 option with the same expiration date which might be selling for 2. You could therefore buy back your 35 option and sell the 40 option for a combined cost of 2½ points, which is to say that you are rolling up for a 2½ debit. Normally in a covered writing program one likes to take in money, but in this instance you are paying out $250 for each 100 shares you own. The reason you do this is that for $250 you have increased the maximum value to you of each share on the expiration date of the option from $35 to $40. Whether you are actually able to benefit from this rolling up or not will depend upon how high the shares are selling at the option's expiration. If they are selling at $40 or better your rolling up has been well worth while, because for a cash expenditure of $2.50 a share, you have increased their value to you by $5.00. If the stock stays at 39, you have increased their value to you by $4.

The danger in rolling up is that if the stock falls back to where it was, you have spent cash and received nothing of value in return. If the stock falls back down to $34, you are left with stock worth that much a share, and you are out the $2.50 a share it cost you to roll up. In short, your roll-up has been a complete failure. This kind of whipsaw will happen from time to time, but the law of averages says that the stock will continue on up at least as often as it falls down. And when it stays at $39 you will come out ahead by $1.50. Thus rolling up does represent something of a risk, because you could lose the entire cost of the operation. But generally it is worth it, and when it works it results in making the covered program far more successful than you originally anticipated.

Let us assume that you sold your original 35 option in this example for $2. That, plus the possible $1 increase in price from 34 to 35, was all that you expected to make from this option expiration period. But by rolling up when the stock went to $39, you were able to squeeze out an additional $1.50 (assuming the stock stays at $39 or an additional $2.50 if it goes above $40), which means that you will realize a 50% to 83% greater profit from this position than you had originally expected. And if the stock goes up to 44, there is no reason why you would not roll up again, with similar gains in potential profit. To conclude our discussion of rolling up, while it requires an expenditure of cash that could be a total loss if the stock comes back down, the roll-up requires taking no more risk than the original covered writing position and offers the opportunity to increase your profit from the position by a very substantial amount.

Rolling down

Rolling down is the saddest of the strategies and the most difficult to do. It is sad because it is done only when the stock has depreciated substantially in price and the position is already a loser, and futhermore, rolling down will not transform a losing position into a winning position. On the contrary, it actually locks in a loss, which is what makes it so difficult to do. Let's use the same example we did for rolling up. You buy a stock for $34 and sell the 35 option for $2. Now let's assume that the stock declines to $29 and the 35 option is at ⅛, and there is a 30 option worth 1½. Obviously you have lost 5 points on your stock and made 1⅞ on the 35 option, giving you a net loss of 3⅛. What do you do?

The easiest answer is to do nothing and hope that the stock will return to $34 or better. This would mean that you would have the profit you wanted, but it depends upon the stock going up 5 points, and the entire point in covered option writing is that you want to minimize your dependence upon the price movement of stocks. Furthermore, the price of the stock could continue downward and you would be left with practically no protection. The only alternative to doing nothing is to buy back the 35 option for ⅛ and sell the 30 for 1½, for a credit spread of 1⅜. Adding this 1⅜ to the 2 you originally took in means that you have taken in a total of 3⅜ in option premiums, while losing 5 points on your stock. You have a net loss of 1⅝, but note that if the stock now goes up over 30, you will get that additional point, meaning that you have a loss of just ⅝ point. While no one wants to take a loss, one can take comfort in the fact that a ⅝ loss when a stock falls 4 points isn't really so terrible.

In short, what rolling down does is to increase the amount of option premium you take in to offset the loss in the price of the stock, and the price you pay for this additional income is a substantial reduction in exercise price. It is never a very appealing choice, and at times you will conclude that it is not worth doing. But it is the only way to get in more option income once your stock has gone down. And just as in rolling up, rolling down can be combined with rolling out. In fact, it usually is, because the additional income to be derived from selling out the longer option helps to make the roll-down more palatable.

Buying in the option. If rolling down is just too depressing for you, then you should consider the fourth alternative of closing out the position and taking your loss. The virtue of this is that there may well be other covered writing positions available which offer better opportunities for profit and downside protection. If you do nothing, but just let your depressed stock stay in your possession, then you are not in an option-writing program anymore, and you are not getting any of its advantages. It's a free world, and you can do that if you want, but you owe it to yourself to make an objective decision as to whether this is what you want to do. There is no place in investing for taking action by default.

COVERED WRITING RULES OF STRATEGY

If you want to avoid disappointments and make money from your covered option writing program, here are some rules of strategy which I have developed from experience.

Strategy Rule Number 1: Figure out exactly what your anticipated return on investment will be. This probably seems like an obvious rule, but there are a number of reasons why it is specifically applicable to a covered write. In the first place, return on covered writing is fixed in advance, and no matter what happens after you have put on your position, your return can never be higher than was predictable from the minute that you completed your position. This is quite unlike buying shares of stock, where the profit you could make is limited only by how high the price of the stock will go. When you buy shares of stock and sell options against them, you are automatically fixing the maximum return you can make, and you ought to know in advance what that maximum return will be. Because once you put on the position things can only live up to that maximum return or they can get worse, and if you didn't do your homework properly beforehand, you are apt to be disappointed even if things work out as well as they possibly can.

The other reason why this rule is specifically appropriate to covered writing is that, since this is a conservative strategy, we are typically looking for a relatively low return over the life of the option. For example, if we sell a four-month option, we might be happy to get a net return on our investment of 8%. This is actually a very small amount of money in absolute terms, and a minor mistake in your calculations could reduce this to the point where you would not be interested in doing it. If you put up $10,000 in cash, you might be able to purchase $28,000 worth of stock on margin, and sell options worth $4,000. These are pretty big numbers to be throwing around, when the maximum you expect to make on it, if everything goes just as you planned, is only $800. It requires far more accuracy than doing out-of-the-money bull spreads (see chapter 6 for a description), where the amount is also limited, but you hope that an investment of $10,000 will bring you a profit of $30,000. If you're off by $800 on your calculations there it wouldn't even be noticed. Here it kills the entire profit of the transaction.

The method for figuring the return from a covered write is given in Appendix J. It should be easy to follow. The reason it is so important to actually go through the form and figure out the return is that if you try to eyeball the figures for the purchase of the stock and the sale of the option, you will invariably be too high in your estimation of the return. Commissions on the purchase of the stock and the sale of the stock when it is called away are extremely significant, and for the smaller investor who is buying a few hundred shares, the commissions can actually be so high that they will take all the profit out of some of the lower-yielding situations and will reduce some of the higher-yielding situations to returns so measly that it may not be worth the risk.

The individual investor needs to keep in mind that in 1977 and early 1978 option premiums began to fall as large institutions began to write options. These institutions have two distinct advantages over the average individual investor: (1) they are satisfied with a smaller return than most individuals are looking for. The mutual funds that have been set up to engage in covered option writing are said to be looking for annual returns from writing against stock which they purchase for cash of 13%. This is hardly what the individual investor is looking for. (2) The institutions operate in such large volume that the commission they pay per share is only a small fraction of what the individual investor must pay. The commission per share to buy 200 shares of a $20 stock is 41.6¢. while the commission per share if you buy 4,200 shares is only 19.7¢. And on top of that the institutions receive substantial discounts from these commission rates. All this points to the fact that when you are looking for covered writing positions you may be competing with an institution which is paying far less in commissions that you are and is willing to get a smaller annualized return. This means that when you find a situation you like, you better examine it very closely to see that on a net basis it is really giving you the return you want.

Strategy Rule Number 2: Decide in advance what you are going to do if the stock falls. If there is one theme I would like to have permeating this book, it is this: Decide in advance exactly what you are going to do if the transaction goes sour. I know that this is difficult to do, because we buy options on a stock only when we "know" that it is going to go up, and we buy puts only when we "know" that it is going to go down, and we do covered writes only when we feel confident that this stock is not going to go very far below the strike price. But the difference between the dilettante on Wall Street and the professional investor is that the professional knows he can be wrong, and he is willing to admit it and to take whatever action he can to minimize his loss; while the amateur is so sure his original views were correct that instead of taking corrective action while he can, he sits back waiting for the gods to reverse the price action of the stock and bring him back into a profit position. When he finally concludes that maybe this time the gods are not going to save him, it is usually too late to take much in the way of constructive action.

This rule is particularly appropriate to covered option writing because the profit potential is limited, and the loss potential is far, far greater. It should be clear that if you can make one dollar on a transaction, but you can lose five dollars, you had better do something to limit your chances of losing that five dollars, or you are not going to come out very much ahead. This is indeed the Achilles heel of covered option writing, as we mentioned with our example of the two $100 stocks, one of which went up by $50 and one of which went down by $50. The way to overcome this is to limit the loss possible when the stock goes down.

Fortunately, there is a very simple and effective mechanism for doing this, and that is to enter a stop-loss order to sell the stock out when it declines to a certain price. As soon as the stop-loss order is executed you must be certain to buy in your options. The basic question is to determine what the price of the stop-loss order should be.

If you are writing in-the-money options, then as long as the stock stays above the strike price, you will make your maximum anticipated profit. So there is certainly no point in getting out of the position as long as the stock is above the strike price. Once it starts to go below the strike price, you may still make money, if the stock does not go further below the strike price than the future time value of the option when you sold it (ignoring transaction costs). And of course, no matter how low the price of the stock goes during the life of the option, there is always the hope that the stock will come back up in price before the option expires, thus saving the position. But this is, alas, more wishful thinking than sound analytical reasoning. When faced with these conflicting forces, it sometimes pays to go back to the original theory behind the position to reach a solution.

Back to the original theory

You originally decided to do a covered write on this particular stock with this particular option because, while you weren't sure that the stock would go up, you felt pretty sure that it would not decline much below the strike price of the option. (If you didn't feel this way, one might wonder why you did the position in the first place.) Now that the stock has gone below the strike price, you have been proven wrong. Since you were wrong in the first place and it went well below the strike price, there is certainly a good chance that you will become even more wrong and the stock will move down even further. When you are wrong, it is often the best strategy to admit it, and then close out the position. Another way to look at a covered write is that you went into it because you did not want to have to worry about whether the stock went up or down, within certain limits. If you wanted to be concerned with the daily movements of the stock you would not have written an in-the-money option. Now that the stock has moved down below the strike price you no longer are accomplishing that objective. You now do have to worry about each move of the stock, because each move down of ⅛ point is costing you $12.50 for every 100 shares you own. Reason number two for closing out the position.

Therefore, the conclusion seems inescapable, that in order to eliminate possible large losses which would wipe out the profits, you must have a program for automatically closing out potential large losers. Placing stop-loss orders is such a program. If you are writing in-the-money options you can place these orders at a point or two below the strike price. Depending upon how much time has elapsed, you might be able to get out of the position at a very small loss, no loss at all, or if a great deal of time has passed, even at a small profit. The disadvantage of closing out the position at the strike price is that you may be taking a loss when the stock is at its low and will soon go back up to a profitable point, or will stay just at the strike price, which is also profitable. In other words, by closing out the position before expiration when the stock is down, you are virtually guaranteeing yourself a loss, whereas if you did nothing there is a fair possibility that the stock will go back up and you will end up with the very profit that you originally intended to get. Is it really, therefore, a good idea to close out the position prematurely?

The answer lies in the basic philosophy of the covered option writer. This is that he is someone who wishes to make his profit primarily from receipt of option premiums and not from the movement of stock prices. The amount of income which can be received is therefore fixed and limited. If you are not willing to close out a position when the stock is falling, then you are taking a chance that you will lose an enormous amount of money, and as we noted above, a large loss on one stock position is not going to be offset by a large gain on another position, because your maximum gain is limited by your sale of the option. This is a completely different method of making money from buying a selection of stocks, and a different method of monitoring must be used. The conclusion to the quandary of taking a certain loss now versus hoping that the stock will go back up is that you must take a certain loss now, because it is a small loss and there is no way that you can afford to take a large loss. If you do nothing now, that small loss might snowball into a large loss and that would be disastrous.

Other stop-loss strategies

Incidentally, closing out the position is not the only action that can be taken when the stock goes down, and I would certainly not preclude taking other actions. Sometimes it might be possible to roll down to the next lower option, or to sell an additional option at the lower strike price if you don't mind changing your position into a two-on-one ratio. (See Chapter 6 for details.) The important rule being stated here is that you must decide in advance exactly at what point you will take action and exactly what action you will take. If you do not, then you are probably playing a losing game, in which the option buyer gets to make all the abnormally large profits, and you get to suffer all the abnormally large losses. When you look at it this way, you realize that there really is no choice.

One example will demonstrate what I mean. On January 1, 1977, Burroughs was selling at 91⅜ and was being recommended as a good buy by a number of firms. Let's assume that you decided to buy 100 shares and write options against them. You might have decided to sell the April 90 for 7⅛. During the next three and a half months the stock market as a whole declined about 8%, but Burroughs stock collapsed with an enormous drop down to

54½. So that when your April option expired you had $712 in income from the option but a loss of 37⅛ on the stock, making a total loss of $3,000, or 35% of your initial investment, and if you had bought the stock on margin you would have lost 96% of your investment. And remember, we are not talking about a particularly speculative stock. With hindsight one can say that the purchase of Burroughs was a mistake, but at the time it could easily have seemed like a very astute move.

Take the small loss

Burroughs is just an example of one stock that had a terrifying drop in price. There are too many other stocks to mention here that had similar drops. And there will be many other stocks in the future that will plummet in what will appear to the people holding the stocks to be a totally "unjustified" and "irrational" manner. The adjectives one applies to such declines are, unfortunately, immaterial. It is the fact of the decline that will affect your profit and loss columns at the end of the year, not your or someone else's opinion that they shouldn't have gone down. Therefore, you should take a small loss in order to prevent a potentially much larger loss. If it helps, you can think of yourself as a forest warden who deliberately burns down a section of timberland in order to stop the possible spread of a raging forest fire, or as the captain of a freighter besieged by raging seas threatening the safety of his ship who throws part of his cargo overboard in order to save the ship, the lives of the crew, and the remaining cargo. Or the doctor who amputates a man's leg in order to save his life. In each case, the common thread is this: There has been a serious occurrence which threatens to become disastrous and perhaps fatal. By taking prompt action, which action admittedly has unfortunate consequences and will obviate the possibility of success in that venture forever, the really serious disaster can be avoided. So, if you want to run your investing program like a professional, take some free tips from some other professionals.

I should point out, furthermore, that a stock's falling further than you had expected is actually to be expected and you must prepare for it. In developing your overall investment goals and anticipated returns you factor in a portion of covered writes that will not work, and you deduct a reasonable loss on these from the others that you expect will work.

The good thing about covered option writing is that at least when premiums are at their normal levels, there is a generous enough return available so that you can absorb the losses from positions which do not work out and still achieve a satisfactory return from the overall portfolio. To do this one cannot seek too high a return. Remember, the average total return to stockholders over many many decades has been 8%. So whatever you can do above that is a plus.

Strategy Rule Number 3: In selecting the stock you wish to write against, carefully weigh the stock's volatility against the premium of the option. This rule is where the entire skill of option writing comes into play, and it is here that the option writer finds his greatest challenge. When options first were introduced brokerage firms started making up lists showing the highest-priced options and how high a return one would receive if one wrote these. Unfortunately, it turned out that the stocks that had the highest options were also the stocks that many people would not want to own if they were the last stocks in the world. The ones with the highest option premiums were always the stocks with the highest price/earnings ratios, the lowest dividends, and the shakiest companies behind them. That is the way it always will be for the very simple reason that when a stock is so speculative that no careful investor wants to own it, there will be a low supply of options available for purchase. Conversely, when a stock is stable, pays a high dividend, carries a low price/earnings ratio, and is one that the conservative institutions would be willing to own, it is easy to find plenty of option sellers, and the price of the option will fall. But this does not mean that that particular option is underpriced, any more than the fact that the option on the opposite type of stock is very high means that it is overpriced.

Over the years that options have been traded on exchanges a great deal of thought has gone into what the theoretical value of an option ought to be. While there are still a number of theories, they all relate option prices to the volatility of the stock and the dividend it pays. The more volatile the stock, the higher the price the option buyer is willing to pay, and the higher the price the option seller demands in return for giving up the upside potential and keeping the downside risk. A dividend reduces the price of the option, because if the stock pays a large dividend, then option writers are more willing to own the stock, reasoning that (1) the return on the dividend itself will help to make money for them as covered writers, and (2) the size of the dividend will give some downside protection, since there is a point below which the stock is not likely to fall because at that level it would be attractive on a yield basis alone.

Whatever theory you choose, the question of whether an option is overpriced or underpriced is not as important to a covered writer as the annualized return you are aiming for, as discussed in Strategy Rule #1. The purpose of this rule is to point out that whenever your stock declines to the point where you are going to take some action in accordance with Rule #2, you have a loss on your hands. You therefore must try to avoid stocks which have a probability of falling to that point. And the more volatile a stock is, the better a chance it has of falling to that point. So your specific concerns as a covered option writer, in order of importance, are (1) determine what the maximum annualized return will be, (2) figure out what your action level is on downside movement of the stock price, and (3) look at the volatility of the stock and perhaps at its recent price action, to estimate what its chances are of falling to that action point.

It is practically a truism that the most volatile stocks are not always the best writing candidates. If you happen to believe in a stock for reasons other than its volatility, then you might be very comfortable in using that stock, even if a straight theoretical evaluation would show that the option is actually underpriced. And the more you believe in a stock, the lower you would be able to put the price at which you would take action in accordance with Rule #1. And the lower you put the action point, the less probability there is that you will ever reach that point and be forced to take a loss.

To summarize this rule, it is not enough for the option writer to look at the annualized rates of return which he can get from various stocks. He must carefully weigh the rate of return against the possibility of the stock going down below a break-even point. Unfortunately there is no easy guide which can be presented in a book to make this weighing any easier. The various formulas which have been developed to determine whether options are "overvalued" or "undervalued" are of only limited assistance, because they are usually on a relative basis, i.e., in relation to what the option usually sells for when the stock is at this price.

But your decision must be made on an absolute basis, i.e., for this particular stock am I willing to take the risk of its declining to my downside action point in return for the return I am going to get? The only help it would be to know that an option was overpriced, if indeed the evaluation turned out to be correct, would be that, if you had to buy back the option later when the stock went down to your action point, you could expect that the option would return to its "normal" price and thus would be relatively cheaper, thereby decreasing your loss. So, basically, in making the decision of what options to write you are on your own, and certainly a subjective view of the underlying stock can be of great value in helping you.

Strategy Rule Number 4: Don't wait until the options expire to write the next options. Some option-writing programs are based upon buying stocks for the purpose of writing a specific in-the-money option and then holding onto the position until the stock is called away. But if you are in a continuous option-writing program against some stock that you want to hold for a longer period, then it is important not to wait until the options expire before you write the next series. If you are writing in-the-money options and you wait until they are about to expire, there is a very good chance that you will be prematurely exercised in the final weeks. This happens when the options are selling at around their actual cash value and is especially prevalent the day before the stock goes ex-dividend. The result is that you lose your stock and have to pay a commission on selling it at the strike price. If you were planning to write another option against the stock, you now have to buy the stock in again. Result: two commissions on the underlying stock which were totally unnecessary.

If you are writing out-of-the-money options, you do not have to be concerned with premature exercises, but there is another reason for not just waiting until the option expires. This is that you originally went into an option-writing program with the idea that the option you had written gave you a certain amount of downside protection against an adverse move in the price of the stock. If you bought the stock for 40 and sold a 40 strike price option for 4, you knew that if when the option expired the stock was at 36, you would break even (disregarding commissions). And you did not mind owning the stock with this kind of protection from the option. If there had been a 45 option available with a price of ¼, you would probably have rejected it because it did not offer the downside protection you wanted.

Now let us assume that you put on the above position, and the option is in its final week. The stock is at 39, the option you originally wrote for 4 has dropped to ¼, and you are happily waiting for the option to expire so that you can sell the next one and take in more money. What I am suggesting in this rule is that you have already strayed from your original philosophy. When you started out you wanted 4 points of downside protection, and now that you have only ¼ of a point, you are waiting for that to entirely disappear! How much downside protection will you have the day before the option is to expire? Absolutely none for all practical purposes.

Let's further analyze the position of a person who owns stock and has an option written that is worth ¼ point. He is still giving up all profit over the strike price, just as if the option were worth 8 points. So the fact that the option is cheap does not decrease what he is giving up. But it certainly does take away any downside protection. So the conclusion is that you should not wait until the last minute to trade in your old option for a new one. One must concede that if the stock stays in the same place, or moves up to the strike price, the maximum return to the covered writer would be achieved by holding onto the option until expiration and then rewriting. But in the real world there is the strong chance that the stock will go down instead of up, and then the urge to squeeze the extra ¼ point out of the old option could have grave consequences. Because if the stock goes down, then the price you will be able to receive for writing the new option could be several dollars less.

Just when should you roll out your old options? There can be no hard-and-fast rule, since this, like everything else in options, is a trade-off. You are trading off a higher possible return if you wait, against a more certain and even return by rolling over. Probably the best method is to decide what you consider a realistic annual return, which should be less than the theoretical return achieved by selling the option and waiting for its expiration. When the option you wrote has declined enough in value over the period of time to give you this annualized rate of return, then you should consider rolling the option out. Your maximum profit may be less, but it could easily be a great deal more. The decision is not unlike that which every car owner must face on when to trade in his old tires. Sure, there may be a few thousand more miles on those treads you're driving now, and trading them in today means that you are losing out on all those miles. But if you should have a blowout next week, the cost could be many times that of getting the new tires a few weeks earlier.

One of the recurring themes of this book is that when you are faced with a question of what to do, go back to your original purpose in taking the position. If your original purpose in covered writing was to get meaningful downside protection, then you've got to roll out when your existing option is priced so low that it is no longer giving you that protection.

Strategy Rule Number 5: Maximize your return by rolling up your options at the proper occasion. Just as you must expect that there are going to be stocks that will decline so fast that you will take a loss on the position, so on the bright side there will be some occasions when you will be able to make more money than you anticipated because you will be able to roll up your options. In deciding when you should roll up you must take the following into consideration:

1. You should try to maintain at least the same downside protection that you had when you first went into the position. Thus, if you initially sold a 40 strike price option for 3 when the stock was 40, and the stock is now 45 with the 45 option at 2, you would not be getting the same downside protection. The big danger in rolling up is always that the stock will fall back down to where it was, and you will be left with a losing position rather than a winner. At least when you go into a roll-up be sure that you are getting the same protection.

2. What proportion of the increase in strike price are you paying to do the roll-up? In the above example, where you roll up from the 40 to the 45 options you are gaining 5 points in the value of your stock, assuming that the stock is over 45 when you do the roll-up. Since a roll-up is done for a debit, it is easy to compare the amount of the debit with the increase in strike price. If the 40 option were 6 and the 45 option were 2, the debit to do the roll-up would be the difference between the two, or 4 points. To pay out 4 points, with the greatly increased risk in case the stock goes down, for the sake of increasing the value of your stock by 5 points is not a particularly appealing move. It is frequently possible to pay out only 60% of the increase in strike price. For instance, if here the 45 option were 3, then the cost of rolling would be only 3 points, and dividing this by the 5-point increase would give you a cost of 60%.

3. Rolling up is often combined with rolling out in order to reduce the

cost of the move and to obtain more downside protection. So, in this example, if the 45 option with the same duration as the one originally written is 3, the next longer duration might be 4. Rolling up and out to this option would cost only 2 points, which means that the cost would be reduced to just 40% of the increase in the value of the stock, remembering of course that we are now also including another three months.

Strategy Rule Number 6: Get out of a stock when it no longer offers attractive writing opportunities. Professional options managers have no loyalties to any stock. And neither should you. A stock is valuable to you only when it can provide you with option-writing opportunities that fit your criteria. When the stock can no longer do so, your response should be to get out of the stock and into something else. A resistance to get out of one stock and into another is often a habit of people who are used to trading or investing in stocks, where there may be a virtue in staying with a stock over a period of time. But in a covered options program, you set your sights at the outset on trying to make money by capturing the future time value of options which you sell. You may also set a goal of obtaining a certain amount of downside protection or the possibility of getting a certain percentage increase in the value of the stock if you are writing out-of-the-money options. But the most important criterion of all is the first strategy rule discussed here, that you be able to obtain a certain annualized rate of return from option income.

It happens frequently that a stock which is just beautiful for your option-writing program when you first sell an option will simply not be appropriate later when the option expires. The most common reason is that the stock moves into a range where there just isn't any option around offering what you want. For example, say you like to write options that give at least 10 percent downside protection and offer an annualized rate of return of 25% when you buy the stock on margin. Let's say stock XYZ is selling for 11, and the six-month option at the 10 strike price is 2, which nicely fits your criteria. You write the option, and six months later, when the option is about to expire, the stock is at 13. Now the 10 option with six months to go is selling at 3½, which is far from enough future time value to give you your desired annualized rate of return. On the other hand, the 15 option is selling for ⅞, which doesn't give either the downside protection you want or the annuilized return. What do you do? Many people would buy in the old 10 option and sell the 15 option hoping that the stock will continue to go up. But that is clearly not within the bounds of your original goals. You have now let circumstances convert you from someone who demanded a 20% downside protection to someone who is accepting a downside protection of only 7% because it was the convenient thing to do. Don't be lazy. If a stock doesn't give you what you want anymore, simply get out of it.

When the stock goes down

Another common example occurs when the stock goes down. Let's say you get into a stock when it is 30 and you write the 30 six-month option for 3. That's a gross potential profit of 11% in six months on your cash investment (30 minus 3, equals 27; 3 divided by 27 equals 11%). The six months pass and the stock is now 26. You have lost money on the transaction and now you are wondering what to do to get even. The 25 option with six months to go is selling for 2½ and the 30 option is now selling for 1. If you sell the 25 option for 1½ points of future time value you have locked in a loss on your overall position, but more important for this discussion is that you can make only 1½ points of future time value on your investment, which comes out to a potential gross profit of only 6.5% for six months (26 minus 3 gives you your investment of 23. Future time value of 1.5 divided by 23 equals 6.5%). If you sell the 30 option for one point, you are getting only 4% in option income, although you have the possibility of making more if the stock goes up.

The conclusion is that neither of these alternatives should be acceptable to you, unless something drastic has happened to premiums of all optionable stocks, which is usually not the case. The problem here is that a stock which was in a good position for option writing when you bought it has now become unacceptable, because the stock is simply not in a good price range, vis-à-vis the option strike prices, and because as the price of the stock has dropped in the last six months the premiums for the options have also fallen. The undisciplined option writer would pick either the 25 option, saying that he will get his 6.5% return with less downside protection because he doesn't expect the stock to drop below 25, while others will choose the 30 option with the wishful thinking that the stock will go back up to 30 and everything will come out all right in the end, just as it does in fairy tales.

But neither of these "solutions" is bucking up to the hard realities of the situation, which are that the stock just isn't right for you anymore as an option-writing situation. If you wanted to get only 6.5% for a six-month option you could probably find a better stock, and if you wanted to write options that were so far out of the money that they gave only a 4% return you wouldn't have gone into this writing program in the first place, when it yielded 11%. So the conclusion is to stick to your original guidelines. Get out of the stock. Get into another one which has downside protection and annualized yields closer to what you are looking for. With over 200 optionable stocks it is sometimes remarkable how many good writing situations there are at any one time. There will almost always be one stock that is just at the strike price, or just one point above it, or whatever you are looking for. But it obviously won't always be the same stock. So don't be reluctant to get out of one and into another when the prices so dictate.

Strategy Rule 7: When initiating positions, buy the stock and sell the option simultaneously. When you buy a stock you know exactly what you are able to sell each of its options for, and you can calculate what your downside protection is and what your potential annualized rate of return will be. That is the time to decide which option to write, and to write it. If you are not satisfied with the rates of return, then don't go into that stock. Wait until the premiums get better, or the stock gets nearer a strike price so that the annualized rate of return gets better.

Unfortunately many people buy the stock now, with the thought that after it goes up by a few points, they will then sell the option for a higher price, having the best of all possible worlds, i.e., a low-cost stock and a high-priced option. The error in this thinking is that it has little to do with covered option writing. What they are doing is simply buying a stock with the idea that it will go up in price. There is certainly nothing wrong with this, and thousands of people do it every day, but it is not a way of rationally writing covered options. Because if these investors are right and the stock does go up, then they don't need to sell an option, they could just as well sell the stock and be out of it completely with a good profit. If the stock goes down, then they have missed out completely on the chance to get the downside protection which selling an option provides, and if the stock stays still, they will never sell the option at the price they could have gotten originally.

What often happens is that if the stock does go up, the investor decides that it is going to go up even further and sees no point in selling an option right now, with the result that he never does sell the option. If the stock keeps going right up, he will be glad that he didn't, but if it turns around he will be very sorry. In any case, he is not in a covered option writing program.

So let's analyze things as they are. If you want to trade stocks by buying stocks that you think will go up, that's fine. But don't delude yourself into thinking that you are in a covered option writing program. You are simply trading stocks and using options as a supplement.

Strategy Rule Number 8: Formulate your objectives when you start your covered writing program and then stick to those objectives. This is a general rule which applies to every covered writing situation. This rule has two parts, and the second is much more difficult than the first, but also far more important. The first is that you should try to quantify your goals when you start your program. Not just that you want to make about 20% annualized by buying stocks on margin and writing covered options. That is not specific enough to be of much help. The specific questions you must answer are: Just how volatile a stock am I willing to buy? With tighter downside cut-offs (e.g. a stop-loss order on the stock) am I willing to buy a more volatile stock? How much downside protection do I want from the options I am selling? How low a rate of annualized return am I willing to accept? Do I want to write out-of-the-money options or do I want the downside protection that only in-the-money options can provide? How little future time value will I accept in an option before I buy it back to roll out, roll up, or close out the position? How low am I willing to let a stock get before I take action, either closing out the position or selling another option at a lower strike price or longer duration? These questions should be carefully thought out before you get into a writing program, and their answers should be written down, so that you can review them from month to month as the program continues.

The second part of the rule is to then follow these guidelines and actually use them as directives for running your program. You will be fighting a constant battle against inaction and wishful thinking. The best example of this is when your stock starts sinking. The normal reaction is to hope that it will move back up. Unfortunately, this is the most dangerous single circumstance in writing covered options, and the one which can destroy the profitability of an entire covered option writing portfolio. So, as difficult as it is, it is imperative to keep it in mind. It is always better to lose a small amount of money now than to risk losing a larger amount later. Those people who bought Polaroid at 140 to write covered options either took prompt, vigorous action when it started going down or their positions got killed. Similarly, when stocks have gone up, the covered writers either rolled their options up or they missed out on what could have been one of the most profitable investments they will ever make. Boeing went from 41⅜ on May 5, 1978, to 71 in three and a half months. Anyone who had written the 40 or 45 options and decided to "wait a while and see whether it's going to keep on going up or whether it will come down" missed out on a one-in-a-hundred opportunity to make an enormous return in a short time.

Develop your own rule. No matter how long or how detailed a book like this is, it cannot answer all the questions that will arise from the actions of hundreds of stocks interacting with thousands of options. The intelligent way of solving problems has always been not to memorize hundreds of little rules, but to understand the general principles and then apply those principles to each situation. That's all that this rule of strategy is saying. First, develop your own general rule of conduct. Then whenever you have a question, go back to that rule. For example, if you are a conservative investor who originally decided that he did not want to write out-of-the-money options, then if you had bought Polaroid at 140, you would have sold the 130 options as soon as they became available, and you would have been selling each new option as the stock went down, at an enormous savings to you. If you were more risk oriented and said that you did not want to ever write in-the-money options, but wanted to write only options that were two points or less out of the money, then if you had written on Boeing, you would have known exactly what to do and when to do it as the stock went up.

No plan will provide the right answers all the time. Sometimes it is going to happen that just after you have rolled up an option at considerable cost to you, the stock will immediately begin to fall back. With hindsight it will be obvious that you have done exactly the wrong thing. But you are going to do the wrong thing a certain percentage of the time no matter what method you follow. By following a consistent procedure you insure your being right at least a major part of the time.

My point here is that with a rational, well-thought-out set of criteria to guide you, you will have a much better chance of fashioning a program for yourself which will fit your objectives, and ultimately be profitable, than with a hit-or-miss approach, where every single decision is based upon the typical question "Do I think that the stock is going to go up or down from here?" An option-writing program is designed to replace that question with "What action should I take now so that this position will meet my original criteria for downside protection and annualized return on investment?"

Covered option writing should be an intellectual, rational pursuit of return on investment, and by applying this rule you will be making it as close to that ideal as is possible.

SELLING NAKED CALLS

4

A highly speculative method for making money

This is the most important chapter in this book, because it describes a method which is usually overlooked or actually discouraged. And it is all done by using a method which wasn't available as a practical matter until April 26, 1973.

The method I am referring to is selling calls on stock that the call writer does not own. In the previous chapter we discussed selling covered calls—calls on stocks that the call seller does own. This was described as a rather conservative transaction, because if the price of the stock goes down, the shareholder is no worse off than if he had never sold the call, and he has the premium from its sale to offset the loss. If, instead, the price of the stock goes up, any loss from the sale of the call would be more than offset by the increase in the price of the stock owned by the call seller. Thus, the seller or writer of a covered call makes money if the stock goes up or stands still and loses less than other shareholders when the price goes down.

In contrast to this, selling a call without owning the underlying stock—a naked call—is extremely risky and speculative, and was even more so before April 26, 1973. Before that date, the seller of an over-the-counter call was almost entirely at the mercy of the stock market. To understand why, let us take a simple example.

Suppose XYZ stock is selling for 50, and the writer sells a three-month option for $5 with a strike price of 50. If the stock goes up to 60, at the expiration of the option the writer must go out into the open market and purchase the shares of XYZ for $60 and deliver them to the call purchaser for $50. He has a $10 loss on this transaction (in addition to the cost of the commissions on the sale of the call and on the purchase and delivery of the stock), which loss is, however, offset by the $5 premium he received from the sale of the call. He thus has a net loss of $5 plus commissions. If, however, the price of the stock goes up to $70, he has a loss of $20 on the sale of the stock, and a net loss of $15. That's a rather steep price to pay for the gain he had hoped to make, which at the very most would have been just $5. But what if the stock goes above $70? In theory at least it could have gone right on up to $80, $90, or $100. If it did go all the way up to $100 (and more amazing things than that have actually happened in the past) the writer of the naked option would be out a net loss of $45 on each call he had sold. Again, this is the risk he was assuming for the sake of making a measly $5.

POTENTIAL LIABILITY

In short, while the maximum profit that could be realized from the sale of a naked call was fixed at the relatively modest premium received, the potential liability was theoretically unlimited. For an illustration of this see Figure 8. There was no way that the writer of a naked call could predict what his total potential loss was. Hence, it could not be used as an investment tool by anyone who did not have large amounts of liquid funds that he could throw into the market in case of a sharp price advance.

If the price of the underlying stock advanced too fast or too high, it was always possible to try to sell the call to someone else. But at that point you would find yourself trying to sell a very unmarketable commodity. There was no organized market for puts and calls. The market as such existed because a number of puts and calls dealers knew each other, and called one another up when they had a call to sell or a customer who wanted to buy one.

You may have heard the story of the man who bought some stock from his broker and was told a week later that the stock had gone up and he should buy some more. He did. A week later the broker informed the customer that the stock had gone up again and that he should buy some more. The investor did. The third week the same scene was repeated. Finally when the fourth week came and the broker said that the price of the stock had gone still higher and suggested further purchases the customer said, "No. The price is high enough now, I want you to sell all the stock." "Sell?" asked the incredulous broker. "Yes, sell," said the customer. "But," asked the broker, "to whom?"

And this was almost the case with respect to puts and calls. As the price of the stock went up, there was no easy way that the writer of the call could even find out what the value of his call was. If he wanted to get out of the deal, it was very hard to find a buyer, and perhaps only at a ruinously high price. So, the selling of naked calls was ruled out as a practical matter for the public.

Now the picture has changed. With the options traded on exchanges, the writer of a call knows every day exactly how much money he will make or lose if he wants to get out of the deal. And not only does he know exactly how much it will cost him, he doesn't have to worry about whom to sell the call to. Because

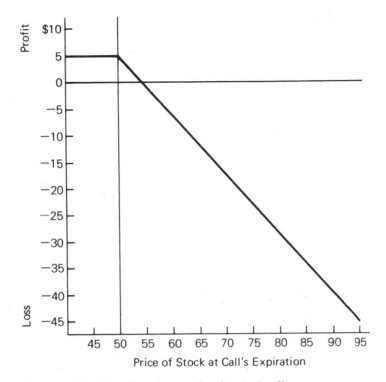

Figure 8. Profit or loss from sale of naked call
Call strike price:$50
Premium received for writing call: $5

This chart shows the limited maximum profit and tremendous potential loss inherent in selling naked options. Thus the imperative importance of Strategy Rule #1.

the options exchanges provide a ready market with a large number of potential buyers for his call.

The real significance of listed options is that now for the first time in history, the writer of a naked call is able to limit his liability and to control his potential loss. For the first time, a person can achieve the advantages that wise investors have always realized could come from selling naked calls, and he can also solve the problem of unlimited potential losses that make it impossible for most investors to realize these benefits.

Suitability requirements

Nevertheless, because naked call selling has traditionally been considered highly speculative, brokerage firms are reluctant to engage in naked call writing for anyone they do not believe can satisfactorily sustain a large loss. Therefore, in addition to the margin requirements discussed in Chapter 8, each firm has its own suitability requirement for naked option writing. Unfortunately in some firms the requirements are very substantial, such as a net worth of $100,000.

If the requirements at your firm are so high as to prohibit you from writing naked call options, and if after reading this chapter you conclude that you do want to write naked options, then there is no reason why you should not open an option account with a firm that is more reasonable. Don't be afraid to call up the other stock brokers in your area or out-of-town firms.

Limiting loss

There are three methods of limiting the possible loss from writing naked options. The first is to carefully watch the price of the option, and to buy it in when the price gets up to a certain point. If you sold an option at 2, and you do not want to lose more than 2 points under any circumstances, you would carefully watch the price of the option, and buy it back as soon as it traded at 4. You could ask your broker to watch the price for you and leave him instructions to buy it in if it ever traded at 4, but he cannot guarantee to do this for you, and if he should be away from his desk when it happens to trade at 4 you will simply miss out. Unfortunately there is no way of placing an order on the floor of the exchange which is the equivalent of a stop-loss order, that is, one which would require the floor brokers to purchase your options when the price got up to 4. You can place a "good till cancelled" order to buy an option at no more than 4 when it is currently selling at more than 4, but you can't place an order to buy the option at 4 or more when the price is now less than that. It would be a very welcome change in the rules if such an order were made possible.

The second method of limiting your loss is to buy in the option when the stock reaches a certain price. For example, if you have sold 40 options when the stock was at 37, you might decide that you want to get out of the position when the stock reaches 41. You would instruct your broker to watch the stock for you and buy back the option when it hit 41. He would do his best to oblige, but again there is no way that he can guarantee that he will be able to do so, and if he is out on the day when the stock goes over 41 you could have problems.

The third way of cutting your losses on a naked option can be done mechanically. That is by placing a stop-loss order to purchase the underlying stock when the stock reaches a certain point, such as 41. When you execute a stop-loss order to buy the stock at a price higher than its current price, that order goes onto the books of the stock specialist on the floor of the exchange, and when the stock trades at the price you have indicated, your order automatically becomes a market order to buy the stock. Therefore, you might buy the stock at a fraction higher than the limit you indicated on your order. Obviously the advantage of this kind of order is that it is guaranteed, and if for some reason your order is not executed, the brokerage firm to whom you gave the order is obligated to make good any loss you may have incurred due to the mistake.

The disadvantage from the point of view of the naked writer is that while you have now bought in the stock and eliminated any chance of loss if the stock keeps going up, you are now a covered writer and subject to the risks of a covered writer, which is that now if the stock goes down you could lose money. So you must weigh carefully the disadvantages of not having a guaranteed means of buying in the option, with the benefits of a guaranteed means of buying in the stock.

RETURNS ON WRITING NAKED CALLS

If, as was recently the case, the price of a certain stock is 60 and that is also the call's striking price, the premium for a six-month option might be 4¼. If one has to buy the stock, even by doing so with the minimum margin requirement of 50%, that means a cash outlay of $30 per share minus the 4¼ received from the option, for a net cash investment of 25¾ in order to earn a maximum income of $4.25, or 16.5%. This is not a bad return for six months, but it is the maximum possible return, and one must expect that in a certain number of cases the stock will go down to produce a loss, so that the average expected return will be quite a bit less.

Now, look at what happens to the percentage return when naked options are used. Because one does not have to own the stock, it is possible to sell the call with a much smaller investment. The current requirement is that the seller of a naked call must have a cash margin equal to 30% of the stock's current market value, plus the amount the stock is above the strike price, or minus the amount it is below the strike price. This means that where the stock is selling for $60, and the strike price is $60, the call writer must put up margin of 30% of 60, or $18, minus the $4.25 received from the option, for a net requirement of $13.75. Simply compare how much less this is than the $25.75 required to own the stock to see the great improvement that this brings about in profit potential. Instead of a return of 16.5%, the return now becomes 30.9%, over 85% more. If the stock was selling below the strike price, the margin required for a naked call would be even less.

If you multiply this 30.9% return by two to get the annual earnings, you find that by maintaining the minimum margin you can earn up to 60% a year on your investment. But even this figure is too low, because if the investor wishes to maximize his profits, he will reinvest not only his original investment, but the earnings as well, thus compounding the rate of return, which gives a profit of 71%. In actual practice, this figure would be much lower because we have not deducted commissions, which can be fairly high, and we are assuming that all the options expired unexercised. In actuality, of course, over the course of an entire year, many of the options will be exercised, resulting in substantial losses to the writer, so that the profit will be considerably smaller. But this shows that it is theoretically possible to make a large profit selling naked calls. Now, you can see why some people are so wrong when they look upon selling calls as only a way to incur unlimited losses while getting the chance to make only a meager profit.

Margin and returns

The low margin requirement is what makes this high profit possible. The effect of this margin requirement is even more striking when you use an out-of-the-money option. For example, on August 29, 1977, a date when option premiums were generally quite low, Houston Oil and Minerals stock was 38⅜ and the October 45 call, with about two months to go, was ¾. The minimum margin required to sell naked calls is computed as follows: 38⅜ times 30% = $11.51. Subtract from this the amount by which the strike price is above the price of the stock. Since we are selling a 45 option, that minus 38⅜ is 6.63, and subtracting this from 11.51 gives us a margin requirement of $4.88. However, to determine the amount of money which must be sent in to do this, we are permitted to subtract the amount of money received from the sale of the option. Subtracting 75¢ from $4.88 gives us $4.13. This is the amount of money required to earn a possible 75¢, which would mean a return of 18%, if the price of the stock does not go up, in a two-month period. This annualizes out to a return of 108%. It must be emphasized that premiums of this magnitude are rare and far between, but this shows what can be done with a stock that does possess such a high option premium.

Another aspect of margins that must be explained is that a naked call writer must "mark to the market." This means that in addition to putting up the required margin on the day that you sell a call, you must meet the margin requirements at the close of each trading day. This can be very expensive, and it is another reason why selling naked calls is only for sophisticated investors who can readily afford to lose all the money that they put up, and also have additional funds which they can apply to their option account in a hurry.

Let us assume that you sell a call with a strike price of $100 on a stock selling for $80. Your margin is 30% of 80, or $24, less the $20 difference between 100 and 80, leaving a margin requirement of $4. You put up your $400. The price of the stock now goes up 3 points to $83. You are now required to put up an additional $390, because you must maintain your margin based upon the current price of the stock. This gets very expensive very fast in the case of a steadily rising stock.

The only encouraging thought is that you are only talking about margin. Any time you do not have the funds to meet your margin needs, you can ask your broker to close you out. And if you don't come up with the requested funds, you will not have to ask your broker to close you out. He will do so automatically, as he is required to. This may be the best thing for you if the price of the call continues to rise.

But in many cases, if the price of the stock is still well below the strike price, you will want to hang onto the call even though the premium has doubled in price. The reason is that if the price of the stock stops rising before it reaches the strike price, the call will be worthless upon its expiration. In such a situation, if you do not have the extra funds to cover the margin call, you may lose money when you would have made a complete profit if you had covered the margin requirement.

We must state again, there is absolutely no guarantee that any results like the 108% mentioned above will be achieved. Even in a bad year when the market as a whole goes down, there are always certain stocks that will rise, and if an option writer has been unfortunate enough to sell these particular calls, he can lose money. Or he may have a very bad quarter, and if the bad quarter is his first quarter selling options, this may wipe out much of his capital, so that he isn't able to continue and recoup his losses. Nevertheless, the purpose of the above example and these paragraphs is to show that on the average the seller of calls will make money. In my opinion the odds are in his favor when option premiums are at their normal levels. You may wonder why this should be.

I think that it is true for the same reason that so many people buy stocks with great expectations, only to be disappointed with their performance later. People are naturally optimistic. And their optimism is fanned by the brokerage firms that are constantly churning out reports indicating that companies are about to enter a wonderful new period of rapid increases in profits, and that their stocks are now a real bargain. The function of brokerage houses is to sell stocks.

As Bernard Baruch said in his advice to investors, don't accept everything the brokerage firms say because they are in business to sell stocks. They sell stocks by telling the public how wonderful a stock is, just as any salesman tries to sell any commodity. In the brokerage business the way you sell a stock is to convince the customer that it is going to go up. And the brokerage firms succeed admirably, both in convincing people that the stock is likely to go up by a significant percentage and in selling stocks to the customers.

If they can sell stocks this way, imagine how much easier it is to sell a call! Who cares if it goes down? The buyer of a call is putting up only a small fraction of the cost of the stock, so if the stock goes down the clever broker tells the customer how smart he was to have bought only a call and not invested really big money on the stock. On the upside, it is so easy to tell a customer that you believe a stock will go up by just a few points. If it does, the buyer will not just have a small percentage gain, but he will be able to double his money. It just all seems so wonderful. And it is—but for the person on the other side who *sells* the call. Because there is no such thing in life as a free lunch. The stock is no more likely to go up "only a few points" in the next few weeks, than it is likely to go up by a much larger percentage over the course of the next year.

RULES OF STRATEGY

Now, we'll get down to actual rules of strategy showing how you can greatly increase the odds in your favor when you sell naked calls.

Strategy Rule Number 1: Immediately after you have sold the call, decide exactly what action you will take if the stock goes up. This is the most important rule of all. Chronologically, it should come after all the other rules that tell you which calls to sell. But I have deliberately placed it first so that you will never forget it. Without a stop-loss decision you could lose your entire investment and more on one call that represented just a fraction of your total investment. Just reread the first few pages of Chapter 2 on the rise of Texas Instruments and you will know what I mean.

If you had sold 10 contracts of Texas Instruments July 90s on July 6, 1973, you would have received $1,375 and have had to put up margin of $17,900. As the price of the stock began to rise, for every rise of $1, you would have been required to "mark to the market" with an additonal $1,300. Perhaps your financial capacity would simply not have been large enough to keep on doing this, and your broker would have had to sell you out long before Texas Instruments got to its high.

But once you have made an investment in selling a call, a strange but compelling psychology takes over. You begin to become convinced that the stock is overpriced. The fact that it has gone up so far so fast seems strong evidence to you that it is headed for a major fall, and headed there fast. Besides, the cost of the option is always going to be more than the amount by which the price of the stock exceeds the strike price, and you may believe that by hanging onto your call longer, you will at least be able to reduce that amount of extra loss.

My point is that sitting back now and knowing from hindsight what happened makes it very easy to think that if you had been so unfortunate as to sell Texas Instruments then, you would certainly have gotten out as soon as it started going up in price. But don't be too sure. When it is happening, it is far easier to think that the price will go down tomorrow.

But as we know, it didn't. And if you had held onto your contract until the end of the quarter on July 30, you would have had a loss of $14,625. That's an unbearable loss to have when the most that you could have gained was a mere $1,375.

Fortunately there is a way to protect yourself from this sort of fantastic loss. That is by instructing your broker what to do immediately upon receiving from him the confirmation that he has sold your calls. You would tell him to close out your position as soon as you sustain a certain loss in your investment. When that point is reached, your broker will buy as many calls for your account as you previously sold. He therefore cancels your short position, and you have closed out your position. You have thus cut your losses to what they were at that point, and no matter how much more the value of the call goes up, your loss is fixed. Normally, your loss will be limited to far less than the amount of your original investment in margin, if you follow the guides in this chapter.

Since the margin requirement is far more than the current premium of the call, even though you may have suffered a large loss when you are closed out, you will usually nevertheless free up a substantial amount of your margin and be able to start again selling another call. For example, let us assume that you have sold a call for $1 and that this requires $5 margin from you. Unfortunately, the stock goes up and your broker executes your instructions, closing out your position by buying the call for $2. Your account was credited with the $100 received from the sale of the calls in the first place, so your loss is just $100. Since you had put up margin of $500, your loss of $100 means that you still have $400 left in your margin account and if you want, you can now sell some calls using that as margin without putting up any additional money.

Stop-loss procedures

There are two kinds of stop-loss procedures, and there are advantages and disadvantages to each of them. The most common is to close out your position when the premium for the call reaches a certain point. For example, let us say you sell some calls for $5 each and you want to make sure that your potential loss is limited to that amount. As soon as your broker has sold the calls you can instruct him to buy the same number of calls for you at the market price as soon as the call sells for $10. Since the market might be rising, it may not be possible to buy the number of calls you need at $10, and the order may have to be executed at a fraction higher, such as 10⅛ or 10¼.

The other method is to ask your broker to buy you out when the price of your underlying stock reaches a certain level. This method can be particularly useful when you are selling a call that has a strike price substantially above the current price of the stock. If you have plenty of reserve margin to cover your margin account in case the premium for the call goes up substantially, you don't have to worry as long as the price of the stock stays below the call's strike price. When the expiration date arrives, your call will be worthless and you will make a profit on the entire premium you received for the call. To illustrate: You sell a call at 100 strike price when the stock is at 88. You receive 2½ for your call. Now, if the stock suddenly shoots up by 10 points to 98, the price of the call would probably rise to 5. But you may conclude that the chances are still very slim that it will go up another 2 points to the level where the option will eventually become worth anything. So instead of closing out your position because the option has doubled, you rely upon the stock price. You ask your broker to close out your position when the price of the underlying stock reaches 100. Because until that happens, you will not be out any money, provided you hold the call until it expires.

The advantage of the first type of strategy, based on the amount of the premium, is that it is a much more precise method of limiting your losses. If you sell a call on a stock that is selling above its strike price, this is probably the kind of stop-loss order you will want to use, because otherwise you don't really know how much protection you are getting against a sudden loss. To illustrate, if you sell a 25 call on a stock selling for 27, you may receive a premium of 3⅝. If you put in an order to cover your position when the stock reaches 30, you really have no idea what premium the call will be selling for.

If the stock jumps up that much in two days, the price of the call will not only increase by three points to reflect the rise in the price of the stock, but it may also increase an additional amount because investors will naturally think that if the stock can move up so far so fast, it will be capable of moving up far more in the remaining period of the option. So, the option may increase to 6⅝ or even 17. You would then find yourself losing more money than you had anticipated.

The big question is—at what price should you close out your position? If you choose a price that is too low, you will be quite safe in never losing a large amount of money, but you might take a loss on a call that later turns out to be worthless. And sometimes this happens even when the price of the stock is higher than the strike price, because the stock will go up briefly and then drop down below the strike price.

On the other hand, if you decide to get out when the stock price is substantially higher than the strike price, you are really going to take a beating if the stock ever gets up that high. This practice should be used only when you have received a healthy premium for the sale of your calls. One fact always to keep in mind when deciding at what price to get out is that when the price of a stock is below the strike price, an increase in the price of the stock of one point results in an increase in the price of the call of only a small fraction of a point. And the farther away from the strike price the stock price is, the smaller the fraction.

As the price of a stock approaches the strike price, on the other hand, it tends to move up faster for every point of the stock's rise. And, of course, once the price of the stock goes above the strike price, the premium for the call must go up virtually a whole point for every point increase in the price of the stock.

Recommended strategy

So here is the strategy I recommend to keep your losses down: If you receive a small premium for a call because the stock is far below the strike price, get out just a point or two below the strike price. In this way you will be getting out when the premium of the call should still be fairly small. The disadvantage is that if, for example, you have a call with a strike price of 40 and get out at 38, but then the stock never goes above 39, you will have suffered unnecessary losses. If you had decided to get out at 40 you would have made money.

But the alternative could have been very expensive, because if the stock did go up to 40 you would have to pay significantly more to buy back your calls. This is a crucial point in a successful naked call program, because each call on which you lose money is a double blow to your profits. It deprives you of the profit you had been hoping for on that particular call, and it incurs a loss that must then be offset by another profitable call. So, the procedure you choose for reducing losses is extremely significant.

Perhaps the best way to get an insight into this problem is to study the price action of a call as the price of the stock approaches and then climbs over the strike price. This example for October 30 calls occurred when premium levels were high, but this trait is even more pronounced when premiums are low:

Date	Stock Price	Premium of Call
September 5	26¼	7/16
September 6	27⅛	9/16
September 17	28	11/16
September 19	29	14/16
September 20	29⅞	1 ¼
September 21	30⅝	1 ¾
September 24	31¾	2 ⅛
September 25	32¾	3
September 26	33⅜	3 ¾

Due to various trading factors, there is not a perfect correlation between the closing premium for a call and the closing price of the stock. Nevertheless, the figures above, and the chart, give clear evidence for my statement that changes in the price of the stock of about a point result in only small fractional changes in the premium of a call when the stock price is well below the strike price. When the price of the stock gets up to the area of the strike price, each increase of a point in the price of the stock is reflected in a much larger fraction of a point in the cost of a call, and when the price of the stock gets more than a point above the strike price, every increase of a point in the price of a stock is translated into an increase of almost a point in the premium for the call.

The moral is very simple, to the shrewd investor. Close out your position between a few points below the strike price and the strike price. You will take losses in a few instances where you would have made a profit if you had held onto the stock, but you will take such a small loss when you do that you will come out ahead. In fact, you may find that in some cases, even where the price of the stock goes up substantially, the price of your call will be no higher when you close out your position than it was when you first sold your call.

The reason for this is that with the passage of time the value of the option automatically becomes worth less and less. To prove this point, let me refer to the stock above. On the first day of the quarter, August 1, the stock was selling at 27, but because the option had a full three months to go, the premium for the 30 call was 1⅜. Thus, an investor who sold that call could have said to his broker that he wanted to close out his position when the price of the stock hit the strike price of 30. The above chart doesn't show the precise price of the call when the stock hit, but you can see that on September 20 the stock closed at 29⅞ and the call was only 1¼.

Reflect on that for a moment. Here we have a stock going up almost 3 points, or more than 10 percentage points, in a period of less than two months. This must be considered an outstanding performance because the stock was not a high flyer but a blue chip industrial. Had an investor sold the stock short, he would be out $3 a share, which could be a lot of money. But if the investor sold

Figure 9. Effect of stock price move on call price

Chart shows the price of a 50 strike price option with six-month duration. Between stock prices of 40 and 41 the option increases an almost imperceptible $1/_{16}$, whereas between 59 and 60 it increases by almost one point. A more technical statement of this is that as the stock moves above the strike price, the hedge ratio approaches 1. Note that the percentage change in option prices, which are what really count to the option buyer, do not change at the same rate as the option price. Thus, between 40 and 45 the option increases by 1,100% while between 55 and 60 it increases only 74%.

a call, and bought it back with the stock at 29⅞, despite the fact that the stock has a gain of over 10% in just seven weeks, our investor actually would get out without losing a dime and would even be ahead by ⅛ of a point, which would cover a large portion of his commissions.

Be wrong and still make money

Herein is the real advantage of selling calls. Can you think of another form of investment involving a high degree of speculation where the investor can be dead wrong and still not lose any money? And let's admit it, anyone who sold the call when the stock was at 27 was dead wrong, because a rise of a full 10% in such a short time is very unusual for a conservative stock. What everyone should have been doing at that time, if they had had actual foresight, was to be buying the stock instead of selling.

Nevertheless. the person who sold the call, being dead wrong, still could

Figure 10. Effect of stock price move on future time value of option

Chart shows future time value for a six-month option with a 50 strike price. With the stock price below 50, where there is no intrinsic cash value, this chart is identical to Figure 9 showing effect of stock price move on option price. This chart is more important to covered call writers, because the only profit they can make is from the future time value shown here. This explains why as an option becomes deeper in the money, thus providing more downside protection, it also reduces the potential profit.

come out of the experience without losing a penny. That in a nutshell is what can make selling naked calls so profitable; when you decide in advance to close out at the right price. When you win, you can get up to 25% return on your investment in three months or less, and sometimes even when you "lose," you can break even.

One must not conclude from this that it is possible to break even every time a stock goes up to the strike price—on the contrary, it usually is not. In the case above two factors were at work that helped. One, the price of the stock went up gradually over a period of seven weeks. As time goes by, the value of an option automatically decreases, unless there is a large offsetting increase in the price of the stock. Had the price of the stock jumped up suddenly to 29⅞ during the first week or two in August, you can be sure that the premium for the call would have been much higher than 1⅜. The second factor was that the stock does not have a reputation on Wall Street for being a big mover. Therefore even when it did go from 27 to 30, the Street was not inclined to think there was a big chance that it would suddenly spurt much higher. So the premium stayed at a fairly modest 1¼. If, on the other hand, this had been a wild action stock well known for its sudden jumps in price, like Texas Instruments, McDonalds, or Houston Oil, the premium would have been much larger when the stock got up to 30, and the call seller would have lost money.

Your choice of a stop-loss method or price is never final, and shouldn't be considered so. For example, if a stock begins shooting up in price shortly after you have sold your call, you might very well want to lower the price of your close-out order—because a quick, high price rise means that when the price of the stock reaches a given level, the premium for the call will be higher than if the stock had slowly ambled up to the same price. Similarly, if you have sold a call and asked your broker to close it out at a low price to be very cautious, and the price of the stock stays where it is for a considerable period of time, you might well want to consider raising your stop-loss order higher. Because as time goes on, even if a stock does get up to a higher price, the call premium will be lower than it would have been earlier.

We can summarize Rule #1 for selling naked calls by saying that you *must* make a stop-loss decision as soon as you have sold your calls. You can do this by requesting your broker to buy you out either when the premium for the call reaches a certain amount or when the price of the underlying stock reaches a certain price. The former method provides more accuracy in limiting your potential losses, but it means that occasionally you will close out your position at a loss when the stock is well below the strike price, whereas if you had held onto the call until its expiration you would have made a profit. The latter method avoids this problem, but you cannot know in advance exactly how high your losses might be.

The stop-loss price of the stock should never be appreciably higher than the strike price (assuming you are selling calls on stock that is below the strike price). When you receive a small premium from your call because the price of the stock is far below the strike price, your stop-loss order should be at a point well below strike price so that when you buy back your calls they will be at low premiums. This simple rule will insure that your losses are limited. You will then be able to enjoy the profits you will make from following the other rules in this chapter.

*Strategy **Rule Number 2**: Sell calls only if the price of the stock is well below the call's strike price.* The reason that this is a successful practice is based upon a simple application of the law of probabilities to the stock market. The increases in stock prices over the long run are so small (about 5% to 8% a year) that in the short run, the three-month periods that we are talking about, they can be ignored. This means that at the end of any three months there is

Figure 11. *Probability of price swings*

Probable stock price when option expires

The probability that a stock will rise greatly during the option period is very small. In this chart there is only a 3.8% chance that the stock will be over 120, thus illustrating the theory behind Strategy Rule #2 for Naked Call Selling. (Note: Since actual probabilities differ with the length of the time period and the volatility of each stock, the figures above can not be applied in each specific situation.)

practically an equal chance that any stock will be down as there is that it will be up.

Furthermore, the odds are greatest that the price will be close to the price that it was at the beginning of the three-month period. This has been established by many serious and painstaking studies of the market. In statistical terms, the probability of any future price for a stock is shown by a bell curve with the current price of the stock at the center and highest point of the bell. (See Figure 11.) This means that in a very small percentage of the cases the stock will go down or go up by a rather large amount, as shown by the very small percentages for prices at the end of the period below 60 and above 140. In a large percentage of cases the price of the stock will end up farily close to the starting point, as indicated by the much higher percentages in the 60–85 and 115–140 area. But the highest probability of all, as clearly illustrated by the chart, is the probability that at the end of the period the price of the stock will be in the 85–115 area. What this means for the practical investor is that by selling a call with a strike at least 15% higher than the price of the stock, the odds are enormously in his favor that the stock will never reach the strike price.

Many years of experience with OTC call options indicated that about 60% of the options issued with the strike price at current market price were never exercised. This is because at the call's expiration almost 50% of the stocks are at the strike price or lower, and another 10% are above the strike price by such a small amount that it would not even cover the costs of commissions to exercise them.

This statistic is derived from the sale of regular OTC options, which are almost always issued at a strike price equal to the market price. Using the knowledge we have about the probability of a price increase in any stock, just imagine how many fewer stock options are exercised when the stock is required to increase just 10% to reach the strike price. And when the price of a stock must go up 15% or more to reach the strike price, the odds that the call will ever be exercised go way down.

Of course, the argument against selling such calls is that the premiums for calls of stocks selling deeply below their strike prices are far less than for other calls. One thing is absolutely certain, and that is that the chances are no greater and no less that a stock selling below the strike price of a call is going to go up in the next three months than that a stock that is selling at or above the strike price of its call is going to go up.

Avoiding loss on small stock increases

Yet, if you sell a call on a stock that is selling at or above the strike price, the value of that call will increase by one dollar for every dollar increase of the price of the stock. This means that the call writer will suffer a direct one dollar loss in his pocketbook for every dollar increase in the price of the stock. But when an option writer sells a call on a stock that is selling well below the strike price of the call, there is no such penalty for having picked a stock that goes up instead of down. Depending upon the length of time left in the option and the distance from the strike price, the increase in the price of the call for each dollar increase in the price of the stock can range from about 50 cents when the price of the stock is close to the strike price, to as little as $1/16$, or even nothing at all.

This often happens when a stock is hopelessly below the strike price and there are only a few weeks left in the option's life. Under these conditions, only a stock move upward of a large number of points can budge the call up from the basement where it is probably selling at a small fraction of a dollar. Therefore, when you are picking the type of call to sell, remember the risks you take if the stock moves against you.

Another good reason for selling calls of stocks selling well below the strike price is related to the margin requirements. The margin formula permits you to deduct $1 from your margin requirements for each $1 that the stock price is below the strike price. Therefore it can be greatly to your advantage to pick a stock selling well below the strike price.

On the other hand, when you sell a call on a stock that is selling above the strike price, you receive a much larger premium, but the option will probably be exercised. More significantly, under the margin formula, your margin requirements go up by a full dollar for every dollar the stock exceeds the strike price. Let me illustrate with an example.

If you sell a call with a 40 strike price on XYZ stock, which is selling for $50, you may receive a premium of $15 for your call. Of this amount, $10 represents present cash value and only $5 is for future time value. This $5 might be said to be all you are receiving for the pure option aspects of the call.

Using the random walk theory, which holds that while it is not possible to predict the future price of a stock, the most probable future price is the present price, the presumption is that at the expiration date of the option the stock will be selling at 50, and you will then buy back the option for $10, which when subtracted from the $15 you received upon sale of the call gives a profit of $5. But note that in order to earn this $5, you had to provide margin of $30\% \times \$50 = \$15 + \$10 = \$25$. Putting up $25 to make a probable $5 means you will make only a 20% profit on your investment.

But this discussion on margin is not at the heart of Rule #2, recommending calls with a strike price above the current stock price. The real reason is simply that most calls buyers don't understand the law of probability as it applies to stock prices. They may believe that because the stock was much higher just a short time ago, it will probably go back up. Or they may believe for various reason that it is an undervalued stock that will go up. In either case they can be wrong.

They are wrong in the first instance because the fact that a stock was selling at a higher price a few months ago has never been shown to have any bearing on the price it is going to be selling at in the future, and wrong in the second instance because no one can predict what the future prices of stocks will be. So, they look at a call on a $45 stock and grab it as a real bargain if it is only selling for $1. My goodness, they say, that's only a cost of 2%, and the option still has a full two months to run. What a bargain.

No. It is not a bargain. Because the strike price is $50. And the charts may show that never in the 60-year history of that company's stock has it ever gone up by 13% in just two months. And it probably never will, either.

So the fact that the premium is a small percentage of the price of the stock completely overlooks one of the essential elements of a call, its strike price. It is almost as if a person went out to buy a house and found a wonderful three bedroom house at a very low price but didn't consider the fact that it abutted on a boiler factory. But let us not complain. Fortunately, a call on a $45 stock looks like a bargain to some people when it is only $1.

Call buyers typically are people who want to double or triple their money in a short time. They think that a $45 stock can easily go up 6 points, at which time they will break even on their investment. Every extra point from then on is money in the bank. And you know how quickly a stock like that can move once it gets going. At least this is the thinking of people who buy such calls. Their thinking is usually wrong, but we won't bother to tell them. The chances of the stock going up 13% are very poor. Period, end of report. If it does go up that much, the shrewd option seller will, by following Rule 1, be out of his position before the stock ever gets that high.

In short, Rule #2 is very simple. Sell calls on stocks that are selling far below the strike price. The reason for this rule is that the price of most stocks doesn't change very much in just three months, and the probability that it will change a lot is inversely proportional to the amount of the change. By selecting a stock that must go up, let us say, 10% to 15% to each the call's strike price, you are greatly increasing the odds that your option will never be exercised. The fact that you receive a smaller premium in relation to the price of the stock doesn't matter to you.

Unlike the seller of a covered call, your investment is not determined by the price of the stock, but by the margin formula. Your objective is to make as certain as possible that you make a profit of 100% of the premium you receive. You accomplish this by picking a stock selling far below the strike price of the call. By following this rule, your rate of unsuccessul options will be very small, normally greatly less than 30%. Therefore, you will make the full profit most of the time, and on the options that are losers you will lose only a limited amount (following Strategy Rule #1), so your rate of overall profits should be good.

Strategy Rule Number 3: To maximize your profits you should constantly reinvest your principal. You might think that an option with a life of only three months is a very short term investment. If you are used to buying and selling common stocks this is certainly true. So, the usual reaction of someone new to options is to sell an option and stay with it until it either expires or goes up in value and his position is sold out. But this is not the way to make the biggest profits in the shortest time. How much can you make in a three-month period? The answer is not easy, since it is a function of the relationship of the premium you receive to the margin you must put up.

If you can sell a call for $5 and are required to put up margin of only $10, you can theoretically make a 50% profit in just three months. If, on the other hand, to sell a call for $5 you have to put up margin of $40, then obviously you are limited to a profit of 12½%. Either one of these is very good, since with compounding, if you actually did make 50% every three months, you would have 406% profit at the end of the year, and a 12½% profit would become a 60% profit at the end of the year. But you can earn more than that by following the strategy of Rule #3.

Suppose that you sell ten contracts for $4. This means that you receive premiums of $4,000, and let us assume that your are required to give your broker $11,000 in margin. Now let us further assume that the price of the underlying stock stays at about the same price for two months and that in accordance with Strategy Rule #2, you have selected a call with a strike price far above the price of the stock. By the end of six weeks or two months, the price of that call will probably have drifted down to $2 or less. This means that your call is now worth half of what you sold it for and that if you get out of your position by buying the ten calls for $2 each you will have made a profit of $2,000. That is 12½% of the amount that you invested and 50% of the value of the premium you received.

Well, you may ask, so what? You could have made a full 25% profit on your investment by letting it alone until the options expired unexercised. But the point is that you now are free to reinvest the entire $16,000 that you had originally invested. And in addition, you have made a profit of $2,000 that you can add to the $16,000 in your margin account, making a total of $18,000. If you can find another call that requires a margin of only four times the premium, you can now sell calls worth $4,500.

This means that if you hold them until the end of the quarter, and none of the stocks go over their strike price, you will have made $4,500 from those options, plus the $2,000 that you made from your earlier options, for a total of $6,500. Compare this to the $4,000 that you would have made had you not reinvested your winnings, and you will realize why this can be an important rule of strategy. Because, with it, you can actually increase your profit by 62% over what it would have been by just a straight investment. It also means that if you are successful in using this technique, you will have received a return on your total margin account of 40%. And that is just in one quarter of a year!

The strategy of not waiting for your successful calls to expire, but buying them out when they have declined by 50% is not limited to one time in an option period. Especially in a falling market it can be done many times. In a declining market it is often remarkable how quickly the value of an option can go down by 50%. For example, on September 27, 1973, the author sold some Avon 120 calls for $1 when the stock was 101½. The next day the stock closed at 100 and the option went down to ¾. On the succeeding trading day the stock fell to 92 and the call closed at $5/16$. This represented 68% of the total possible profit in just two trading days. With this kind of luck, there is no reason why one should not close out the transaction right then and there, take one's profits, and reinvest them in something else.

If this can be repeated a number of times during the option period, there is actually no limit to the amount of money that can be made. The reason is that each time you close out your position at a profit you can actually increase your future profits because the profit from the first sale has increased the amount of your margin account so that your next sale can be larger than the first.

Thus, toward the end of the option period you will have the accumulated cash profits that you made during the period, and the final amount you have invested will be far higher than the amount you started out with. If you are successful, the entire amount invested at the end of the period will be net profit.

Strategy Rule #3 can then be summarized by saying that if you are in a profitable position from writing calls, don't just sit there and contemplate your profit. Close out your position and reinvest by selling a different option. This operation can be repeated as many times as you wish as long as the market value of your options falls by 50% and as long as there are other options that you would like to sell. The potential for increasing your profit is almost limitless.

Strategy Rule Number 4: Avoid disasters by diversifying your call-writing portfolio. Rule #1 explained how to limit your potential loss. But when a stock does go up above its strike price, the chances are that in spite of that rule you will lose money. Frequently a call will double between when you sold it and when you are closed out. Your cash loss then might equal the amount of the premium at the time you wrote the call, but it could be much higher. Therefore, everyone who decides to go into a call-writing program must obey Rule # 4, which is to protect yourself to the greatest degree possible against major losses by diversifying your investment.

The temptation to ignore this rule can be very strong. Before selling any naked calls you will carefully examine every call offered on the exchanges and subject them to the various tests outlined in these rules of strategy. After you have reached your conclusions on the probability of each call making money for you, you may wish to write down the calls in order of preference.

Very often, there will be one call that for various reasons will seem to stand out head and shoulders above all the others. The stock may be selling at 20% below its strike price, and the call may still be fetching a premium of 4% of the value of underlying stock. The next best call may be a stock selling only 15% below its strike price and paying a 3% premium. You may conclude that your first choice is so much better a selection than even the second best that most, if not all, your money should be invested in it. Don't do it.

No call looks so good as when its stock is down. Let the price of that stock go up about 5 points and it won't look quite so attractive. Let is go up another 10 points and you will be wishing that you had never sold it. And then if it should go over your closeout price, you will thank your stars that you did follow this rule.

Remember that there is absolutely no way to predict the future action of a stock price. All the rules that you can read or even imagine can do no more than tell you the probability of what might happen in the future. And the important thing about selling a call is not what it looks like when you sell it, but what happens to it when the expiration date comes or when you are forced to buy it back. And when you sell your call you just don't know what is going to happen. The law of probability is only effective in telling you anything about the future if you can utilize it over a large number of different situations. The law of probability is of no value to a person who puts his entire savings into selling one call, if it happens that that one call rises over its strike price, with resulting heavy losses to the call writer.

So, when you find your "perfect" call, the one that shouts out at you to sell it, the one that says this is a "can't lose" situation, remember that there is no such thing, that no past history can tell you what is going to happen in the future, that stocks have gone up by 15% or more in a single day, and that the prices of calls have a way of increasing at a greater rate than the price of a stock when it is rising. When you sell calls, be sure that you diversify. I recommend that at the very minimum, no matter how little you invest in writing calls, no more than 20% be invested in any one call. For larger investors, 10% would be a better rule.

Diversification is a good rule for every kind of investment with high risk. Where the risk is as great as it is for selling naked calls, the need for diversification is imperative. But let me point out that even diversification cannot protect the call writer when the entire market begins to rise. What it will do, however, is to force him out of his positions at various times, so that if he senses disaster coming, he may have enough time to close out voluntarily his remaining positions before being forced out at a more costly level.

To summarize Strategy Rule # 4: Selling naked calls is a risky business, and one way to make it slightly less so is to make sure that you never put all your eggs in one basket. Even though diversification cannot save you from heavy losses if the entire market advances, it will help a great deal. No investor, no matter how small, should ever have more than 20% of his funds invested in one call, and more substantial investors should make certain that no more than 10% of their money is invested in any one call. Remember, no matter how good a call looks when you sell, there is no guarantee that its stock won't suddenly go up. Don't trust any stock to stay down.

Strategy Rule Number 5: Learn all you can about the stock's price history. You are making a big investment, and a very risky one. The buyer of a regular common stock will investigate carefully before he invests. You should investigate at least three times as hard, because you are taking at least three times as great a risk as the buyer of the common stock. Whereas a stock can only go down in price to a fraction of the original investment, so that the potential loss is limited to the investment, you as the seller of a naked call are risking perhaps many times your investment.

Furthermore, the purchaser of common stock can afford to be wrong, at least for a while, because if his stock goes down he can always make the decision to hold onto it, and hope that it will go back up in the future.

You do not have the luxury of a second chance. You are betting that, during the period of your call, the stock will not go above a certain price. If it does, you are out. Out of the game, out of the ball park, finally and irrevocably out of business in that call. There is no extension possible. Thus it behooves you to study carefully the nature of the movement of the stock's prices.

For purposes of selling a call your analysis of a stock should be somewhat different from that of the buyer of common stock. If the purchaser of common stock is buying the stock for investment purposes (as opposed to trading purposes) he is interested in the future action of the stock over a period of a year or longer. For this reason, he can consider future changes within the industry, the next recession, future progress of inflation, the likely political climate in the next few years, and many other long-range factors that may affect the stock in the future. You shouldn't be distracted by these factors.

If you are selling a call that has only three months to run, there probably won't be time for any long-range effects to make themselves felt on your stock. So, I would strongly urge you to minimize the consideration that you give to the fundamentals of a stock. Concentrate instead on its past price movement.

By this I do not mean whether it has been in an upward trend or in a downward trend. This doesn't indicate which way it will move in the future. Similarly, I am not impressed with the work of chartists who can discern "head and shoulder" patterns, "double lows," and so on—all of which prove, at least to the chartists, the likely resistance levels, breakout points, and probable highs and lows of a stock.

But there is something that I believe you can learn from the past, and that is the nature of its price movements, That is, is the stock volatile or not? Does its price fluctuate by large amounts quickly, or has it always changed only slightly, achieving large price changes only gradually over long periods of time? American Tel & Tel, for instance, is the classic example of a stock which never moves much in a single day. Over the course of a few weeks, like the giant tortoise, it may manage to lumber up an aggregate of a whole point, and over the space of a month it can on rare occasions actually move three or four points, but normally it is quite happy to inch along a few eighths of a point one way or the other.

In general you can apply the same methods of studying the movements of a stock for purposes of selling a call as one uses in buying one. Thus, the reader should review Strategy Rules # 6 and 7, set forth in the chapter on buying calls. The only difference is that, naturally, you must deduce exactly the opposite conclusion. For instance, while the chapter on buying calls says to check the Beta factor to be certain that it is high, the call writer checks that it is low. The premiums received for selling a stock with a low Beta will necessarily be much less than for a stock with a high Beta, but the results to the call seller can be just as rewarding and less risky.

Stop-loss strategy

When selling a naked call, you must always ask what the consequence will be if you are wrong and the price of the stock goes up. Presumably you have decided on a stop-loss strategy. How much money will you lose when the stop-loss order goes off? In the case of a stop-loss order computed on a certain price per call you know exactly, but you don't know what the price of the stock will be.

With a stock of a low Beta you have a better chance of not being forced out when the price of the stock is still low, because the premium for a call on a low Beta stock will tend to rise more slowly and more directly in proportion to the price of the stock. Since the investor community knows that the stock is a slow mover, a move up of a few points will not start a wave of wild optimism that in the next few days the stock can easily move another 4 points to get over the strike price.

Rather, investors will calmly reflect that since the stock is now 2 points higher, it has 2 points less to go to get over the strike price and therefore the call should be worth slightly more. Thus, a stop-loss strategy based on the price of a call will tend to work out better on a stock with a low Beta.

A stop-loss order based upon the price of the stock is also likely to cause smaller losses because, while even a stock with a low Beta can rise over the strike price, it is probably going to take longer to do so. And time works in favor of the call seller. So, like the example of the stock given earlier in this chapter, if you can sell a call at the beginning of an option period for a premium of perhaps 2, when the low Beta stock finally climbs up to the strike price there will be little time left in the option period. Investors will realize that at its slow pace of increase it will not get too much farther during the life of the option and therefore the premium will not be much more than you received upon the sale of the call.

Thus a low Beta stock is good for the call writer. The obvious disadvantage is that with the small premium, it is not practical to sell calls when these stocks are very far below the strike price, because the premium will be too low to make the sale practical.

The call writer will carefully check the chart to see the stock's weekly performance over a long period, and just as the call buyer looks to make sure that many times in the past the stock has gone up enough to make his hoped-for gain a good possibility, the option writer checks to make sure that the opposite is true. Just one word of caution. When selling calls you must be more cautious than when buying them because the potential risk is higher. Thus, the fact that a particular stock has never gone up 12% in a three-month period cannot be taken as any assurance that it will not do so this time.

If you were thinking of buying the call you would assume that it would be impossible and shun the call. But as a call seller you must be far more open to the unusual and unexpected. Because in this case the premium is probably going to be very low, and you are therefore taking a large chance that a quick rise will produce a dramatic increase in the premium of the call. So, if a stock has never gone up the percentage required to get over the strike price, that is indeed a positive sign to the option writer, but it is far from any assurance of success.

The easiest facts to learn about a stock are its high and low points for the year, and for the past five years. Stock information booklets containing these facts are available from most brokers, and they are entitled to some consideration. But just as sports records are consistently broken, so too stocks climb over their highs with even more ease than a high jumper clears a bar higher than any many before him ever cleared.

The price/earnings ratio is another factor that everyone takes into consideration, but it is difficult to place any real importance on it for the call writer. The fact that a stock has a high P/E means indeed that it can fall farther than one with a low P/E, but as a call writer you are not really so interested in how far or fast the stock can fall. If it just stays where it is that will be fine, thank you. What you are concerned with is whether it is likely to go up, and if so by how much.

Here it is, surprisingly, probably an advantage to be dealing with a low P/E stock. The reason is that if investors already believe that a stock is worth 20 times earnings and for various reasons the investing community comes to believe that the stock should be worth more, there is nothing to stop them from believing that it is worth 25 or 30 times earnings. Once a stock gets up into that rarified atmosphere it is not judged by the usual rules of performance. It has become a full-fledged glamor stock and is rated more by emotion than by logic. It may well be a unique company for many reasons, such as a strong patent position, or an unassailable market share in a growing, profitable industry. Therefore, it cannot be compared directly with any other company, and no one can easily prove that its price/earnings ratio is too high.

A more mundane stock, such as a steel company for example, is simply one of a large number of steel companies, and its stock ratio is not going to get far above that of all the other steel companies. Therefore, the high price/ earnings ratio is a double-edged factor for call writers, and in fact does not make as attractive a vehicle for the conservative writer (and that is not very conservative) as a stock with a low P/E ratio.

On the other hand, since most stocks with high P/E ratios are more volatile than others they tend to command a higher premium, which can more than offset the volatility.

So Strategy Rule # 5 may be summarized by saying that the call writer is taking a tremendous risk in the hope of a fairly large gain in a short time. It is therefore extremely important that he study the movement of the stock carefully before investing in the writing of a call. The type of business, dividend rate on the stock, and other fundamentals of the stock are of no importance to the call writer because he is interested only in the probability of a large price increase in the next few months and not in any long-term trends. Therefore, he studies those things that tend to indicate how much the stock will be likely to move, including the Beta of the stock, price history as shown on charts, its highs and lows for the year, and its price/earnings ratio.

In general, the less volatile and more stable the price movements of a stock are, the better the vehicle for the sale of a naked call. The reason for this is that the naked option writer should not be interested so much in making a quick profit on a stock that will go down, as he is in not losing money on a stock that will go up. What he wants is a stock that will stay just about where it is, or go up so slightly that it does not reach the strike price. With this kind of price action the call seller will earn a very handsome profit.

Strategy Rule Number 6: Never leave well enough alone. This is an overall procedural rule. It may be particularly difficult for investors who are used to buying stock. Good conservative stock brokers for generations have advised their clients to buy stocks in good companies and hold onto them. The thought was that if the company was solid, profitable, and growing, the stock would take care of itself, and only an impatient investor who sold too early would lose out on an almost inevitable profit. As subsequent events have shown, this concept of "one decision stocks" often does not fit the realities of the market, but it was a highly respected position, espoused by many of the leading and most successful professional stock investors.

The stock option market is totally different. One might almost say that a stock option is the opposite of the "one decision stock." For whereas a person can buy a stock for long-term investment, there is no such thing as a long-term stock option, since the longest option available is only nine months. This means that the investor has great freedom of movement, because the hardest part of investing in stocks has always been the agonizing decision of when to sell. How many investors, amateur and professional alike, have said that they are good buyers, but bad sellers?

They know a good buy when they see one, but they can't decide when to sell. And logically so. When a stock goes down, it appears to be even a better value than when it was purchased, and if only it is held for a while longer the market will surely recognize how badly underpriced it is. On the other hand, if the stock goes up, why then you certainly don't want to get out of it, because nothing succeeds like success, and as the Swiss bankers are quoted as saying, "Cut your losses short and let your winnings ride." No one wants to part with a winner, so the tendency is always to hold, with the expectation that it will increase even more in the future. So whether your stock goes up or down the temptation is to hang onto it.

The person who sells a naked call cannot fall victim to these fallacies and traps for two very good reasons. The first is that he is dealing in an investment with an additional dimension, the dimension of time. An investor in a stock may have personal investment goals for his stock to achieve in a given time. But time itself is not a dimension of the stock. The stock is a permanent certificate representing a share in a corporation with a perpetual life.

On the contrary, a call exists only for a finite period of time. Since the seller of a call knows that his call is going to expire, it is much easier to decide to close out his position and move on to another investment. Instead of making the big decision whether or not to get out of the investment, as the owner of a share of stock must make, the seller of a call need only decide *when* to get out of the investment. By taking no action at all he will automatically get out on the expiration date of the call, and anything he does will change only the date, not the fact of getting out.

The other factor that makes it so much easier for the option writer to get out of his position is that he is dealing with a very limited potential gain. If he sold the call originally for 1½, the highest possible gain that he can make is just that little 1½. It matters not whether the stock ends up just ⅛ below the strike price, or crashes to almost nothing. In either case, the maximum that the call seller can make is his original 1½. Thus there is not the great temptation to hold onto a call through thick and thin. Whereas the person who has bought a stock may well believe that if he just holds onto it for a little while longer, it could increase by 200%, our option seller knows that he can only get his little 1½.

So, the result is that the option writer has great actual and psychological freedom to move fast. In Rule # 3 I have already suggested that the option writer can make more money by not holding onto his options until they expire, but rather covering his positions when they decline to half their sale price. But this is just one rule. The astute option seller will be constantly reassessing his position to determine whether he can make any trades now.

He should confer with his broker at least once a week to learn what his free margin balance is. He should decide what the maximum is that he wishes to invest and if his total margin requirements go down, he should immediately make a decision as to whether or not he should invest more.

What this rule is saying is that an option writer must be constantly flexible. He must be ready to cover his position an any time when he feels that his money can be better utilized in another call situation. Not only must he be constantly reassessing the positions he has taken, but he must constantly think of how much money he wants to have invested in selling calls in total. For example, if a person has committed $10,000 to writing options, it might be that if all his calls are doing well, and there are still some good opportunities around near the end of an option period, he will decide that for the period of one month he will invest additional funds.

In summary, Strategy Rule # 6 says: realize that a call is a temporary, fleeting object that exists only to cease existing in a short time. Thus there is no loyalty to be expressed, no fixed position that must be adhered to. Calls are traded in a very fast moving market, where premiums can easily rise 100% or fall by over 50% in a day. Thus the person who wishes to trade in call options should keep a daily lookout, and he must take stock of his position at least once a week to know where he stands. He must be able to act decisively, closing out positions where he can take a good profit, plunging into positions that look promising. The sky is not the limit. But by moving in and out adroitly the call writer can make a very generous return on his money.

SUMMARY

Let us summarize the strategy principles that have been laid down in this chapter:

Rule 1. Selling naked calls is made possible for the average investor by the new liquidity created by the options exchanges that permit an investor to limit his risk when he sells a call. But this risk limiting is not automatic. The only way that it can come into play is for you, the option writer, to tell your broker at the time you sell the call that you want to take stop-loss action. This may be to close out your position either when the underlying stock reaches a certain price, such as the strike price, or when the price of the call itself reaches a certain level. In either event, once the price you have selected is reached, and your broker executes the order, you are out of the market. The importance of this rule cannot be overstated, because without it the seller of a call is at the mercy of the gods.

Rule 2. Sell only those calls where the stock is well below the strike price; the minimum would be where it is 5% below the strike price, but 10%

or 15% is better. The reason for this is that the odds against a stock's going up to the strike price are much greater than the price of the premium usually justifies. Furthermore, such a call offers a great deal of insurance in case of an upward price movement, because the price of the call does not increase in proportion to the increase in the price of the stock. Although you will probably lose a substantial amount of money in those cases where the stock does go over the strike price, this should be more than offset by the other calls for which the stock does not. Furthermore, this can be reduced by putting in stop-loss orders for prices well below the strike price.

Rule 3. You can greatly increase your profits by not waiting until your successful options expire. Take advantage of the fact that the premiums have gone down by buying the calls when the price goes down to less than 50% of what you sold them for. This will increase your potential profits from the sale of calls. Since the very nature of calls limits your possible gain to the amount that you have received from the sale of the original call, this method is vital to the investor who really expects to do well. By closing out your position as soon as your net investment has gone down 50%, you will immediately increase your earnings potential.

And of course if this technique can be done twice in an option period, the profit will go up even more. This is not impossible, because if you follow Rule Number 2 and sell only calls on stocks that are below the strike price, the price of the call will constantly fall, even if the price of the stock rises slightly. Over halfway through the option period the price of the call will have fallen by about one half if the stock price remains stable. You can then close out your position, and sell options on another stock, which in turn could fall to one half its value in about three or four weeks, thus enabling you to repeat the procedure.

Rule 4. To maximize your chances for making a profit, you must diversify. This is made imperative by the highly risky nature of option writing. The option that you think looks the most promising may turn out to be the biggest disaster. The stock may simply go up far faster and higher than the rules of probability ever said that it should. But that is no consolation when it happens.

No call writer should ever have more than 20% of his money tied up in one call, and as the investor expands his account, the amount ideally should fall to no more than 10%. In selling a call, the profit is limited for each call. The only way to make money is to have enough calls so that if you do lose on a few, they will not be able to drag your overall profit down to a loss.

Rule 5. This is the most obvious one—learn all you can about the stock you are dealing in, especially with respect to its price movement. Since an option exists for only a short period, it is my belief that you can ignore the fundamentals in your determination. They won't be very likely to influence the movement of the stock price in the few months of interest to you.

Do concentrate on its past price habits as shown on ten-year charts. Find out its Beta to learn whether it is a fast mover. Look up the high for the year and the low. Analyze its price/earnings ratio. In general, the higher the P/E ratio the more movement there can be in a stock. And of course you are looking for the factors that indicate that the stock is not a fast mover. You are looking for a stock with a good premium, but even more importantly, for one that does not move fast. Because even if the premium is small, if the stock never gets to the strike price, your profit is still 100% of the premium you received.

Rule 6. To make the maximum profits at writing options you must be constantly on the alert. Option writing is not for the person who wants to make an investment and forget it. Due to the limited time period of options, they change constantly and rapidly. The successful option writer must be able to get out of positions fast when he has a profit, get into new ones, perhaps committing a bit more money in the final month of the option period, letting some options ride, selling out others because he sees better alternative investment opportunities.

Writing options is a highly risky business. But unless the market as a whole rises by an unusually large amount, the option writer who follows these rules should come out ahead. He must, however, use all the rules given above. Because some options are bound to go sour and knock out two or three that are winners, you must seek to make the most out of the winners. But if the market does not rise spectacularly and if you keep reinvesting your winnings and cutting your possible losses by a consistent stop-loss program, you should come out a winner.

BUYING AND SELLING PUTS

5

Buying them, selling them, and how to make your own

As we have seen in the preceding chapters, a call is the option to *buy* a share of stock for a specified price within a given duration of time. It is purchased by a person who believes that the stock will rise in price, and that his right to purchase the stock for the specified price will become a valuable right as the market price of the stock moves up above the specified price.

A put is the option to *sell* a share of stock for a specified price within a given duration of time. It is purchased by an investor who believes that the stock will decline in price. If he is correct, and the stock has declined to a point far enough below the strike price of the put to cover the costs of commissions, the put owner will go into the market just before its expiration, purchase the stock at the low market price, and then immediately sell it to the put issuer for the strike price, or, of course, the owner could simply sell the put instead.

Puts have all the characteristics of calls, that is, they have an expiration date and a strike price. As this book is being written, puts are being traded on only a limited number of stocks, but it is anticipated that eventually there will be puts for every stock that has calls.

To find which stocks have puts you can look in Appendix B or check a newspaper listing for those options which have the letter "p" after the name of the stock. For example, if a stock is selling for 47, you may see that the four-month put with a 50 strike price is selling for 4. The 50 put already has an intrinsic cash value of 3, because the put takes on value when the stock goes down below the strike price, and this stock is 3 points below the strike price. The extra point in the price of the put is the future time value of the put. If you look for the price of the 45 put it may be 1. Since the current price of the stock is above the strike price of this put, the put is out of the money and the $1 price of the put is therefore entirely future time value. If there is a 40 strike price option it might be selling for just ⅜ point because it is far out of the money. A 60 strike price put would be selling at 13¼, because it is deep in the money.

The 13 points represent the large intrinsic value of the put, and put buyers are willing to pay only an additional ¼ point for the future time value of the put.

As the price of the stock goes down, the price of the put will increase. At 43, upon the expiration of the option, the 50 put will be worth 7. It will be worth more if the stock reaches that price before the expiration of the put. The 45 strike price put will be worth 2 upon the option's expiration, and at 40, the 45 put will be worth 5. Since it could have been purchased for 1, it is clear that puts can be a very profitable speculation on a stock that declines.

But until puts on the stock you want are traded on an exchange there are traditional over-the-counter (OTC) puts available for those who want to use them. Of course, the OTC puts are subject to the same disadvantages that make OTC calls less desirable: high commissions, uncertainty as to the price, and almost no liquidity. In other words, once one has purchased an OTC put, or sold one, it is extremely difficult to close out the transaction until it is about to expire.

MAKING YOUR OWN PUTS

Nevertheless, it is possible for investors to obtain most of the advantages of exchange puts even before they are actually traded on an exchange. The method is to make your own puts. This is done by simultaneously buying a call on a stock and selling the same number of shares of stock short. Just how does this work? Let's take a specific example. Assume a stock is at 69⅞, and the January 65 call is 9¼. The investor sells 100 shares of the stock short, which requires that he deposit 50% or more of the current market price of the shares with his broker as margin, and purchases a call.

Possibilities

What are the possibilities? First let's take the hoped-for outcome: the stock falls. If the stock falls to 55 by the expiration date of the January call, here is the result. The call that the investor purchased is now worthless, so he has a loss of $925. But the short sale has been profitable. He sold the shares for $6,987.50, and now when he covers his short position by buying the shares back, they cost him only $5,500, for a profit on the short sale of $1,487.50. Subtract from this the loss of $925 on the purchase of the call, and we have a net profit of $562.50.

Since all the profit was made on the short sale, and the purchase of the call was a significant loss, you might wonder why it was necessary to purchase the call at all. The answer is that the call is what limits your risk of loss and transforms the ordinary short sale, which has an infinite capacity for loss, into a fixed maximum loss situation. This can be easily illustrated by looking at what would happen if the stock had gone up instead of down.

Let us assume that at the call expiration date the stock is worth 100. If the investor had sold the stock short without buying a call, his loss would be the cost of covering his short position, $100 times the 100 shares he sold short for a cost of $10,000, minus the amount he received when he originally sold the stock short of $6,987.50, giving a loss of $3,012.50. And of course, if the stock had gone higher, his loss would have been even greater.

Now let's see what happens when the investor sells the stock short and buys a call. As the stock rises and he loses money on his short, his call automatically becomes worth more as it rises above the strike price. For every dollar that the price of the stock exceeds the strike price on the expiration date, the investor will make an additional dollar on the call and lose an additional dollar on the short sale. Thus, the two balance each other out, and the final loss will be the original cost of the call, minus the amount that the price of the stock was above the call strike price when the call was originally purchased. In other words, the cost of the transaction will be the future time value cost of the call on the date it was purchased. In our example the call cost $925, but when we bought it the stock was 4⅞ above the strike price. Subtracting $488 gives a net loss of $437.

Capital requirements

Thus the "homemade" put works just as well as one that you would buy, except for two disadvantages. The first is the amount of capital that is required. In addition to the cost of the call, the regular margin requirement for selling stock short must be deposited. This margin requirement is currently 50% of the market price of the stock, with many brokerage firms requiring more. If the price of the stock goes up, the investor will be required to mark to the market by depositing additional funds. This large amount of cash means that a person using a homemade put can never earn the large rate of return on capital that he could earn from a real put.

Another major disadvantage of a homemade put is that when you short stock you are required to pay any dividends which are declared on the stock. The reason for this is that the stock is borrowed from someone who may not even know it had been loaned out, and he is entitled to its dividends. But when the stock was sold short it was purchased by someone else, who doesn't know it was borrowed stock, and since he now owns the stock, he also is entitled to its dividends. Thus one share of stock must now pay dividends to two people, and it is the short seller who must provide the additional dividends.

CONVERSION-HOUSE PUTS

Fortunately, there is a way of overcoming the capital requirement that your broker may be able to arrange for you. There are some large brokerage and investment banking firms that are willing to act as conversion houses and are willing to convert calls into puts. In order to do this they purchase calls on an option exchange and then sell the stock short themselves. As a result of this they have a homemade or synthetic put, and they are then willing to sell this put to an outsider. So what, you may ask, you can do this yourself. Well, the big advantage is that these conversion houses will sell you the put for its current cost, without requiring you to deposit the margin required for a short sale of the stock. So, you are getting the advantage of a homemade put without the disadvantage of having to deposit margin and incur the risk of being required to deposit additional margin if the price of the stock increases.

What price does the conversion house charge for this put? The price is the actual cost of the put to them, plus a nominal service charge such as 25¢ per share. To determine the cost of such a put, take the strike price of the call that the conversion house will have to purchase, add to the strike price the price of the call, and subtract the price of the common stock. For example, if you want to purchase an April put on Sears with a 50 strike price, and Sears stock is selling for 52 and the April 50 call for 6¾, the price of your put would be: $50 plus $6.75, minus $52, giving $4.75 plus the 25¢ fee, for a total of $5.00, plus all the dividends that it is anticipated will be paid on the stock between the time you buy the put and its expiration.

You might wonder why the conversion house is being so accommodating as to perform this service for you at such a small profit. Since this is Wall Street and money is the name of the game, you may think that they are not doing this as a public service—and right you are. The reason that a conversion house is willing to do this is that you are paying for the call that then enables them to sell the stock short without taking any risk. When a brokerage firm sells a stock short it has borrowed the stock from a customer, which it does without paying the customer any interest, and it sells the stock on the open market, putting the proceeds from that sale into its own bank account until the short sale is covered.

In effect, therefore, the firm has created a balance in its bank account equal to the current price of the stock. And of course the conversion house is free to earn the interest on this bank balance, and that is the reason that they are so willing to be of service to you. Wouldn't you, if you could generate interest without any risk or cost?

Cost of synthetic puts

However, another disadvantage of a homemade or synthetic put as opposed to an exchange put is simply that it frequently costs more. Traditionally, puts cost less than calls, often about two-thirds as much. The reason for this is that investors in general are an optimistic lot, and they usually believe that there is a greater chance that stocks will go up than that they will go down. Furthermore, there is the obvious fact that a stock can only decline to zero and in practice, if we are talking about a healthy company, to a floor that is substantially above that amount, while a stock may go up to any amount. Thus, it does make some sense that the right to participate in a stock's rise should be worth more than the right to share in its decline. Unfortunately, whether you "make your own" put or use a conversion house, you are buying a put, but at the price of a call!

FUNDAMENTALS OF PUTS

For those who are used to calls, the "upside down" concepts of puts can be a bit confusing at first. Thus if a stock is selling for 57, a 60 put is 3 points "in the money" and if the put is worth $5, then it has 3 points of intrinsic cash value and 2 points of future time value. Similarly, when a stock is 63, the 60 put is 3 points out of the money and has no intrinsic value. As the price of a stock goes up, the value of any given put declines, and as the price of the stock goes down, the price of the put will increase.

But, of course, puts are not the mirror images of calls. For instance, one cannot offset a call position with a put position. If one is short a call, being long a put is not going to cancel out the risk of that position. In fact, being long a put when one is short a call is only adding to the risk, because both positions are on the same side, that is, they will both make money when the stock goes down. If you are short a call, and you want something that will counteract that with a put, then you must find a put position that will make money for you when the stock goes up. The proper position is to be short a put, because if you sell a put and the stock goes up, then the put will expire worthless and you make a profit of the amount for which you originally sold the put. But, please notice that even this is not a way to cancel your risk from selling the call. For example, if you are short a 50 call, which you had sold for $3, and the stock is now 47, you might decide you want to offset the risk on the call. You could sell a 50 put (remember that's in the money) for $4. Does this now mean that you have no risk on the upside? Not at all. Let's see what happens if the stock goes up to $60 upon expiration of the option. The put expires worthless, and you have that profit of $4. But what happened to the call? You must now buy it back for $10, and since you originally sold it for $3, this leaves you with a $7 loss on the call. Thus, the $4 profit on the put does not cancel out the loss on the call, and if the stock had gone higher, the loss obviously would have been even greater. The moral of the story is that while a put increases in value when a stock goes down, and a call increases in value when a stock goes up, they are not exact opposites, and you cannot assume that a put has the reverse effect of a call.

Now let's discuss the basic uses which investors and traders can make of puts. The most obvious is to purchase a put when you think that the stock is going to go down. Another use is to purchase a put on stock which you own, or buy simultaneously, because although you hope and expect that the stock will *not* go down, you want the put to protect you in case you are wrong. A third reason to purchase puts is simply as insurance in general in case there is a decline in the market. Selling puts can be used in a manner somewhat like selling naked calls, except that writing puts will be profitable if the stock does not go below the strike price. Then there are many combinations of puts with other puts and puts with calls which can be used, and these are discussed in the chapter on spreads.

Buying puts as a speculation

The easiest use of puts is to buy them on a stock that you believe is going down. The similarities to buying a call on a stock when you think that it is going up are very close. The selection of the strike price depends upon the same factors as in a call, except of course that everything is upside down. The put most people will find the best to purchase is just slightly in the money or slightly out of the money, because you are looking for a put that will make a profit for you on a minimum downside movement in the stock. If you take a put that is already deep in the money (where the stock is substantially below the put strike price) you will be paying a lot of money for the put, and you will not be able to make a large percentage gain on the cash you put up even if the stock moves down by a generous amount. On the other hand, if you buy an out-of-the-money put (where the stock is far above the put strike price) you run the risk that even if the stock moves down, it will not quite get to the strike price, and your put will expire worthless.

There is one basic difference in the pricing and profitability of puts as compared to calls. This is that the dividend is working with you, and the higher the anticipated dividend, the better off you are. The reason is that the amount and date of a dividend are usually well known on Wall Street weeks before the actual ex-dividend date. Therefore, the stock price already fully reflects the fact that everyone who purchases the stock before the ex-dividend date is entitled to the dividend, and anyone who purchases the stock after it has gone ex-dividend will not get that dividend. The result is that stocks normally open on the day that they go ex-dividend at a price that is reduced from the previous closing price by the amount of the dividend. For example, if a company pays a dividend of 50¢ a share and the stock closes at 47¼ the day before it goes ex-dividend, it will normally open the next morning at 46¾. In the case of certain dividends, this change can be quite significant. For instance, General Motors has in the past declared special year-end dividends of $3 a share. What this means is that any in-the-money put should start appreciating in value before the ex-dividend date, and the day before the stock goes ex-dividend, the in-the-money puts ought to be selling at almost $3 more than their normal value.

When you are buying puts you certainly are going to take a close look at the price of the put. Here again, all the factors that influence the pricing of a call will have the same effect upon the price of a put, if for no other reason than that brokerage firms and arbitrageurs can easily convert calls into puts and vice versa if it is worth their while. So that volatile stocks with high Betas, high P/E ratios, and low dividends will command the highest prices, while low prices will prevail on stocks with the opposite. As the table in Appendix D shows, the ease of conversion from put to call means that there must be comparability of the prices of puts and calls in any stock. The reason that the price of a put is not the exact equivalent of the price of the call is due to the dividend and to the cost of money.

Converting calls into puts

Once one understands how these two factors affect the conversion, one can figure out what the exact price should be. To create a put, a firm must first buy the call and then short the stock. As you remember from our discussion of synthetic puts, when one shorts one must pay all the anticipated dividends. Therefore, if one is converting calls into puts, one must include the cost of all anticipated dividends, and the presence of dividends will tend to make the puts more expensive in relation to the calls. If you look at the relationship of put prices to call prices, you will usually find that the put prices are relatively highest on those stocks with the biggest dividends. The second factor is that when a brokerage firm shorts stock and is protected by a call option, it usually does not have to put up any margin, and the amount of money received from shorting the stock is used by the brokerage firm to invest at interest. So, creating puts is a money-making operation, and firms are happy to do it even if they must take a small loss on the exchange, knowing that they can make this up on the interest. That is why the puts of some expensive stocks like I.B.M. appear so cheap in relation to the cost of the calls. But if you will figure in the money that a firm receives from the short sale of the stock, and multiply this by the brokers' call rate of interest times the amount of time remaining, you will understand why puts are cheaper. So, from the viewpoint of creating puts from calls, the higher the dividend, the more expensive the put; the more expensive the stock, the more money is created by shorting it, and the cheaper the put will be.

This conversion process can work the other way too. A firm, or you yourself for that matter, can buy a put, buy 100 shares of the stock, and voilà! You have created a call. Since you own the stock you receive the dividends, and the higher the dividends, the lower the cost of the call. You also must put up the money to buy those 100 shares of stock, so the more expensive the stock, the higher your cost of money, and the more expensive the call will be. Thus the cost factors for conversion from a call to a put are exactly the same as for the reverse conversion.

Since there is such ease in converting calls into puts, it is axiomatic that the pricing will be comparable, and that is why it is so easy to apply the rules of strategy for buying calls to buying puts. The future time value will be greatest for those puts which are at the strike price, and will decrease as the stock moves away from the strike price in either direction. The longer-duration options will be more expensive, but less expensive on a per-unit-of-time basis.

So in purchasing a put, you can comfortably use the rules outlined in Chapter 2 for buying calls.

Buying puts to protect a stock investment

If you own stock there may be many reasons why you are afraid of the downside risk but do not wish to give up ownership of the stock. One frequent problem is that you have owned the stock for so long, or perhaps you have even inherited it, that its tax basis is so low that a sale would result in a very large capital gains tax. So you are in practice prevented from selling the stock. And yet you may have serious grounds for believing that the stock may decline precipitously. Or you may want to hold onto a stock because you believe in it for the long haul and do not want to sell the stock now, incur sizable commission costs, and then buy it back later, also at sizable commission costs. In any situation where you do not want to sell your stock for some reason such as these, but do want to get absolute protection against a decline in the price of the stock, the purchase of a put is the perfect solution.

Before we discuss this in more length, let's look at some instances where it is not necessarily the answer. If you are going to sell the stock at some future date in any event, and you want to hold onto it now because you believe the stock still could go up, but you do want that downside protection, then buying a put is an answer, but it may not be the best answer. The reason for this is that an equivalent of being long stock and long a put is to be long a call. Strange as this seems, in both cases on the downside all that you can lose is the premium on the option, whether it be the put or call, and on the upside there is unlimited potential. Being long a call instead of being long the stock and a put has one big advantage, namely that you have freed up all the cash you had invested in the stock. So if you can have exactly the same position by being long a call, you should carefully consider selling your stock and buying a call, so that you can then invest the money from the stock in something that can be of more potential profit to you than simply substituting for a call.

But if there is a legitimate reason for not selling the stock, then the purchase of a put will provide you with absolute protection against a downside move. In fact, it is no exaggeration at all to call the purchase of a put in this case insurance against any price decline, because no matter how low the price of the stock goes, down to and including zero, the put will give you absolute and complete protection against loss. The only catch is that you will be out by the part of the put's price that was its future time value. This will be a direct cost to you no matter what happens to the price of the stock. So when you buy the put, you must realize that the future time value of the put will never be recovered, whether the stock goes up or down, that it is simply a loss like the premium on a fire insurance policy. It may save you many times its cost, but it is still a cost. For example, if you own a stock which is at 63 and you buy a 70 put for $9, you are paying $2 for its future time value and this money will never be recovered. The other $7 represent the intrinsic cash value of the put, and they will be recovered when you sell the put, regardless of what happens to the stock. If the stock ends up at $53 when the put expires, your stock is down $10, the put is worth $17, meaning that you have a profit of $17 minus $9 = $8 on the put, offset by the $10 loss on the stock, giving a net loss of $2. This is the future time value of the original put.

If the stock goes up. Let's see what happens if the stock goes up. Remember that your put gives you protection up to the strike price, and not beyond. So, if the stock goes up $10 to $73, you should be making a profit of the amount by which the stock goes up over the strike price of the option, which would be $3. But you have a profit of $10 on the stock, while the put has become worthless with the stock above its strike price. Since it cost you $9, the loss on your put subtracted from the $10 profit on the stock, gives you a net profit of just $1. This is the $3 profit you should have made minus the $2 originally paid for the future time value of the put. The moral of the story is that if you have the choice of buying two out-of-the-money puts to protect your stock position, you will wind up paying less if you get the one with the higher strike price (the one deeper in the money and hence with the lower cost for future time value). This must be carefully weighed, however, against the fact that once you buy a put on stock you own, you cannot make any money until the stock goes up above its strike price. So the higher-strike-price put will prevent you from making a profit until your stock goes above its strike price.

Tax problem

One point to keep in mind in buying a put on stock you own is that if you have not held the stock long enough to qualify for long-term capital gains treatment (one year as of 1978), then the purchase of the put will completely eliminate the holding period you already have and will stop the holding period from running until you have sold the put. For example, if you have owned some stock for ten months and you then purchase a put on that stock to give you downside protection, then hold the put for five months, your holding period of the stock when you sell that put will be zero for purposes of computing whether the stock qualifies for long-term capital gain. You must therefore own the stock for an entire year after you have sold the put to qualify for long-term treatment. Thus, the time you held the stock before you bought the put, and the time you owned the stock while you owned the put, are both completely lost.

Interestingly enough, once you have attained long-term status with your stock, then you can buy a put and it will have no effect upon the status of the stock. So if you are considering buying a put to protect your stock, you ought to do it promptly after you have acquired the stock, or else wait for your year to run out, when it becomes long-term. Selling a put after you have owned a stock for eleven months could be a very expensive move in terms of taxes.

After this long discussion, it might occur to you that another method of getting downside protection, without having to pay out any money but in fact getting money in, is to sell a call against the stock. This does take in money and can be profitable, but it is *not* insurance against a decline in the stock's price. It is protection merely to the extent of the money you take in from the sale of the call. If the stock goes down by more than that amount, you are on your own. If you are really worried about a stock falling out of bed, a call is not going to be a very good substitute, even though a deep-in-the-money call can give a great deal of protection. It is not the same as being insured.

An expensive practice. One further word should be said about the concept of buying puts on stocks you already own. It is the view of the author that this should be done only on a temporary basis. Even when premiums are low, the cost of continually buying puts on a stock one owns is very likely to drain out all the potential profit from owning the stock. Just as constantly buying calls on the same stock is unlikely to be profitable over an extended period of time, so buying puts on a stock is also likely to end up losing money. If you feel so uncomfortable owning a stock that you feel the need to constantly have the protection of a put, then perhaps you shouldn't own that stock at all.

A possible compromise would be to buy out-of-the-money puts. If these are available, they will be very cheap, because their strike prices are so far below the current price of the stock. They will not provide you any help if the price of the stock dips slightly, but in that infrequent time when the stock just crashes down, the put will be there to save you like the safety net under the trapeze artists at the circus. Perhaps such a program is worth its slight cost for the peace of mind it gives.

An alternative means for having some security in owning stocks has always been to put in a good till cancelled stop-loss order at a price well below the current price of the stock. When the stock reaches the indicated price, the order automatically becomes a market order and the stock is sold. But there are two big differences and advantages which puts have over stop-loss orders. The first is that a put provides a continuous protection from the day the put is purchased until it expires. The bane of the stop-loss order is that the stock may go down to the level of the order, touch off the sale of all the stock, and then the price of the stock can soar back up to more than the purchase cost, without of course the person who was taken out of his position by the stop-loss order. This can happen no matter at what price you put the stop-loss order.

With a put working for you, you can simply wait until the put is about to expire and then cash it in. You will continue to own the stock for the entire period, and you cannot be faked out by a sudden dip in the stock. The stock can go up and down by any amount in any sequence, and you will come out owning the stock and making the profit if it is up while being fully protected against any loss because the stock is below the strike price of the put on the final day of the put's life.

The second big advantage of the put is that it is actually insurance, meaning that a put will give you the amount of money necessary to reimburse you for a loss on the stock. A stop-loss order gives you nothing. It simply is a means of limiting your loss. Thus, while a put is like a fire insurance policy, a stop-loss order is simply like a sprinkler system. It may limit the loss, but it doesn't pay the bills for you.

Buying puts to protect a portfolio

We have already discussed buying a put to give you downside protection on a specific stock. Another very helpful use of puts can be as insurance against a decline in the value of your entire stock portfolio. Since puts are now available on only a very small percentage of the stocks a person might have in his portfolio, it is invariably impossible to provide insurance against a decline in the very stocks which a person owns. But, by carefully selecting puts on a representative list of stocks, or on stocks that match the ones you own, it may be possible to come up with a list of puts that roughly resemble the type of securities in your own portfolio.

Since the typical portfolio is long stock, it makes a good hedge to own some puts in case the market goes down. If the market goes up, you will make so much money on the stocks you own that you shouldn't mind the loss of the money you spent for the puts. But if the market really goes down, the puts will produce many times their cost. For this type of scatter insurance, it might be wisest to use out-of-the-money puts, which are inexpensive. They will not become profitable until the market, or the particular stocks you select, have a substantial decline, but that is when you really need the help they can give. You are probably willing to wait out a small decrease in stock prices or you wouldn't be in common stocks in the first place. So an out-of-the-money put could be just right; low cost in case the market goes up, but emergency insurance in case it drops severely. You could think of it as collision insurance with a large deductible. Unless there is a major accident, the puts aren't going to help you, but when you really need them in a disaster, they'll be there.

Some of the brightest money managers I know make extensive use of puts for just this purpose. Especially when combined with a covered call writing program they make sense. As one money manager who uses covered calls pointed out, "I can absorb a decline of about 10% with my calls, but beyond that any loss goes right down to the bottom line. That's why I need the protection of out-of-the-money puts." A comment well worth considering. One final note: The time to buy puts is always when the market is going up, everyone is bullish, and you are absolutely certain that you will not need them.

Selling puts

When we discussed selling calls, we used two different chapters, selling covered calls and selling naked calls. We needed two different chapters, because although both strategies involved the sale of calls, they are totally different in result and could not be discussed together. The interesting thing about puts is that there is literally no method of selling a covered put against stock. At first glance one would think that selling a put against a short stock position would be the sale of a covered put, and I suppose theoretically that is correct. But although you may be protected in the downside from a loss on your naked put, you are totally exposed on the upside to a loss on your stock short position. So, the OCC prospectus states quite clearly that the only way to sell a covered put is to be long a put on the same stock with a longer or similar expiration period and with a lower or equal strike price. Thus, there is no put equivalent to selling a covered call. So this chapter is perforce limited to a consideration of naked put writing.

Fundamentally, selling uncovered puts is quite similar to selling uncovered calls. You take in the premium from the put, are required to have on deposit the proper amount of margin, and the original price you received is your profit as long as the stock stays out of the money at the expiration date (i.e, above the strike price in the case of a put). A put seller is basically an optimist about the stock market, at least to the extent that he does not expect the stocks to go down below the strike price. As in selling naked calls, however, no matter how right he is and no matter how far up the stocks climb, he can make no more than the amount of the premium he originally received. His loss is limited to only how low the stock can go.

For example, if a stock is now 37, and you sell the 35 put for 2, you are betting that, upon the expiration of the put, the stock will be at 33 or better. At 33, the put will be 2 points in the money, and thus have a cash value of 2, so that if you buy it back for its cash value on the last day, you will break even. If the stock is 34, the put will be worth $1 on the last day and anywhere at 35 or better it will be worthless, giving you a profit of $2.

Typically, the naked put seller will be selling out-of-the-money puts, and the amount by which they are out of the money will be determined by the amount of premium which can be obtained, and probably by the extent to which the put seller is bullish on the market.

Like his cousin, the naked call seller, a naked put seller will probably also be interested in maximizing his return on a per-week basis by selling only the shortest-term puts, almost never with more than three months of life left, and usually with about six to eight weeks left.

His selection of the proper stock will be determined by his quest for the highest premium possible and by his distaste for selling a put on a stock that could plunge rapidly in price. As is the case in every other aspect of options, so here too these two conflicting goals will result in a subjective decision which will not be the same for the many different naked put sellers. One factor which will undoubtedly influence decisions on which stock to write puts is that put premiums will tend to be higher on stocks which are moving down. This is because so many Wall Street aficionados are chart followers or technicians of one sort or another. Without trying to oversimplify a very complicated group of theories, it can be said that in general most chart watchers believe that if a stock is going down, it is likely to continue to go down, and if it is already reaching new lows, then it is even more likely to continue going down, because it has now passed its downside support area. Therefore, these true believers in the validity of technical analysis of stock prices will be rushing in to buy puts on stocks which are making new lows. The result is that these puts should be selling for more than their normal value given the volatility of the stock, the amount of time remaining in the life of the put, and the relationship of the price of the stock to the strike price of the option.

Finding the overpriced put. The true option believer, who is interested in whether an option is over- or underpriced, and not in what some chart watchers say about the stock, will quickly spot such a situation as one that is made to order for him to sell the puts which the chart watchers are so eagerly seeking to buy. In fact, if the naked put seller partially believes stock prices move in an unpredictable manner, this is the position of the "random walk" believer, the purest form of option investor; but also looks at fundamental statistics of the stock such as price/earnings ratio and dividend yield, he might conclude that now that the stock is at a lower price level than it was before, demand for the stock should increase, and it should be even less likely to fall in price than when it was higher in price. And so one word of advice I can give the naked put seller is to look for those stocks that have been falling recently if he wants to spot the overpriced put.

Just as in selling naked calls, the naked put seller needs to have on deposit the required amount of margin. This margin is computed in exactly the same manner as that required for calls. First, you must know what percentage requirement your brokerage firm is requiring of you. The lowest percentage permitted now by federal regulations is 30%, but many firms require more. In many cases the requirement is 50%. Step one is to take that percentage of the current price of the stock. Step two is to subtract the amount by which the stock is out of the money, i.e., the amount by which the current price of the stock is above the strike price of the put, or add the amount by which the put is in the money, i.e., the amount by which the current price of the stock is lower than the strike price of the option. Finally, to determine the amount of money which you must deposit to do the naked sale, you can deduct the amount of the premium which you take in.

Computing the margin requirement. For example, if a stock is currently selling for $66 and you think that it would be profitable to write the nearest duration $60 put for a premium of $2, the margin would be computed this way: (1) Assuming that you are permitted to use the minimum rate of 30%, you would multiply the present price of the stock, $66, by 30%, getting $19.80. (2) You next determine whether the put is in the money or out of the money. Here it is out of the money, so you can deduct the difference between the current price of the stock and the strike price. That difference is $6, and subtracting $6 from $19.80 leaves us $13.80. (3) Finally, to determine how much money you must add to your account to carry this position, you can deduct the full amount of the premiums you took in. Subtracting $2 from $13.80 gives a total margin call of $11.80. Therefore, for the opportunity of making $2, you must invest $11.80, which means that your maximum return from this trade would be 16.9%. If the option had two months to go, you would multiply by six to get the annualized rate of return, which turns out to be a 101% return on your money. Since that figure seems unusually high, remember that you will make that much money only if you can reinvest the entire amount at the same rate of return every other month, and only if all the trades you make during the year turn out to be completely successful. These are very large "ifs" indeed, and provide the basis for the SEC rule that annualized returns cannot be used by brokers to describe how profitable a particular trade is, but may be used only in a comparative sense so that equivalent option trades of different durations can be analyzed with a common standardized means of measurement.

But there is an even more important reason why that rate of return is highly questionable as a realistic measurement of rate of return. This is that, just as in naked call selling, the amount of margin required for selling naked puts is marked to the market every day. This means that every time the price of the stock falls by one point, if you have only the minimum margin on deposit, you will be required by your brokerage firm to come up with more margin money. The amount of money required for each decline of one point can be determined as follows: (1) Recompute the requirement for a percentage of the current price of the stock. Since the price of the stock is falling, this amount will be less. If you are on a 30% requirement, then each decline of a point will reduce this part of the margin requirement by $30 per put, and if you are on a 50% requirement, it will be reduced by $50 per put. (2) Add one point for each point decline to make up for the fact that as the stock gets closer to the put strike price, the difference between the two, which you subtracted from the margin requirement, is reduced. (3) The result is that if you are on a 30% requirement, your margin requirement will increase by $70 per put, and if you are on a 50% requirement, then it will increase by $50 per put for each one-point drop in stock.

When one originally sells a put it is impossible to tell whether the stock will go down or not, and therefore it is not possible to state that the original amount of margin is the amount which will be the maximum requirement later on. Therefore, if a person has $10,000 to use in writing naked puts, he cannot with any prudence write enough puts to use up his $10,000 in initial margin requirements, because if any of his stocks start to go down, he will get a margin call, which will result in some of his position being liquidated, probably at a loss. Anyone contemplating selling naked puts must have some additional capital in reserve with which to provide additional margin. Of course, it is possible that the stocks can go up. If this happens, exactly as much margin is released as was required when they went down, i.e., $70 per put if you are on 30% margin requirement, and $50 if you are on 50%.

One final similarity between writing naked puts and writing naked calls is that it is just as dangerous and speculative to write puts as it is calls. Stocks can fall even more rapidly than they rise and when they do it can mean quick losses for the put writer. In fact, since put premiums appear to be usually less than call premiums, the price of a put will increase proportionally even more rapidly than a call once the put becomes in the money. Thus, it is imperative to have a method of making sure that your loss is held to a reasonable limit. Otherwise you will be in the situation of trying to make money from a transaction with a very modest possible gain but an almost infinite possible loss. And you know that it is hard to make money from that kind of a game.

Limiting your loss. The best method of limiting your loss is to watch either the price of the stock or the price of the put and decide to buy back your put once the stock gets below your limit or the price of your put exceeds your limit. Unfortunately there is no automatic method of doing this and so you must rely upon the attention of your broker. But please make sure that as soon as you have sold your naked put, you decide exactly when you are going to close out your position. If you do not, you are going to be tempted to fall into the treacherous trap of inaction, which means that when the stock falls by 3 points you hesitate to close out your position because you will be creating an irrevocable loss, whereas if you let things alone the stock might go back up and you will have a wonderful profit, just as you had originally expected. Believe me, with this kind of thinking you can watch a stock go from 105 to 55 and not close out your position, with a resulting loss that will be staggering. Of course, you might be lucky and the stock could go back up. But don't bet on it. The entire purpose of this book is to suggest methods of substituting action which will give you the best probability of making money and will reduce your dependence upon luck. If you want to trust lady luck, don't be surprised if she turns out to be a fickle lady indeed, and you are later forced to close out your position by the ever-increasing margin requirement at a much larger loss than you would have had earlier.

In all seriousness, writing naked puts should be done only by someone who is willing to decide upon his stop-loss limits before he writes the put and is then willing to stick to his decision exactly. It seems hard to do at the time, but life sometimes requires difficult action. One way of making it easier is to have a number of partial limits. If you have written ten puts, you might decide that you will buy back two when the stock gets to 45, two more at 44, another two at 43, and so on. This eliminates the terrible feeling when you buy in your puts that you are converting what might have been a handsome profit into a sure loss. By closing out only a portion of your position at a time you are never converting your entire position into a total loss at once.

Selling puts as a means of acquiring stock

So far we have considered selling puts only as a means of making money on a margin balance. If the stock went down below the strike price, we assumed that the put writer would buy back the put before he was exercised. He obviously doesn't want to be exercised and have to pay commissions on purchasing the high-priced stock upon the exercise of his put, and then pay another commission when he sells the stock out at the market price. But there is another type of put writer who would not complain if his put is exercised. This is the type of person who likes the underlying stock. He is not selling the put because it is necessarily overpriced and he feels confident that the stock will not get below the strike price. Rather, he likes the stock and would be happy to purchase it if he could get it at a discount from its current market price. He therefore sells a put, taking in premium income, and if the put is exercised he has bought the stock at a price which is reduced from today's price by the amount of the future time value in the put when he sold it.

This type of put writer can write either in-the-money or out-of-the-money puts, depending upon how badly he wants to own the stock, and how he feels about making money simply by being a naked put writer. Let's take the same example we used before; the stock is now $66 and the nearest-term put at the $60 level is $2. Our put writer may decide to write this put, and if the price of the stock stays above $60, he is pleased to have made a good return on the sale of the naked put. He is not sorry that he didn't buy the stock, because he only wanted to buy it at a price below $60. In this respect he is identical to our naked put seller above. But if the price of the stock should drop to $55, he would behave differently. Unlike the regular naked put seller, who would set a level at which he would buy in the put, this put seller sets no such level. He doesn't care how low the stock goes, because he is quite willing to have the stock put to him at $60. With the premium of $2 he received for selling the put, his actual purchase cost for the stock is just $58. A large discount indeed from the cost of $66 which he would have had if he had purchased the stock in the open market originally.

This type of put seller could also sell an in-the-money put. Let us assume that there is a put with a 70 strike price and that it is selling for $6, consisting of $4 cash value, and future time value of $2. If the put seller were more interested in acquiring the stock, this is the method he would use, because he is going to have to buy the stock unless it goes above $70 a share on the put's expiration date. If the stock goes up to $69, the put will be exercised and he will have to buy the stock for $70. Since he originally received $6 for the sale of the put, his actual cost for the stock is $64, which is a discount of $2 from the price of the stock on the day that he sold the put. Note that this in-the-money put seller is much more likely to end up as a buyer of the stock than the seller of the 60 strike price put. And if he does not end up buying the stock, it is only because it has gone up above the $70 strike price. The result of this is that the entire $6 which he took in from the original sale of the put is his profit. So this person either gets the stock at $2 below the market, or he makes a whopping profit on his naked put. Either way he should be happy.

No assurance of actually buying the stock. A word of warning is in order here. Selling naked puts is not a way of acquiring stock if you really want to get the stock. If you really want to own some stock the only way to be sure of owning it is to either enter a market order to buy the shares, or else to buy a call and exercise it at some future date. Selling a put gives you no assurance that you will own the stock, for the simple reason that if the price of the stock goes above the strike price, it will not be put to you. And this is the very time when you want to own the stock, when it is going up! So, don't think that selling puts is the miraculous method of always buying stock at a discount.

If you are right, and the stock goes up the way you think that it will, you will not buy it. But if you are wrong, and the stock goes down, then you will be forced to buy it, probably at a higher net price than it is currently selling for, all your kicking and screaming to the contrary notwithstanding! This is not following Will Rogers' advice on how to get rich on Wall Street. Said he, "It's very simple, you just buy a stock that's going to go up. And if it doesn't go up, then you don't buy it in the first place." A naked put seller is often doing just the opposite. But it is the perfect strategy for the person who would like either to get a stock at a low price or to make a good return on his money from the put premium.

SPREADS, STRADDLES, AND COMBINATIONS 6

A spread is a position which consists of being long one or more options on a stock and short one or more options on the same stock, but of a different series, i.e., a different strike price or expiration date. Thus, if one is long 5 RCA October 30 calls and is also at the same time short 5 RCA July 30 calls, that is a spread. There is an enormous variety of spreads available, but they all have in common that one position is long and the other is short. Spreads can involve calls or puts but, where both puts and calls are involved in a single stock, that is a called a straddle or combination.

Now that we have learned that one can make a great deal of money buying a call if the stock goes up, and a lot of money buying a put when the stock goes down, you might wonder why we have to fool around with a combination of being long and short the same options on the same stock at the same time? Isn't that contradictory and self-defeating? In a way yes, but in another way definitely no. Spreads are extremely popular because they serve a very useful purpose. If we have firm convictions that a stock is going to move a large amount in a specific direction, we will always be better off simply buying a call or a put as the price direction indicates.

But in the real world, clouded as it is in uncertainty, we often do not have a firm conviction as to what is going to happen, or we believe that a stock will make only a relatively modest move. It is in these circumstances that spreads are made to order. One can say that the purpose of a spread is to increase the range of prices under which a person can make money, but this is done at the cost of limiting the potential profit which can be made. In other words, there is a larger range of stock prices in which some profit will be made, but there is no longer the possibility of infinite riches as there is in simply buying an option.

An example would be a bull spread, which is a spread one uses when one is expecting a stock to go up. If a stock is now selling at 41, and the 40 strike price option is 4, the purchase of the call will not be profitable on expiration until the stock reaches 44. Of course it is profitable at any level above that, and if the stock really takes off, say to 55, there will be a profit of 11 on the 4 investment. On the other hand, a bull spread which consists in buying the 40 call and selling the 45 call, may cost as little as 2, which means that the position breaks even at just 42. Thus the break-even point has been reduced by 2 points, which is a substantial reduction. On the other hand, the maximum profit is reached when the stock gets to 45, and no matter how much higher it goes above the level, it does not add one penny to the profit of the bull spread.

Vertical spreads and horizontal spreads. Spreads are divided into two major groups. There are the vertical, or price, spreads, and the horizontal, or calendar, spreads. Vertical spreads consist of two options of the same expiration date with different strike prices. Since the options are listed in the newspaper columns with one strike price under the other of the same month, it is easy to see why these are called vertical spreads, and one can find them just by looking at the option above or below any other option. For example, a spread involving an October 25 and an October 30 option is a vertical spread.

Another reason that tyus type of spread may be called a vertical spread is that the price of the stock must move vertically in order to make money, and hence they are also sometimes called price spreads.

In contrast to the vertical spreads, the horizontal spreads, can be found in the newspaper columns by reading across a line. For example, a spread involving an October 25 and a January 25 option is a horizontal spread. Because these involve spreads of different expiration months, they are more frequently called calendar spreads or time spreads. Unlike vertical spreads, which make money primarily from the movement in the price of the stock, calendar spreads rely upon the effect of time upon the relationship of the option prices.

Volatility and nonvolatility spreads. Another classification of spreads which is useful is a volatility spread. This is a spread position in which one will make money if the stock moves in either direction, provided only that it moves far enough and soon enough. The opposite of this is a nonvolatility spread, in which one makes money when the stock stays right where it is now. An example of a volatility spread is being short an in-the-money 20 option for a price of perhaps 3, and then being long three 25 options at a price of perhaps ½ each. In this case the spread is done for a credit of 1½. If the stock declines below 20, all the options become worthless and the spread is profitable. On the other hand, if the stock goes up far enough above 25, each of the three 25 options begins to make enough to offset the loss on the single 20 option.

The best example of a nonvolatility spread is an on-the-money calendar spread because it is the most profitable when the stock ends up right at the strike price. Thus, if a stock is now 60, and you put on a calendar spread involving an April 60 and a July 60, you will make the most money when the stock stays just where it is, and hence this is called a nonvolatility spread.

Then there are also an almost infinite number of complex spreads, including the butterfly or sandwich spread, the diagonal spread, and the domino spread (see Fig. 12). But one should remember, in options as in life in

	Cost	Profit
Out-of-the-Money Bull Spread	$ .12½ to $2.00	$4.87½ to $3.00
On-the-Money Bull Spread	$1.00 to $2.50	$4.00 to $2.50
In-the-Money Bull Spread	$2.50 to $4.75	$2.50 to $ .25
Out-of-the-Money Calendar Spread	$ .12½ to $1.50	$ .25 to $3.00
On-the-Money Calendar Spread	$1.00 to $3.00	$1.00 to $3.00
In-the-Money Calendar Spread	$2.50 to $4.75	$2.50 to $2.25
On-the-Money Bear Spread	$1.00 to $2.50	$4.00 to $2.50
In-the-Money Bear Spread	$ .25 to $1.50	$ .25 to $1.50
Out-of-the-Money Bear Spread	$ .12½ to $2.00	$4.87½ to $4.87½
Butterfly Spread	$0 to $2.00	$5.00 to $3.00

Figure 12. *Profitability range of spreads*
Area of box indicates profit zone

Figures, which are only approximate guidelines, are for spreads of options with strike prices $5 apart. Double figures if strike prices are $10 apart. Cost is also the amount at risk, all of which can be lost. Profit is the potential profit if stock ends up at proper price.

general, the theory of Ockham's razor applies. This theory holds that where there are two methods of accomplishing the same objective, the simpler method is preferred. This is especially true in options for three reasons. One, the amount of commissions is greatly increased by using complex spreads. Two, complex spreads are much harder to execute and "take off" (get out of) than simpler spreads; and three, a complex spread will usually involve being short more options and each option you are short involves the danger of unwelcome exercise which is the bane of the option trader's existence. So before you put on a complex spread, try hard to know whether it is possible to accomplish the same thing, or almost the same thing, with a much simpler spread. You don't want to be in the position of accidentally having done an alligator spread. What's that? That's the phrase brokers use for a spread in which the commissions eat you alive.

Executing the spread order

Now let's talk about how spreads are executed. When you buy a share of stock, if you are a careful investor, you may put in a limit order, i.e., to buy the stock at any price up to 25½, but you will not pay any more for the stock than that. The same thing is true when you buy options. Now, when it comes to doing a spread, where you are simultaneously buying one option and selling another, how can you be sure that they will both be done at prices which give you the spread you want at a price you are willing to pay? If you put in an order to buy an option for no more than 3, and then sell another for no less than 1 (if you are trying to do a spread at a cost of 2), you might find that the stock was going up, and you had no trouble in selling an option for 1, but you couldn't buy the other option for 3. So instead of having a spread, you are left being short a naked option, which is the last thing in the world you wanted to do.

The answer to this dilemma is resolved by the fact that you really do not care at what prices the individual options are bought or sold for, it is the net difference between the prices of the spread that you are interested in. And the exchanges all accept spread orders to be done at a certain difference in spread i.e., for a debit of 3½ or for a credit of 9. When you put in an order of this type, it must be done either at the debit you request, or lower, or for the credit you asked, or for more, or it will not be done at all.

This brings us to another point about spreads. You may think that if you are doing a bull spread you will make money for an increase in the price of the stock. And this may be correct. But to option professionals, the way they describe making money on a spread is from a change in the spread. That is, they talk about a spread increasing or a spread decreasing. If you have put on a debit spread, that is, one that cost you money, you want that cost to increase so you can sell it for a profit. Thus, in a debit spread, you want to get in for a low debit and have the spread increase, so you can sell out for a high credit. A bull spread done with call options is a typical debit spread. You might go in with a debit of 2, i.e., a cost of 2, and come out with a credit of 5.

A credit spread is where you take in money when you put on the spread. A bear spread done with calls is an example of such a spread. When you do a credit spread, you naturally want to take in as much money as possible when you do it, that is, to get as high a credit as you can. Then when you close out the spread, it is done at a debit, and you have to put money in. Therefore, when you close out a credit spread you want to close it out for as small a debit as possible. For instance, if you are doing a bear spread with calls, you might put it on a credit of 4½. This means that you took in $450 per option when you did the spread. Now as time passes and the stock moves down, you might be able to close it out for a debit of only $100, and you have made money from a decrease in the spread.

In summary, a debit spread is closed out for a credit, and a credit spread is closed out for a debit. Both orders can be entered as spread limits. It is very easy to remember what you want the spread to do. If it cost you money originally, you want that cost to get higher, because you will be selling it out at the close, and you want the spread to widen. If you took in money when you originally did the spread, you will have to buy it back for a debit at the close, and you want the spread to be as small as possible.

It was George Fugler, president of Pi Corporation, who I first heard mention that in a call option spread if it is a bear spread, you want to squeeze the spread in a "bear hug" down to as tiny an amount as possible. On the other hand, bulls are famous for pushing things over in wild charges, and so when you do a bull spread with calls you want to push the spread as far apart as possible.

CALL OPTION SPREADS

Bull spreads

As we said, a spread is basically trying to accomplish what could be done by other means, but with an increase in the price range of the stock in which it is profitable. In a bull spread we are attempting to make money when a stock goes up or stays up. Thus, what we are trying to do is very similar to what one does when one buys a call option. And a bull spread is basically buying a call option. This is always the principal part of the bull spread, which means that you are always buying a relatively expensive call option. It is from the increase in price of the call option you buy that you usually expect to make your profit.

So the first step in putting on a bull spread is buying an option, let's say at the 30 strike price. The second step is to reduce the cost of this call by selling a call of the same expiration date on the same stock, but with a higher strike price. The option you sell is always worth less than the one you buy because it is always at a higher strike price.So if you bought the January 25 option, you might sell the January 30 option.

In describing a bull spread we pointed out that you sold the option with the higher strike price. You might have remembered the chapter on selling naked options and wondered whether you could sell an option without owning the underlying stock, as in covered writing, without putting up the required margin, as is done in selling naked options. The answer is that when the price of the stock goes up, so that you might lose money on the January 30 option, you know that the January 25 option will also have to go up in price, and that, indeed, it will be worth 5 points more than the 30 option at expiration. Thus, you are always fully protected against any loss by reason of the stock going up too far. Therefore, the January 25 option serves as your margin here, just as owning the underlying stock itself serves as the margin in covered writing.

Margin rule in spreads. The rule in spreads is that the option you own provides the margin for the option you are short, *provided* that it is (1) of the same or longer duration, and (2) is of the same or lower strike price. Both these requirements must be present, or the short option will be treated for margin purposes just as if it were a naked option (subject to a limitation we'll describe later if you own an option of the right duration but a higher strike price). So if you are long a January 25 option and short an April 35, the January option cannot provide margin for your short option because the January option is not of the same or longer duration. And there is no point in arguing that it is much more expensive and will certainly go up in value if the stock increases in price. The rules are the rules, and you do not have a spread in the margin sense of the word. To repeat, the option you own must be of the same or lower strike price, *and* must be of the same or longer duration than the option you have sold. Thus, if you are long the April 25 call, that would provide margin for being short the January 30 call, or the April 30 call, but not the July 30 or the April 20.

A bull spread requires buying an option with a low strike price, which is always the more expensive option, and selling an option with a higher strike price, which is always the cheaper option. Since you are buying something expensive and selling something cheap, this spread always ends up costing you money, and therefore it is also classed as a debit spread, since it results in a debit to your account. The general rule is that there is no margin requirement to a debit spread. You simply pay cash for the amount of the debit plus transaction costs. On the way out, whatever can be realized from the sale of the position is yours to keep, and if it brings in more than your original cost, you have a profit.

Now let's examine in detail a bull spread where you buy a January 25 option and sell a January 30 to see just what benefit you will derive from selling the 30 option. Assume that the stock is at 26, and that the January 25 is 3 and the January 30 is 1. If you buy the January 25 option for 3, it is obvious that the stock must increase to 28 before you can break even at expiration, and that in order for you to double your money it must go up to 31. As the stock goes up above that price, your option goes up point for point. The big disadvantage is that if the stock stays where it is, your call will be worth just 1 at expiration, and you will have lost 66% of your initial cost. Furthermore, an increase of 2 points just to break even isn't very tempting, and a 5-point increase, a 19% increase in the stock price, just to double your money is quite a bit to ask. The purpose of a bull spread is to make all three of these situations more favorable for you.

So you decide to use a bull spread, and at the same time that you buy the January 25 option for 3, you sell the January 30 call for 1. Immediately this does one thing. You take in $100, and reduce the cost of your position by exactly one-third, from $300 for one call to $200. The first thing you notice is that this reduction in cost is a great blessing if you are wrong, and the stock goes down in price rather than goes up. As with buying a call, it is also true in a bull spread that you cannot lose more than you initially spend. Therefore, no matter how far down the stock goes, you will never lose more than $200, and that is just two-thirds of what you could have lost in buying the option. So the first benefit of a bull spread as opposed to just buying the call is greatly reduced losses in case the stock goes down.

Now let's see what happens as the stock goes up. If the stock is at 27 upon the calls' expiration, the 30 call you sold will be worthless, and the 25 option you own will be worth 2. You would sell it and realize 2. Since the entire spread originally cost you 2, you have broken even, less transaction costs. Compare this with the purchase of the 25 call option alone. That would have cost you 3, and by selling it for 2 you would have lost 33% of your money. So, clearly, advantage number 2 is that at this price you are much better off with a bull spread because you have reduced the break-even level by a whole point.

Let's continue up the price scale at expiration. If the stock is 28 upon expiration, the January 25 is worth 3 and the January 30 expires worthless. If you had put on the bull spread for 2, you would now sell out the 25 option for 3, and find yourself with a profit of 1, for 33% profit. Very good. Now, let's see what would have happened if you had just bought the January 25 option without doing the bull spread. You would have paid 3 for it, and at its expiration, with the stock at 28, the option would have been worth 3, and you would have broken even, ignoring transaction costs. There is the big difference. Which would you rather have? A 33% profit or a mere break-even?

If the stock goes up. But the benefits of the bull spread do not stop here. Let's assume that the stock goes up to 30 at the options' expiration. Here again the January 30 option expires worthless. The January 25 option is worth 5, and if you have just bought the option for 3, you would have a profit of 2, which is a 66% profit. Not bad, but let's see what kind of a profit you would have with the bull spread. You originally bought the January 25 call and sold the January 30 for a cost of 2. Now with the stock at 30, and the January 30 expiring worthless, you sell the January 25 option for 5, giving you a profit of 3. But a profit of 3 on an investment of 2, comes out to be a profit of 150%. Just compare a profit of 66% with one of 150% and you will see that the benefits of the bull spread are way ahead of a straight option buy at this price.

But we can continue on further. As the stock goes higher and higher, the January 25 option purchased by itself will keep on advancing, point for point, with the stock. The higher the better. But the value of the bull spread cannot increase beyond the 5 points that the position has when the stock is at 30 upon the options' expiration. To see why this is so, one must only consider that as the 25 option which one owns goes up point for point with the increase in the price of the stock, the 30 option which you are short is also increasing point for point with the stock's price rise. And since you are short the 30 option, you must buy it back when you close out the position. So each additional point in the price of the 30 option is costing you a point. Thus each point gain in the value of the 25 option is exactly offset by a point gain in the price of the 30 option once the stock gets above 30, and accordingly the value of the bull spread cannot increase once the stock gets above 30.

The maximum value that a bull spread can attain is the difference between the strike prices of the two options. Here the difference between the 25 and 30 strike prices is 5, and so the spread can never be worth more than 5. Of course, the profit on the spread is limited to the difference between the original cost, here 2, and the maximum value of the spread, here 5. Thus the maximum profit this spread can generate is 3. One of the nice things about a bull spread as compared to the outright purchase of an option is that you can have an idea of the maximum profit, so that you need not be disappointed by a failure to reach some exaggerated goal.

But back to our example. We left the bull spread when the stock was 30 and pointed out that at this point it had reached its maximum profit potential, whereas the option by itself would keep on becoming more and more profitable. Does this mean that at 31 the option is more profitable than the bull spread? Definitely no. Doing the arithmetic shows that the January 25 option is worth 6, with a cost of 3, giving a profit of 3 for a 100% profit. But as we already saw, the bull spread achieves a profit of 150%. So, even above the strike price of the short option, a bull spread can be more profitable than the outright

Figure 13. Profitability of bull spreads compared to buying calls
Initial prices of options—Jan. 25: $3; Jan. 30: $1
Initial stock price: 25

Note that at any price from 25 to 32 a bull spread is more profitable, but beyond 32 the purchase of either option makes more money, with the 30 option increasing the fastest.

purchase of an option. See the table for a complete comparison, including the purchase of the 30 option alone.

Just how high does the price of the stock have to go before the option is the better investment? If we increase the stock price one more point to 32, we can get an idea. At 32, the January 25 would be worth 7 at its expiration. Since it cost 3, we have a profit of 4, which is 133%. And as we have previously seen, this is almost the profit on the bull spread. So the answer to our question is that in this case the stock had to rise more than 2 points above the strike price of the short option in order to become as profitable as the bull spread. And of course it would have to go higher before it became more profitable.

Incidentally this is not a particularly exciting bull spread, but I used it as sort of a minimum. You may be able to find bull spreads which are much more advantageous, that is, where there is much stronger ratio between the price of the higher option to the lower one. If, in our example, the January 30 option were priced at 1½ instead of 1, it would greatly improve the performance of the spread. That would mean that the cost of the spread was 1½ instead of 2, and the profit which could be achieved would be 3½, or 233% rather than 150%. To equal the potential gain of the bull spread, by buying the January 25 option alone, the stock would have to climb to 35 instead of 30. This means that it would have to advance by 9 points instead of just by 4 in order to make the same percentage profit. In other words, the stock would have to increase by 125% more just to make the same percentage return on your money, and at any point below that the bull spread would be more favorable. When premiums are high it is often possible to find bull spreads where the price of the upper strike price option is about one half the price of the lower.

Here is the lesson of a bull spread. Under the right circumstances, it can clearly be the preferable investment. Consider our original case. Comparing percentages, and forgetting absolute amounts, we find that at 25 and below both strategies are equally bad, i.e., they both are worthless and we have a loss of 100%. But from 26 on up, the bull spread is clearly superior, and above 27 it begins making a profit while the option is losing. It is superior all the way up to 32 which means that at any price of the stock from 26 to 32, or any increase of from 0% to 23%, the bull spread is superior to the purchase of the option.

Buying an option vs. a bull spread

The next time you are tempted to purchase an option, work out the relative prices and profits of a bull spread versus the purchase of an option the way we did here. You may be surprised at how high the stock has to go before you make more money with the option by itself. And then there is always the psychological point, that if you do make 150% or 233% profit on a bull spread, isn't this enough? Would you really be disappointed because you might have made even more by buying an option? Not me. If I made a profit of 233% on my investment in just a few months I would thank my lucky stars that I had done so well.

Types of bull spreads

Bull spreads may be subdivided into three basic types, although there are no hard-and-fast categories. The first type could be called an *out-of-the-money bull spread*. This is when the price of the stock is below the strike price of the option you are buying. These spreads should cost very little, just a point or two, perhaps as much as three points when you are using strike prices 10 points apart. They are highly speculative and are the most similar of the three types of bull spreads to just buying options. They are speculative because just a small drop in the price of the stock will make them worthless. On the other hand, because of their small cost, the potential exists for quite a large percentage profit. Thus, if a spread between the 40 and 45 options costs $1, it could be worth $5 at expiration for a profit of 400%.

Since these are out-of-the-money bull spreads, in many cases the price of the call to be sold will seem quite insignificant, and the question will arise whether it is worth limiting the profit potential in order to take in the small amount realized from selling the higher strike price option. Typically one might be able to buy a 40 option for 1½ and sell the 45 for ½ or just ¼, or maybe ⅜. Should one sell this higher strike price option for such a small amount and thus limit one's profit?

My personal conclusion is yes, and here's my thinking. While the money you take in is not a large amount, in terms of percentage cost of the spread it is substantial. If you can get only ¼ for the 45 option, you will be saving 16.6% of the cost of buying the 40 option. That may not seem like a lot but in buying options or spreads you should be just as cost conscious as in any other purchase you make.

The benefit of selling the higher strike price option. Think of the last time you bought a new car. You may have trudged from dealer to dealer, getting the best deal you could on the car you wanted. It took a lot of work, discussing installment terms, trade-in allowance, cost of various options, etc., but after spending a lot of time and effort you felt that it was all worthwhile because you were able to save $450 on your $6,000 car. And that certainly was a worthwhile saving. Yet it amounted to just 7.5%. Here you have a chance to save over twice that percentage without any work or time at all, and you can't decide whether it's worthwhile? The money you save on a bull spread will buy you the same things as the money you saved on your new car. But what about the limitation you are putting on yourself in case the stock goes up above the higher strike price? Of course there is some price at which it might just be absurd to sell the higher option, such as if it were $^{1}/_{16}$, but in that case you would probably be paying very little for the lower strike price option you bought, and it still might be a worthwhile percentage. But, in general, my way of looking at this is that if the stock should ever get up to the higher strike price, you have won a maginificent victory, and you should be pleased as can be. In over 80% of the cases this will not happen, and you will be better off having sold the other option. In the few cases where you are not, you still have a wonderful profit. So why not be happy.

You will note that in talking about profit, I have always described option prices at the expiration of the option. This is because when the options still have some time to run, both the option you are long and the one you are short will be worth more than their cash value, but it is not possible to know exactly how much more. As the price of the stock goes up and the option you are buying becomes deeper in the money, the option you are shorting will tend to have more future time value to it, whereas the one you are buying will tend to have less and will be selling for a price close to its intrinsic cash value. This situation is very good when you are putting on the spread, and it is why the two other types of bull spreads which we are going to discuss are such favorable situations. The option you are buying represents solid cash value of the stock, but the one you are selling is the froth of future speculation. It's always good business to buy the solid and sell the problematical.

But there is a disadvantage to this when we come to close out the position. The problem is that the pricing of the options works exactly against us. Let's say we want to close out a 40–45 bull spread when the stock is at 45, and the options have about two months to run. You might think that with the stock at 45, you could close out your spread for approximately 5 points, congratulate yourself for having made a super trade, and go on to the next moneymaking opportunity. If you check the prices of the options, you will find to your sorrow that the 40 option may be at 5¼ and the 45 option may be at 2, which means that the spread you thought would be worth 5 is worth only 3¼. This is the nature of bull spreads, and there is nothing you can do. You must decide either to get out with whatever profit you will make from a 3¼ spread or wait until the expiration of the options. Then, if the stock is still at 45 or higher, you will indeed get the approximately 5 points to which you are entitled.

On-the-money bull spread

This leads us directly into the second type, which is an *on-the-money bull spread*. It occurs when the stock is approximately at the midpoint between the two strike prices of the options in the spread. We are now talking about a spread which will cost you far more than an out-of-the-money spread. Generally, depending upon how high option prices are and the volatility of the stock, as well as the time left for the options' expiration, the cost of the spread will be approximately equal to the cash value of the option you are buying. If it is less than the cash value of the option you are buying, that is a favorable spread. To illustrate with an example, let's assume that a stock is selling for 95, the October 90 option is 7 and the October 100 is 2. The cost of the bull spread is 5, and this is exactly the actual cash value of the 90 option.

The disadvantage of the on-the-money as compared to the out-of-the-money is that the percentage return is necessarily much lower. In this example, where the cost of the spread is 5, the most that the spread can be worth is the difference between 90 and 100, or 10. Thus, no matter how high the price of the stock goes, you cannot make more than 100% profit. And the risk of total loss is still there too. If the stock goes down below 90, you have lost every penny you put into the spread.

The advantages are that you are getting into a position which is quite rare in the world of options. That is, you are obtaining a situation where you make money as soon as the stock moves up by even the smallest fraction, and you do so with limited risk. If you put on a bull spread for a debit equal to the cash value of the lower strike price option, you have in effect purchased an option for its actual cash value. This is something we would all like to do and usually can't. So this type of spread is ideal when you expect the price of the stock to go up, but not necessarily by any large amount. If it just goes up 2 points by expiration, your spread will be worth 7, giving you a profit of 2, which is a 40% profit. The out-of-the-money options which we discussed previously are almost always done at a debit above the current cash value of the lower strike price option, if indeed it has any cash value at all.

These on-the-money bull spreads are not quite as speculative as the out-of-the-money, because the stock can go down somewhat before you lose all your money, but make no mistake about it—they are still speculative on any absolute scale.

Another disadvantage of these on-the-money spreads is that since they cost you comparatively so much to put on, you will be even less inclined to take them off until the options are about to expire. So when you are deciding about which duration options to use, consider that you will probably be locked into the position until the expiration date of the option.

In-the-money bull spread

The third and final type of bull spread is the in-the-money spread. This spread is done when the stock is at or above the higher strike price. For example, the stock might be 47 and you are planning to buy the 40 strike option and sell the 45. The only reason that this type of a spread can work at all is that the future time value of the higher strike option exceeds the future time value of the one you are buying. Unlike the out-of-the-money or on-the-money spreads, the movement of the price of the stock is not what makes this work. The stock has only to stay somewhere above the higher strike price. Rather, it is time that makes the spread work.

In the example above, if the 40 option were selling for 7¼ and the 45 option were selling for 2½, you would have a debit of 4¾. The most that the spread could be worth at expiration is 5, so your maximum potential profit would be just ¼. When you consider that you have two commissions in and two commissions out, it is easy to see that if you were to put on this spread it could only result in a certain loss, even under the most perfect conditions. And remember, too, if the stock goes down in price, you could lose your entire debit of 4¾. So, please avoid.

But, on the other hand, if this were a volatile stock, and options were selling at good prices, the 40 option might still be 7¼ but the 45 option might be 3¼. Now, the cost of putting this on is 4 points, and if you got out at 5 points you would have a 1-point profit, or 25% on your cost. This is the type of situation in which you could consider an in-the-money bull spread. You put on an in-the-money spread when you are quite sure that the stock will not fall below the upper strike price, and when the debit to put it on can give you a fair profit, and when you are willing to hold the spread until almost the very last day of the options' duration, because unless you wait until then you will not be able to realize your anticipated profit.

To conclude our discussion on in-the-money bull spreads, remember they should be done only when option premiums are fairly high. If this is not the case, then the future time value of the upper strike price option will not be enough higher than the future time value of the option you are buying. And it is this disparity in future time value that makes the in-the-money bull spread possible. Second, they are not a chance to hit it rich. Rather, they are a chance to make perhaps a 25% profit or less on a stock. On the other hand, the stock does not have to go up in order to realize that profit, and on the contrary there is even some downside protection because the stock can fall to the upper strike price and you will still realize the full profit.

These are the three types of bull spreads. They all have some things in common. In all of them, every penny that you put up is at total risk, and that is something of which you must never lose sight. It is especially dangerous in the in-the-money bull spreads because they cost you so much. Second, the potential profit is always limited to the difference between the debit you must originally pay and the difference between the two strike prices of the options you use. Third, you must usually stay with the bull spread until almost the last day of the option in order to realize this maximum profit. Therefore, if you are a quick trader, who wants to be able to get in and out of a situation within days, you should carefully consider to what extent a bull spread will limit your mobility. The out-of-the moneys are the least confining in this respect, the on-the-moneys fairly difficult, and there is almost no possibility of getting out of in-the-money options until the very end. The one exception to all these statements is if the stock really takes off, rising substantially above the higher strike price. Then the future time value of both the options will rapidly decrease, and you will be able to get out sooner. For example, if you go into a 50 and 60 option bull spread, and you pay 13 for the 50, and are able to sell the 60 for 6 when the stock is 62, you have a 7-point debit. That spread is not going to increase very rapidly as long as the stock stays at 62. But, should the stock suddenly go up to 72, you will find that the 50 option may be at 22½ and the 60 at 13, for a debit of 9½. If there is still plenty of time in the options' lives, you might just as well put in a closing order for a credit of 9½. If the order gets executed, you can surely find something better to do with your money than tying up $950 for weeks in expectation of making another possible $50. Remember, there is no guarantee that even on the expiration day you will actually be able to get 10 points, and in fact you should expect to have to take a small discount to get out.

Bull spread strategy

Here is a strategy tip for bull spreads: Think in advance of what you are going to do if things go wrong especially for in-the-money and on-the-money options. This is my standard first rule, and it should be your first rule, because it is not only the most important, but also the one most frequently overlooked. Each week I talk with many investors who tell me that they think a certain stock is going to go up, and they ask my advice on the best way to utilize current option prices to realize that greatest profit. After I find out the time frame in which they expect the rise, and the approximate magnitude of the increase, it is a relatively easy task for me to recommend the appropriate option strategy. Rarely indeed does anyone ask how we can get protection in case the stock goes down. So we execute and wait for the stock to go up. If it does, the rest is easy. The hard part unfortunately often faces us, because the stock goes in the wrong direction. And the reason that this is the hard question is that there is no easy answer. No matter what you do, you will probably be losing money, and you will be taking the chance of preventing yourself from ever recouping the loss if the stock comes back.

For example, let's say you put on a bull spread between the 60 and 70 options when the stock is 65, and the spread costs you 5 points. The stock moves down to 60, and the spread is now worth 3 points. Your choices are (1) to stay in your position and hope that the stock moves up before the expiration, in which case it must go up over 63 in order for the spread to be worth what it is now, or (2) you can close out the position for 3 points, realizing a loss of 40% of your investment, plus transaction costs. The obvious advantage of the latter is that now, if the stock continues to move down, you are out and have salvaged most of your investment for what it is hoped will be a more successful investment in the future. But if the stock should start going back up, you have irrevocably lost the chance to recoup your loss, and what may hurt even more, the chance to make a good profit if the stock should go back up to 70. One word of advice is easy to give. If you do get out of the spread, and the stock starts going up, *do not* go back into the spread at the higher level. You are just begging to be a whipsawed. Go on to another stock or wait until there is another strategy available for this one.

Now we see why it is so hard to decide what to do when things go wrong. But unless you do make some decision in advance, then you will just let the spread drift down in value until it expires.

Bear spreads

A bear spread is a spread that will make money when the price of the stock goes down. Just as you sell a naked call to make money from the decline in the price of a stock, so a bear spread using calls is basically the sale of a call which brings in a substantial amount of money. Then, in order to obtain the advantages of a spread, and to eliminate some of the strong disadvantages of selling a naked call, you buy another option on the same stock. But the option you buy is worth much less than the one you sell, so you are basically selling the option mentioned above. You hope to make your money from the decline in the price of the option you have sold, and you are willing to take a small loss upon the expiration of the option you bought in order to get the advantages of a spread.

Let's take an example. Suppose a rather nonvolatile stock is now 69 and you believe that it is going to go down. You could sell the nearest-duration 70 option, which might be selling for 2 with about two months to go. If the stock stayed below 70 you would pick up the $2 as your profit. But you would have to put up margin of as much as $32 to do it, so your percentage return would not be very good. But even more important is the tremendous risk you would be taking. If the stock went up, you might be forced to buy back the option at $3 or $4, thus losing as much as you could have made, and furthermore there is always the possibility that the stock might go up so fast that you miss the chance to buy it back at $3 or $4 and have to buy it back for more. Finally, you just might not want the risk hanging over your head which a naked option entails, or there might be reasons why you cannot sell naked options, i.e., you are not approved for naked option writing by your brokerage firm. All these problems are solved by using a bear spread instead of selling a naked option. And if the stock goes down you can make a much greater return on your investment.

In this example, let's assume that there is a 60 option available of the same duration, and it is 9½. The bear spread consists of selling the 60 option for 9½ and simultaneously buying the 70 option for 2. The result of doing this spread is that you have taken in a net amount of 7½. Since you have more money in your account when you are finished with the spread than you had before, it is called a credit spread. All bear spreads are credit spreads, and the amount of the credit is always the difference between the amount received for selling the expensive lower strike price option and the amount spent to buy the cheaper higher strike price option. Since they are done for a net credit, the way to execute such orders is to request your broker to try to do it at a credit of a certain amount.

Instant credit? Some of you who are used to dealing with brokerage firms must find it a refreshing change to be able to do something that will immediately make your account richer. Your next question is probably whether you can withdraw this credit from your account, immediately, and if the answer to that question is yes, then you will want to know how many of these you can do and when the next plane leaves for Brazil. Unfortunately, although probably not unexpectedly, the answer is that you cannot withdraw the credit from your account until after the transaction is closed out. But even worse is that, despite the fact that this is called a credit spread, you have to send in money to do it.

The money required is the difference between what you take in as a credit, and the difference between the two strike prices. So, in this bear spread, where you are using the 60 and 70 strike prices with a difference of 10, and you are putting the spread on for a credit of 7½, you must have margin of 2½ in your account or send it in.

The profit potential of a bear spread arises when the stock declines below the level of the lower strike price option, and both of the options used in the spread then expire worthless. When this happens, your spread will have no value, and it will expire without anything being expected of you. At that time the entire credit for which you originally did the spread becomes your profit on the transaction. Here you would make $750.

The investment required was the amount of margin required, namely $250. You therefore would have a profit of 300%. Thus, in deciding whether to do a bear spread, you first figure out the credit you are looking for, (here 7½), then subtract it from the difference in strike prices (here 10) to determine the amount of margin you have to use up to do the spread (2½), and then you divide the credit by the amount of margin to determine your maximum rate of return. Here you would have divided the credit of $750 by $250 to get the maximum rate of return of 300%.

The three types of bear spreads

Bear spreads can be roughly divided into the same three subtypes as bull spreads, i.e., out-of-the-money, on-the-money, and in-the-money. The big difference is that the prices of the stocks are in the other direction from the option strike prices than they were for the bull spreads. While in an out-of-the-money bull spread the stock price is below the lower option strike price, the out-of-the-money bear spread has the stock price above the higher option strike price. If you are thinking of doing a bear spread with the 45 and 50 strike price options, and the stock is 54, that is an out-of-the-money bear spread. But once you get that difference digested, the result in the bear spread is quite similar to a bull spread. The out-of-the-money is the one that requires very little money to do and can give a high percentage return if it is successful. The on-the-money spreads require more money to do and cannot make as high a percentage return, but do not require the stock to move as far to make a profit. Finally, the in-the-money spreads take a lot of capital, can result in a relatively large loss, and have limited profit potential.

In the example we started with, the stock was 69 and we did the bear spread for a credit of 7½. To find the break-even point, you add the credit onto the lower strike price. Hence, the stock must move down a point and a half to 67½ just to break even. And of course that is before transaction costs. If the stock stays still you will lose 1½ points, which is a very substantial amount relative to your cost of putting this spread on, which was just 2½.

Out-of-the-money bear spreads

Now let's take a look at each of the subtypes of bear spreads. First is the out-of-the-money, which is the most popular type of bear spread and is the most similar in result to selling a stock short. If a stock is 64 and you want to do a bear spread selling the 50 call option and buying the 60, that is an out-of-the-money bear spread. With three months to go, the 50 option might be 14½ and the 60 might be 5½. Thus, you would be putting this spread on for a credit of 9, which means that you would have to put up $100 for margin, and you could make a profit of $900. But there are two problems. The first is that the stock will have to move down to below 59 before you even break even. At any point above 60 you will lose your $1 per share. Of course, once the stock does get down to 59, you will be increasing your profit by 100% for every additional point that the stock declines. But that's a problem which you should be prepared to face before you put on the spread.

The second problem is a bit nastier, and you might not be prepared for it. That is the danger of being exercised on the deep-in-the money option which you have shorted. Here you shorted the 50 option with three months to go when the stock was 64 and the option had a future time value of only ½ point. As time moves on and the expiration date of the option comes closer, the future time value will naturally decline. Two other factors may hasten its decline. First, if you should be wrong about the future price action of the stock, and it goes up further, the future time value of the option will certainly go down. Second, if the stock is a dividend-paying stock, the future time value of the option will decrease very rapidly as the ex-dividend date of the stock nears.

This is easily explained, but not so easily counteracted. As the stock gets closer to going ex-dividend, the price of the stock may slightly increase in anticipation of the dividend, but it will certainly decrease in value on the ex-dividend date by the amount of the dividend. Naturally, all option buyers realize that the stock is going to decrease by the amount of the dividend, so on the day before the stock goes ex-dividend, the option will decline even further than normal to reflect this anticipated decline in the price of the stock.

Thus, if GM were paying a quarterly dividend of $1, its in-the-money options would decrease by approximately that amount from their normal price on the day before the stock went ex-dividend. And if the amount of the dividend is greater than the future time value which the option would normally have, the option might be selling for less than its intrinsic cash value, that is, at a slight discount from cash value. Once that happens, arbitrageurs will buy the option and exercise it, and sell the stock at the same time, making the ¼ point profit. Since they pay no commissions, it is profitable for them to do this.

Premature exercise. The unfortunate result is that you may be exercised on your short deep-in-the-money long before the expiration date. When this happens, you no longer are short your deep-in-the-money. Instead you must pay a sales commission on the sale of the stock at the exercise price, and you are now short the stock, which may take more margin than you have. You can buy in the stock to cover your short position, but now you are long the higher strike price options and have no short position. This is exactly the opposite of what you want! You could sell the deep-in-the-money option all over again to reinstate your position, but before you do so, check the future time value of the option. If it isn't more than a small fraction, you are letting yourself in for an unwelcome exercise again. The conclusion is that before you put on a deep-in-the-money bear spread with calls, you must check the lower strike option (1) to make sure that there is still a decent future time value and (2) that if an ex-dividend date is coming up before the expiration date of the option, the dividend will not be great enough to more than offset the amount of future time value.

On-the-money bear spreads

The second subtype of bear spread is the on-the-money. This is something like shorting the stock, in that you can make quite a bit of money if the stock goes down, and something like selling a naked call, in that you may be able to do it in a situation where you can have the odds on your side, that is, you can make money if the stock stays still. For example, if a stock is 55, and you are selling a three-month 50 option for 6, you might be able to buy the 60 call for ½. This means that you are putting this on for a credit of 5½, which gives you a break-even point of 55½. Thus, the stock can actually go up ½ point before you begin to lose money, and if it stays still you will be making ½ point. The spread is done for a credit of 5½, which means that you are required to put up 4½ as a margin call. Thus, you could make a profit of 5½ on your investment, or a profit of 122%. Notice that the potential return is much less than from the out-of-the-money, and note also that you are putting up much more money per spread. All the money you have to put up as margin is money you can lose. So, whereas you could have lost $1 per share on the out-of-the-money spread, here you can lose over four times that amount. Thus, this type of bear spread is not as popular as the other two subtypes.

In-the-money bear spreads

The third subtype of bear spread is the in-the-money, which means that the price of the stock is already near or below the strike price of the lower strike price option. For example, where a stock is 69, you may sell the 70 option with three months to go for 4 and pay ½ for the 80 option. Your credit for doing the spread is therefore 3½, which is the maximum profit you could make, and your cost of margin required, and also the possible loss, is 6½. So you have a chance to make about half the amount you have to put up, while risking the possibility of losing twice that amount. Doesn't sound too appealing to you?

It can be, but it must be approached with the right expectations. This type of bear spread is actually very similar to selling naked options, but for margin purposes and suitability purposes it is not treated that way. Therefore, it can be very valuable for accounts which for either of these reasons cannot or will not do naked option writing. At many brokerage firms, a person who is approved to purchase calls and write covered calls can do bear spreads. And if you shy away from naked options because of the unlimited potential losses and the risk of mushrooming margin requirements, out-of-the-money bear spreads provide an alternative. The margin is fixed when you put on the spread and can never get any higher. The loss is limited to the amount of margin you put up. Therefore, for those who are reluctant to get into the water of naked option writing, in-the-money bear spreads provide a good wading ground in which to experiment before taking on the currents of the deep water.

The other benefit of an in-the-money bear spread is that, depending upon the price of the stock, it is possible to give yourself quite a bit of upside leeway. Thus, if the stock were only 66 when you did this spread, and you received a credit of perhaps 2 for the spread, your break-even point at expiration would be 72, which means that you have 6 points or almost 10% upside protection. And if the stock stays below 70, which doesn't sound too unlikely, you would have a profit of 2 points on your margin requirement of 8, for a profit of 25%. Furthermore, unless the spread turns out to be a disaster because the stock goes up too far, you don't have to worry about the short option being exercised prematurely.

The strategy for handling these spreads after they have been put on should be very similar to the strategy for naked calls. That is, one shouldn't just sit there and let the option go up and up. Decide upon a price at which you will close out the position and if the stock gets up that high, do it! If you have any luck, the option you own will have increased a little and will provide a small profit to offset your loss on the option you are buying back.

This concludes our discussion of bear spreads. While each of the three subtypes was a bear spread, in actual practice they are more different than they are alike. The out-of-the-money bear spread involves little risk and can result in a great profit if the stock moves down, but it must make that move in order to just break even and make a bigger move to give you a profit. These spreads also have the unwanted problem of early exercise of the deep-in-the-money you have shorted. Next were the on-the-money bear spreads, where the stock is between the two strike prices. Here you can make about as much money as you can lose, but it may not be necessary for the stock to go down in order to break even. Finally, we looked at the in-the-money bear spread, where the stock was already below the lower strike price. This spread entailed quite a bit of margin and thus risk of loss, and had the promise of a smaller profit, but the stock could actually move up and the spread could still result in a profit. Thus, the in-the-money bear spread is very similar to selling an out-of-the-money naked call, and the strategy for following them once they are on is quite similar.

Calendar spreads

The most difficult type of basic call spread to understand is the calendar spread. What is difficult to comprehend is how it is supposed to make money, and at times people who have done calendar spreads have asked themselves that very question after the spreads were completed. Hopefully, that will not be your predicament after you have read this section. The big advantage of calendar spreads is that they are much more hedged than either bull spreads or bear spreads and it is therefore unlikely that there will be a complete loss of the cost of doing a calendar spread.

A calendar spread consists of buying an option and simultaneously selling a shorter-duration option at the same strike price on the same stock. For example, let us assume that it is now January 20, and you buy the July 35 Polaroid option and sell the April 35 Polaroid option. That is a calendar spread. If you paid 3 for the July option and sold the April option for 2, your cost of doing the spread would be 1, and it would be a debit spread. Thus, there is no margin required, simply payment of the difference between the option prices, here $1, plus transaction costs.

Now for the more difficult question of how you make money on this spread. Let us assume that Polaroid stock was at 35 when we put on this calendar spread, and to make matters easy, let's assume that it is 35 three months later, when the April 35 option expires. The April option therefore expires worthless, and we have a profit of $2 on the April option. We close out the calendar spread by buying in the near-term option if this is necessary (and here it is not since it expires worthless) and at the same time selling the long-term option. The big question is what the July option will be worth with the stock at 35 and three months left to go. This the question we must answer when we put on the spread, because the answer to that question will tell us whether or not there is a chance that the spread can be profitable.

The best way to estimate when we are putting on the spread what the July option will be worth when it has three months to go is to see what the current option with three months to go is worth. On January 20, when we put on the spread, the stock was at 35, and the April option, with three months to go, was worth 2. Therefore, we can make an estimate that if three months later the stock is where it is now, the option at that time which has three months to go will also be worth 2. We must remember that this is only a rough estimate, and the actual price of the July option three months from now could vary widely due to many factors such as the tone of the market in general and the level of option premiums on other stocks. But this rough estimate is probably as accurate as any.

So we estimate that at the expiration of the April 35 call the July 35 will be worth 2. We sell it for 2, and thus a spread which cost us 1 to put on is taken off for 2, for a 100% profit before transaction costs.

The mathematical theory behind the potential profitability of a calendar spread is related to the price action of options with the passage of time. This action is that as the price of the underlying stock stays constant, the price of options does not decrease equally for equal-duration options. Rather, the price erodes very slowly for the long-term options, and becomes a more and more pronounced decline as the option gets closer to its expiration, until in the final weeks and days, the decline is extremely rapid. Obviously, an option with just one week to go will lose 100% of its value in that week if the underlying stock stays below strike price, whereas an option with three months to go will suffer an almost imperceptible decline. The principle behind calendar spreads is that you sell an option which, if the stock stays where it is, will decline 100%, and you buy an option which under the same circumstances will decline by only a small percentage. You must pay careful attention to the fact that a decline of 100% in the near-term option may not be so much more than a decline of 30% in the long-term option, since the price of the long-term option is so much greater to begin with.

Estimating profitability of calendar spreads. Obviously the most important aspect of calendar spreads is whether they can be profitable, and if so, under what circumstances. Both these questions are difficult because both involve an estimate of the price of the long option upon the expiration of the short option. And unlike the bull spreads and the bear spreads we discussed, there is no method known to man to come up with an estimate that is more than a rough estimate. This inability to predict what the longer-duration option will be worth when the short-duration option expires makes calendar spreads a less accurate spread than the others. However, there are two basic rules which can help.

The first is that a calendar spread is always worth the most when the underlying stock is at the strike price upon the expiration of the underlying option. As the stock goes up above the strike price, the short-term option begins to pick up a large amount of intrinsic cash value, and as its price goes up, the difference between it and the longer-duration option starts to decrease. In our Polaroid example, if the stock had gone up to 40 when the April 35 expired, the April 35 would have been worth 5, and the July 40 might have been worth 6. The spread would then be 1, and there would be no profit on it. Even worse, if the stock went to 45, the April 35 would be worth 10, and depending upon the level of option premiums in general, the July 35 Polaroid might be worth only 10½, for a loss of one half of your investment before transaction costs.

But calendar spreads are like Icarus, the Greek mythological figure who put on wings and attempted to fly. When he flew too high, the sun melted the wax that held on his wings, and when he flew too low the waves knocked him into the water.

So, too, a calendar spread is in an equally unhappy situation when the stock goes too low. Let's say that Polaroid goes down to 30, and the April option expires worthless. What will the July option be worth? It's anyone's guess, but certainly 1 is not improbable, especially since the stock has gone down 5 points from where it was. Thus, again, the spread is not a profit maker. Obviously, if the stock goes down to 27, the July 35 option is worth even less and we have a loss situation. So the first rule to apply when thinking about a calendar spread is to project what the prices of the two options are going to be if the stock is at the strike price when the near-term option expires. This will give you the *maximum* potential spread. If you can't see a really good profit at this price of the underlying stock, after deducting your estimated transaction costs, then for heaven's sake don't do the spread. Because your chances of having the stock end up just on or around the strike price are no better than your chances that the stock will go up when you do a bull spread, or that it will go down when you do a bear spread. And for every point that the stock is above or below the strike price you diminish your profit very significantly.

The second helpful rule to keep in mind is the mathematical formula which tells you the correct theoretical relationship between options of different durations. This theorem was discovered by the French mathematician Louis Bachelier in 1900. It is that the price of an option varies with the square root of the time remaining in its life. Therefore, if there is an option with 4 weeks left, and another one with 16 weeks, the correct mathematical relationship between the option prices should be the square root of 4 (2) to the square root of 16 (4), so we have a ratio of 2 to 4, or 1 to 2. The short-term option should be at least

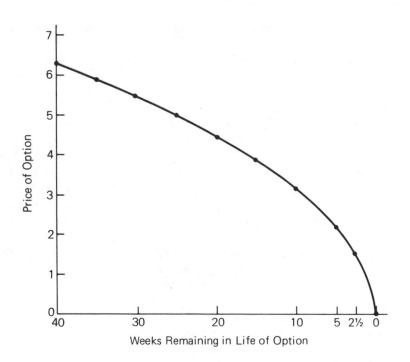

Figure 14. Effect of time on theoretical price of option
Chart assumes that the stock remains at the same price and the option is on the money

Note that in first ten weeks the option price declines $.82, whereas in the last ten weeks it loses $3.20. This provides the mathematical basis for profiting from calendar spreads.

one half the price of the long-term option. Note that if you simply took the ratio of the time periods, that is, 4 to 16, you would come up with a ratio of 1 to 4, and if you noticed that the options acutally had a relationship of 2 to 4 you would be overjoyed. But you would be wrong.

In doing a calendar spread one is always looking for a relationship where the near-term option seems overpriced in relationship to the longer-term option. But many times, what seems upon casual observation to be an over-priced near-term option, when subjected to Bachelier's theory, is really not overpriced at all. The way to use his theory is with a pocket calculator that has a square root key. If yours doesn't and you intend to do calendar spreads, I would advise you to buy one that does. It's very simple to find the square root of the times left in the various options, and then divide the one number by the other to get the ratios of the proper mathematical price relationships. If your near-term option is priced higher than it should be, then the odds are on your side. If not, then the odds are not on your side.

Advantages of the calendar spread. So far we have discussed when it is possible to make money from a calendar spread, and you will have correctly gathered that in certain situations there is simply no way to make money from a calendar spread. In fact, you may be wondering what the point of a calendar spread is at all. The big advantage of a calendar spread over either the bull or bear spread is that you are not likely to lose all your money. Properly set up, a calendar spread has a good probability of making money and a very small chance of losing more than a fraction of your money. Remember, with a bull spread, if the stock is below the lower strike price upon expiration, you lose all your money. Every single penny. And the same thing is true with a bear spread when the stock goes above the higher strike price. But with a calendar spread this is most unlikely to happen. Because when it is over you are left with a three-month option. If the stock is way down, it may not be worth very much, but it still will have some value. And if the stock has gone up dramatically, the difference in the price between the option you are short and the one you are long may not be a very big difference, but in only extreme circumstances will there be no difference, and of course this difference is the value of the spread. The calendar spread can be said to be the most conservative of the three types of spreads we have discussed, because it is the only one in which you are not likely to lose all your money. And the right calendar spread can also make a lot of money on a percentage basis.

Calendar spreads may also be divided into three categories: in-the-money, on-the-money, and out-of-the-money. Just remember that in every case, a calendar spread is its most profitable when the stock is at the strike price, and you will have no trouble in remembering how you make money from these three different types of calendar spreads.

In-the-money calendar spreads

In an in-the-money calendar spread, the stock might be at 30 and you are buying and selling options at the 25 level. Presumably you are putting them on for a very small debit spread, and of course your risk is limited to the amount of the debit you put up, since under normal circumstances the difference between the two options can never be less than zero. Your objective is to have the stock fall to 25. If the option you sell is at 5¾ and the longer-term option is 6¼, you hope that the stock will be at 25 upon the near-term option's expiration, and that then the options' prices will be 0 and perhaps 2. Your spread will have increased from ½ to 2, which is a 300% profit.

Nevertheless, these in-the-money spreads are the least frequently used of the three types. One reason is that the commissions are quite large. While the spread of ½ is very reasonable, if you were doing 10 options, the commission on the 5¾ option would be 13.3 cents per share, and the commission on the 6¼ option would be 13.9 cents, for a total commission of 27.2 cents, which is a commission cost of more than 50% of your cost of the spread! Worse, if the stock stays where it is, your commission costs for coming out of the spread will be approximately the same. This means that even if the spread stays at ½, so that you theoretically will break even, you are still losing your entire investment in commission costs! It is spreads like this which led to the invention of the phrase "cemetery spread". That is a spread in which you get buried by the commissions.

On-the-money calendar spreads

More commonly used are the on-the-money spreads, where the stock is just about at the strike price. Here the biggest concern is whether it will be possible to make a profit. The difficulty is that the stock is already at the point where the spread is the largest, and the only element that can improve your spread is the passage of time. Any movement of the stock price either up or down will decrease your spread. So carefully figure out your maximum profit by the method outlined above, and then be realistic with yourself and concede that it is not too likely that the stock is going to end up exactly on the strike price. Your most difficult aspect is to estimate how much of a decrease there will be in the spread for every point that the stock is above or below the strike price. While there is no easy way of doing so, the example below might be of some help. It is a computer projection of what a Polaroid 30 calendar spread would be upon expiration of the near-term option with the stock at prices ranging from 20 to 40. Of course, different stocks will react in different ways depending upon the volatility of the stock and hence the amount of future time value given to the premiums, but the general result will be similar.

Prices when spread was transacted:

Stock   28 ⅝
July 30 calls: 1 $^3/_{16}$
Oct. 30 calls: 1 ⅞
Cost of spread: $^{11}/_{16}$ or $.6875

Estimated price of spread just before expiration of July calls

Stock Price	Spread	(Loss) or Profit
24	$.07	(.61)
25	.19	(.49)
26	.38	(.30)
27	.58	(.10)
28	.89	.20
29	1.36	68
30	1.64	95
31	1.54	86
32	1.22	54
33	.91	23
34	.60	(.08)
35	.28	(40)
36	0	(68)

Out-of-the money calendar spreads

Probably the most popular calendar spread is the out-of-the-money, which is really very much like a bull spread in its purpose. The purpose is to make money when the stock goes up, and the benefit over a bull spread is that if the stock stays where it is, you may be able to get out upon the expiration of the near-term option with a break-even, instead of losing all your money, as you do with an out-of-the-money bull spread. The biggest disadvantage is that if you are too successful in your prediction, and the price of the stock goes up over the strike price, the spread begins to lose value, and it could happen that if the stock goes up far enough you would actually lose money on the spread.

As an example, let's say your stock is at 30, and you sell a three-month 35 option for ¾ and buy the six-month 35 option for 1½, giving a spread of ¾. You hope that the stock will be at 35 in three months, at which time the near-term will expire worthless, and you will sell the longer-term option for a price you estimate at about 2. This would give you a profit of 166%. If the stock just stays where it is, then in three months, when the near-term option expires, the longer-term option should still be worth about ¾, and you get out at a break-even. Of course, if you are really wrong, and the stock goes down, then the long-term option could decline to any amount, and there would be a loss. Finally, in the unlikely situation that the stock goes up to 40, the near-term option will be worth 5 at its expiration and the long-term option might be worth 5¾ for a break-even. One big advantage of the out-of-the-money calendar spread is that the commissions going in are so much less. In this case, if you were doing ten options, the total commission costs are only 15.4 cents per share, and on the way out, with the stock at 35, the total commissions would be just 6.3 cents.

Calendar spread strategy. Strategy tip. The biggest cause of losses on calendar spreads is not treating them as calendar spreads after the near-term option has expired. Remember, a calendar spread exists only as long as there are a long-term option and a short-term option. When the short option expires, or loses so much value that it is providing no meaningful downside protection to the long-term option, then you don't have a calendar spread anymore. If you went into the spread because you liked the hedged concept of a calendar spread, then for heaven's sake when the calendar spread is over close it out! This may seem easy, but in practice the temptation to hold onto the long option can be almost overpowering. It takes strong willpower, but I can tell you, from seeing many, many calendar spreads, that the big losses always occur when people are unwilling to close them out when they should.

What typically happens is that the stock will float downward somewhat, accompanied by what seems like an inordinately large loss in the price of the long-term option. Thus, if you have put on a spread at the 50 strike price for a debit of 2, when the near term option expires the long term option may be just 1¾ with the stock at 48. You now are in the position of owning a three-month option at what seems to you to be a ridiculously low price. How can the option be worth so little when this is a great stock, and it's only 2 points away from the strike price? Of course you know that you really should close out the spread and take your loss of a quarter of a point, but in this case the option seems to be so seriously undervalued that you decide to wait just one week to see if the stock won't rally a couple of points so you can get out with a small profit at least. So one week goes by, and the stock sinks to 47, the option declines to 1½, and now you really are determined not to sell it out. And so it goes. Three months later the option may expire worthless and you will swear that you will never do a calendar spread again as long as you live. But was it the fault of the calendar spread or was it that you didn't treat it as a calendar spread? Of course, it was your fault, and the ¼ loss you should have taken when the calendar spread was over would have been negligible, while the loss of your entire spread is both substantial and insulting.

So please remember: When you go into a calendar spread, you are doing so because you want the downside protection of a spread, and you want the relative safety of a calendar spread. Therefore, when the near-term option expires, be consistent in your thinking and get out of the spread! Take your loss now, and hope that the next spread will make more than enough profit to make up for it. As tempting as it is to stay with the long-term option, remember that you could have bought an option in the beginning. But you chose not to do so and to do a calendar spread instead for very good reasons. Stick to those reasons! Once you become the holder of an option, you are subject to all the hazards of that position, including not getting out until the option expires worthless.

Some people look upon out-of-the-money calendar spreads as a means of buying longer-term options for a lower price. While this may be correct in some instances, one must always keep in mind that if the stock does move up over the strike price before the expiration of the near-term option, you will not make nearly as much profit as you would have with a bull spread.

Using ratios on call spreads

There is a virtually limitless number of call spread varieties possible. Some of the most interesting ones involve simple variations on the three basic spreads we have already discussed. The simplest variation concerns buying a different number of options than you sell. For example, a bull spread which involves buying 10 May 40 options and selling 10 May 45 options can be varied to buying 15 May 40s and selling 10 May 45s. The purpose of this variation is to allow 5 of the 40 options to keep on increasing in value once the stock gets above 45 without having the profit increase cut off by the 45 options that were sold. In this case there would be an increase in the cost of the spread on a per-share basis, because you would not be getting the benefit of selling the 45 options on 5 of the options. This is the trade-off against the greater profit potential.

Or if you wanted an even lower cost, you could sell 15 of the 45 options and still buy only 10 of the 40 options. In this case you are taking in 50% more money from the sale of the extra 45s, thus reducing your cost accordingly. The risk is that now if the stock goes above 45, you will begin making less money because you actually have sold 5 naked options. In putting on this spread, you must be approved for writing naked options, and you must supply the margin for selling the 5 extra options.

Let's say that you bought the 40 options for 3 and sold the 45 options for 1, for a 2-point debit on a one-for-one basis. By selling the extra five 45 options, you took in 5 points more, which reduced your cost per spread by 50 cents, meaning that you were able to put on the spreads for a 1½-point debit instead of a 2-point debit, for a meaningful savings of 25%. Now let's see what happens when the stock starts going up. At 45 all is well, because your 40s are worth 5 points, and the 45s expire worthless, so you are making 3½ points profit on each spread. If you had not sold the additional 5 options and your cost for the spread had been 2 points, you would have made a profit of 3 points per spread. The percentage profit on your investment when you sell the extra calls is 233%, but the percentage profit on the regular bull spread is only 150%, so the sale of the additional 5 calls can really pay off.

As the stock starts going up above 45, the ten 40 options which are covered by the ten 45s continue to be worth exactly 5 points. But you also have 5 naked 45 options, and as the price of the stock goes up, you must buy them back at some point. At 46 you are buying them back for 1, which is exactly what you paid for them, but for every point that the stock goes above that you are losing an additional point. Since you sold an extra half an option for each spread, you are losing ½ point for every point that the stock goes above 45. Since your maximum profit per spread was 3½ points at 45, and since you are losing ½ point per spread for every 1 point increase in the price of the stock, you see that at 7 points above 45 you will break even on the spread, and that at any stock price above that (52) you will begin to lose money on the spread.

The general rule for determining how high the break-even point is in a spread where you have sold additional options is to figure out the total profit at the maximum profit point, which in this case was 45, and then to divide that by the number of naked options. Here your total profit on the transaction when the stock is 45 at expiration is $35 (disregarding hundreds). You are short 5 naked options. Dividing 35 by 5 gives 7, which you add to the strike price to get a break-even point of 42.

The two-on-one bull spread

In fact, one of the most popular variations on a bull spread is the two-against-one spread, which involves buying one lower strike price option and selling two of the next higher strike price options. There were times when option premiums were fat and juicy that this could be done for almost no debit at all, or for only a very small fraction of a point. Those prices are hard to find today, but they may come back. And if they do, this can be a very interesting play. Let's assume that you do find such a zero cost two-on-one spread, perhaps buying the 45s at 4 and selling the 50s at 2 when the stock is 47. Note that in order to do this you must have the margin for selling the naked 50 options, and that as the price of the stock goes up you will be marked to the market on your margin and may be required to supply more margin.

The first advantage of this spread is that since it cost you nothing to put on, there is absolutely no risk on the downside. If the stock goes down to 45 or less, all of the options become worthless, and you simply walk away without any profit or any loss. It is on the upside that this strategy becomes profitable. If the stock is at 50 upon expiration, your 45 options are worth 5 points each and the 50s are worthless. So something that cost you no cash at all to put on is now worth 5 points a share. It's hard to compute a percentage return on zero, so let's take the margin you need. At 50, if you are on 35% margin, you would have to have $17.50 for each share, which means that a profit of $5 would be a percentage return of 28%.

The real risk in this type of spread is that the stock will go up too far. Since you have written two for one, you start reducing your profit one whole point for every 1-point increase in the price of the stock over 50. Applying the general rule, your maximum profit was 5, and therefore your break-even would be 5 points above 50, or 55. Above 55 you begin to lose an entire point for each increase in the stock price, so that at 60 you are losing 5 points, which is as much as you could ever have gained, and above that the loss just continues to mount. Obviously the proper strategy to use is the same one that is urged so strongly in the chapter on naked option selling: Decide in advance exactly what you will do at exactly what stock price, and then do it. You could decide to close out the entire spread when the stock got to a certain price or you could just buy back the naked options, leaving yourself with a straight one-on-one bull spread, which you hope would increase in value with the passage of time, provided only that the stock does not fall back again.

Although the unlimited theoretical liability of the two-on-one spread means that it is not everyone's cup of tea, it can provide a very wide band of potential profit. In the example we have studied, there is a profit anywhere from 40 up to 50, and there is no loss below that. The only risk is if the stock actually goes above 50, and you can judge for yourself just how often a stock goes from 42 to 50 in three months or so. If it happened very often there would be a lot of rich stockholders out there, and I'm sorry to say that at last count there weren't that many.

Ratio bear spreads

Bear spreads can also be done in a ratio, but this is not as common. If you don't buy as many higher strike options as you have sold lower strike options, you face a serious risk of loss if the stock goes up, and those higher strike price options are usually pretty cheap anyway. On the other hand, if you buy more higher strike price options, then you are really offsetting the bearish nature of the spread and perhaps converting it into a neutral or bullish spread. If you buy two out-of-the-money options for every in-the-money option that you sell, you can probably still do this at a credit, but you will have transformed your bear spread into a volatility spread. This is a spread in which you will make money if the stock moves far enough in either direction. The big disadvantage is that if the stock stays within a fairly wide band in the middle you will lose.

Suppose you sold ten 20 options for 4 when the stock was 23 and you bought twenty 25 options for 1, for a credit of 2 points for each spread. If the stock goes high enough you will make enough money on the ten extra 25 options to offset your loss on the 20 option. Specifically, at 25 you would have a loss of 5 points per spread (1 point on the 20 option, which you would buy back for 5, and 2 on each of the 25s, which are worthless). You have one extra 25 option per spread, which will make you 1 point profit for every 1 point increase in the price of the stock, so that you start to make money above 30. On the downside, since you did this for a credit of 2, you will begin to make money below 22 (at which point you would have to buy back the 20 for 2) and your maximum profit on the downside would be the 2 points that were your original credit. Thus, your loss band is from 22 to 30, your profit below 22 is just 2 points, while your profit above 30 doesn't really get attractive until you reach 32 or 33. Of course if premiums are different you might be able to find a combination that has a slimmer band of loss range, but often there are more direct ways of putting on a volatility spread. (See the sections on straddles and combinations at the end of this chapter.)

Ratio calendar spreads

Calendar spreads also lend themselves very well to a ratio variation. If you are bullish on the stock, you can buy more of the long-term options than you sell of the short-term. Then if the stock goes up over the strike price, your profit continues to gain, instead of being reduced as in the regular calendar spread. The disadvantage is that you lose downside protection, since obviously if you use a two-to-one ratio you will have only half the downside protection. When you consider that in some calendar spreads there isn't very much downside protection in the first place, I can only urge you to consider very carefully what you are doing.

A calendar spread that has a two-to-one ratio of long-term options to short-term is actually a substitute for a bull spread and can be preferable. Sometimes, such a spread will make as much money when the stock goes up to the next higher strike price as a one-on-one bull spread would, and will continue to make more money as the stock goes up further, while it will perform far better than a bull spread on the downside. In a bull spread you have to suffer a total loss when the options expire with the stock below the strike price, but with a two-to-one calendar spread you still have three-month options, which should be worth something. So the next time you're inclined to do a bull spread, work out the figures first on a two-to-one calendar spread.

Selling additional short-term options in a calendar spread is not very popular because of the margin problem that arises on the naked options, plus the fact that you begin to lose money rapidly once the stock goes over the strike price.

Complex call spreads

In addition to the bull spread, the bear spread, and the calendar spread there are a number of complex spreads used by options traders which deserve mention. Perhaps the most exotic is the butterfly or sandwich spread. This is a theoretically beautiful spread which should appeal to the mathematician in everyone. When properly done, one theoretically cannot lose, and can make a very good return on a fairly broad band of stock prices at expiration. A butterfly spread consists of four options on the same stock with the same expiration time, with three different strike prices. You sell two options at the middle strike price of, say, 40, and then you buy one option with the higher strike price, here 45, and you buy one below, 35. The name sandwich spread is derived from the fact that the short options are sandwiched in between a long option above and below. The beauty of the spread is that the long options give you protection against any excessive loss on the short options.

The ideal butterfly spread is done for a zero debit, but depending upon the difference between the strike prices of the options (whether at the 5- or 10-point level), the time left before expiration (the less time the more you should be willing to pay), and the volatility of the underlying stock (the more volatile the less you should pay), it may be acceptable to pay up to 2 points for one of these spreads. To understand how a butterfly spread works, let's take an example. Suppose a stock is at 45, and you buy one 40 option for 6, sell two 45 options for 3½ each (taking in 7), and buy one 50 option for 1. You now have a zero debit for the spread. Let's see what happens to you at expiration. When the stock is at 40 or less, all the options expire and you are out with nothing.

As the stock goes up above 40, the 40 option you are long begins to increase in price, until when the stock reaches 45 it is worth 5 points. All the other options expire worthless, so the spread that cost you zero to put on is now worth 5. But, as the stock advances above 45, each of your two short 45 options begins to increase in value, and you will have to buy them back. So, for example, at 47, your 40 option is worth 7, but each of the 45s has to be bought back for 2, making a cost of 4, which reduces your profit to 3. At 50 you have to repurchase the two 40 options for 5 each, making a total cost of 10, which just exactly cancels out the value of your 40 option, so the spread is worth zero for a break-even. At any point above 50, the 50 option you own begins increasing in value, so both your long options are going up in value point for point with the stock while the two 45s are going down, with the result that at any point above 50 your spread is worth exactly zero.

A BUTTERFLY SPREAD

Cost to Do   *Value at Options' Expiration*

	Stock at 45	Stock at 40 (or less)	Stock at 40	Stock at 50 (or higher)	
Buy 1 50 option @ 1 =	−1	0	0		0
Sell 2 45 options @ 3½ =	+7	0	0	2 @ 5 =	−10
Buy 1 40 option @ 6 =	−6	0	+5	1 @ 10 =	10
	0	0	+5		0

This table shows that in theory one cannot lose money, and that there is a maximum profit of 5 points. For every point that the stock is either above or below 45 at expiration, the value is reduced by 1, e.g., at 47 or 43 the spread is worth 3.

Actually, a butterfly spread is just a bull spread (that is, buying the 40 and selling the 45 options) with a bear spread added on top (selling a 45 option and buying a 50 option). This is the reason that the butterfly spread is so beautiful from theoretical viewpoint. When you are making a lot of money in the bull spread, it offsets the loss from the bear spread, and vice versa. And it just happens that if the stock ends up at the middle, or near the middle, you can make some money on both of them, or make much more on one than you lose on the other.

Butterfly spreads do require margin in addition to whatever they cost. The amount of margin is the difference in strike prices for the bear spread on the top. Since there are 5 points difference between the 45 and 50 strike prices, we get a margin requirment of 5. This does not change with movement in the price of the stock and is a relatively modest requirement considering the profit possibility of the spread and the very limited risk.

Thus, it is clear that a butterfly spread is a nonvolatility spread that reaches its maximum profit at the strike price of the middle options and decreases in value to zero as the stock reaches each of the outer strike prices. Still, if butterfly spreads offered a chance to make a profit without any chance of losing any money, there are many people who would use them all day long. Unfortunately three practical considerations have a severe negative impact on the attractiveness of butterfly spreads, and we will discuss them here.

Disadvantages of the butterfly spread. The first drawback is that the premiums, at least when this revised edition was being prepared, are a long way from making it possible to do many spreads at a zero or small amount of debit. There is simply no point in doing a butterfly spread unless you can do it for a very low debit. But premium levels could improve in the future, and for that reason it is worth discussing butterfly spreads.

A second and more inherent problem is the difficulty of executing butterfly spreads at costs close to the prices you see in the newspaper. The newspaper shows only the last price of the option, but it does not tell you at what price you could have bought the option when that final sale was made. To illustrate, you could be trying to buy an option for $1, but there are many people ahead of you, also trying to buy that option for a dollar, and it has been trading at $1 \frac{1}{16}$ all day. When someone finally comes along who is willing to sell the option for one dollar, the first buyer in line gets it. If you had been trying to get it for a dollar, your broker would have told you that it could not be bought for that price.

Every option is quoted in three important ways. The price of the last sale, the bid price, and the offering price. The bid price is what the brokers on the floor of the exchange are willing to pay right now for at least a small number of options. The offering price is what they are willing to sell you a small number of the options for right now. Thus, an option may show last trade 2⅜, bid 2¼, offered at 2½. If you come in with a market order to sell the option, you will receive 2¼. If you enter a market order to buy an option, you will pay 2½. If you are willing to be patient, and don't expect the stock to move in the near future, you could enter your order to buy or to sell at 2⅜, and the chances are that if the stock does not move, you will eventually be able to execute your order, but you also may not be able to do so. The only certain way of getting an order executed is to be willing to buy at the offering price and be willing to sell at the bid price.

This discussion is appropriate to our consideration of butterfly spreads, because this is the first spread we discussed which uses three different options. Now, when you are buying one option you may not care very much whether you pay 1⅜ or $1^7/_{16}$. At the end, the option will probably be worth either zero or perhaps 5 and it won't make any difference whether you paid one-sixteenth of a point more or less. But where you are dealing with four options, and trying to put on a spread for a fraction of a point, it can make an enormous difference. Let's use the example we started with of buying one 45 option for 6, selling two 45s for 3½, and buying one 50 for 1, which came out to a zero debit. If these were not too actively traded options, we might find that the 40 options were offered at 6¼, the 45s were bid at 3¼, and the 50s were offered at 1⅛. Putting these prices together means that you would have to do this spread at a debit of not zero but ⅞. That's an enormous difference from zero. Of course, butterfly spreads are always entered as spread orders, but because there are so many different things to do, there is no way that anyone on the floor can hope to pick up more than one of the three options for the last sale price. He must be willing to execute the other two at market order prices, because when he fills one part of the order, he must know that he can immediately fill the other two parts, or he will be stuck with the loss. So there is really no way that you could do this spread unless you were willing to pay at least ⅝, and from my experience even that is rather unlikely. The question then becomes one of judgment as to whether you are willing to do it at ⅞.

The problems in closing out a butterfly spread. But unfortunately putting on the spread is only half of the execution morass. At least when you put the spread on you can decide upon the maximum debit you are willing to pay, put in the order with that debit, and if it isn't executed you can go on to something else with nothing lost. But once you have the spread on, you eventually will have to take it off. And there you are in a position with almost no room for maneuvering. They've got you. As expiration comes close you must get out of that spread or pay enormous commissions when your short options are exercised. So your hands are tied. While in theory you should always be able to get out of a calendar spread for zero at expiration, this just isn't always the case. Typically, the deep-in-the-money option you are long is selling at a discount, while the two options you have to buy back are selling at a premium over their cash value. But you are in no position to argue.

So you take off the spread, and if the in-the-moneys are at a ¼ discount, and the middle options are at a ¼ point premium, and then you have to sell the in-the-money at the bid price and buy the middle options at the offering price, you might have to tack on another ¼ or ⅛ to the price of each. So you could easily have to pay a debit of a point or more to take off the spread. When the maximum theoretical profit was 5 (and this only if the stock ends up exactly at 45 and you risk not buying back to 45 options) you can see that paying over a point to close out the position really hurts. Thus, while in theory you should be able to put on and close out a butterfly spread for zero cost, in the real world you might have to pay almost 2 points to do this.

A final problem, especially for the smaller trader, is commissions. We saw how troublesome commissions could be in spreads involving two options. Naturally they are about 50% higher when the spread involves three options. The cost of doing the spread we used as our example is 40 cents per share if you were doing ten options. Naturally if you did less, the cost per share would be higher. When you are trying to keep the cost of the spread down to about zero, commissions of almost half a point are very substantial. If the stock goes up, let's say to over 50, your commissions will be substantially higher, so that commissions could easily total over one point. Thus, between the costs of doing your spread at the bid and asked prices and commission costs, your transaction costs could easily be 2½ points per share. When you consider that the maximum possible profit is 5, you realize that fully half of your greatest profit is consumed by transaction costs.

It is due to these three practical problems, finding the right option prices, getting executions at good prices, and commissions, that butterfly spreads are not as good as their excellent theoretical properties would suggest.

Diagonal spread

One popular variation of bull spread is to purchase a long-term option, and then rather than selling an option of same duration, sell one of the shorter-term options. For example, in May you purchase a January 40 option and sell a July 45. The advantage of selling the July option compared to an October or January 45 is that your premium income on a per-week basis is probably going to be higher between now and July. The July option will lose all its future time value, while the January might decline only very slightly. The theory is that if the stock is around 44 when the July expires, you will sell an October 45, let that expire, and then if the stock is in the right place, sell a January 45 option. This way you have three chances to take in premiums from the near-term option which should be the one with the highest future time value in it.

On the other side of the spread, the advantage of buying the long-term option as opposed to a short-term one is that you should be paying less future time value on a per-week basis, and also, if the stock should decline within the next few months, you will have something that will retain a portion of its value much better than a short-term option. In fact, when declining stock markets have caused very low premiums on short-term options, it is sometimes surprising how well the longer-term options have maintained their levels due to the fact that option buyers often get somewhat pessimistic about near-term prospects but continue to believe that there could be an upturn in about six months.

Another way of perceiving a diagonal spread is as a calendar spread that uses two strike prices. The benefit is that if the stock stays up near the strike price of the short option, the spread should result in a bigger profit than a regular calendar spread could.

There is even another way of looking at a diagonal spread, which should appeal to the more conservative traders. This is to think of it as a substitute for covered writing. In covered writing you buy the stock and write an option on it. Here, in lieu of buying the stock, you buy a long-term in-the-money option, which is the closest that you can come to actually buying the stock in the option world. These long-term options typically have a very low percentage of their value tied up in future time value, which means that they are quite similar to the underlying stock itself, and because of their long duration you don't have to trade them as often. The obvious advantage over covered writing is that it requires so much less money, since even these options cost much less than buying the stock on margin. And less capital tied up means greater leverage and the chance for a much higher return. If you want a higher return than a covered writing program can give you, consider diagonal spreads.

Selling two different options against one option

Earlier we discussed buying one 40 option and selling two 45 options. This section discusses buying one 40 option and selling one 45 option and one 50 option, and perhaps even one 60 option, all with the same expiration dates. This type of spread works best when option premiums are high, but it offers a great advantage over the two-on-one option positions we discussed earlier, namely that since you are short only one of the 45 options you do not begin to lose money at expiration until the stock gets up to the strike price of the next option, which here is the 50. Therefore your band of profitability is greatly enlarged. Instead of having a spread that is a break-even at 50 after declining in profitability every point up from 45, you have a bull spread which will stay at its maximum profitability all the way from 45 to 50. Only when the stock reaches 50 at expiration does the spread begin to lose in value, and then only on a point-for-point basis, so that your break-even is reached at 55. On the downside, your loss is limited to the debit at which you did the spread, and your spread is worth one point for each point that the stock is above 40.

Principles of complex spreads. It is impossible to discuss very possible spread, for the reason that the variety of spreads is limited only by the imagination of the trader who wants to put them on. But there are certain basic principles which should guide the option spreader. The first is that every complex spread is a combination of the three basic spreads: bull, bear, and calendar spreads. When you are considering a fancy spread you should ask yourself why you are combining these basic spreads, that is, what advantages you seek that you cannot get from the basic spreads. As we noted, a butterfly spread is simply a bear spread on top of a bull spread, but there was a very good reason for combining the two. In theory, because they counterbalanced each other, there was no potential loss, and there was a possibility of a good gain. Therefore, one could logically decide to put on a butterfly spread.

The only real answer to the question of why spreads should be combined that I have learned is that it makes sense if in one way or another the combination provides greater range of profitability than a single spread. That is, if one spread works better over a long period, and another over the short period, you might have a valid combination. Or if one works beautifully when the stock moves up, and the other when it stays still. For example, I have often combined a bull spread with a calendar spread done on the lower strike price of the bull spread when I thought that there was little likelihood the stock would go down very far, but I was quite concerned that it might not move up above the level of the lower strike price in the bull spread. In that case the bull spread would be worthless, but the calendar spread would be producing a fat profit. On the other hand, if the stock goes up, the calendar spread will start to show reduced profits, but the bull spread will be coming on strong.

When you consider complex spreads, therefore, it pays to take them apart in your mind, reduce them down to their basic components, and then ask yourself whether the different parts complement one another. If they are just two different ways of doing the same thing, or if they are diametrically opposed, then maybe you shouldn't be doing the complex spread at all.

The other basic rule in considering complex spreads is that in options as in everything else in life, the best is the simplest. You should strive to keep your spreads as simple as possible, consistent with accomplishing your objectives. We have seen how complex spreads cost money in three distinct ways: (1) They are more difficult and expensive to execute; (2) commissions are higher; and (3) the more options you are short, the greater the danger of an unwelcome exercise. Each of these three will take money right out of your pocket. So consider carefully. There are many benefits to complex spreads, but they frequently are outweighed by the practical problems and costs associated with them.

Put spreads

To summarize puts spreads, you can do anything with puts that you can do with calls. Sometimes you may feel as if you were standing on your head and looking at them from upside down to figure out what's going on, but put spreads can be done, and often with distinct advantages over doing the same thing with calls. In this section we will not bother explaining each spread in detail, since that would just duplicate what we said about call spreads, but will limit ourselves to pointing out the differences between call and put spreads and emphasizing when it is advantageous to use the put spreads.

Put bull spread. The first put spread we will consider is the put bull spread, which is what you do with puts if you think a stock is going up. If that sounds self-contradictory, remember that we had bear spreads done with calls. The simple way to remember what a put bull spread is, is to remember that in a bull spread you always buy the lower strike option and sell the higher strike option. This is true whether you are doing a call bull spread or a put bull spread. Thus, in a put bull spread you would buy the 40 put for 2 where the stock is at 40, and sell the 45 put for 6, for a credit of 4. One difference between a call bull spread and a put bull spread is that whereas the call spread results in a debit, as you will recall, a put spread results in credit. Since it is a credit spread, you have to deposit margin. The same rule applies as in a call credit spread; the margin call is for the difference between strike prices, minus the difference between the prices of the two options. Here the difference between strike prices is 5, and since we took in a 4-point credit on the spread, the margin call is for 1 point.

Just how does a put bull spread make money? Let's take a look at the example where the stock was 40 and we bought the 40 put for 2 and sold the 45 put for 6, for a credit of 4. If we are right and the stock goes up to 45 or higher, the 40 put will expire worthless, and the 45 put will also expire. Thus, it will cost us nothing to get out of this position, and we are left retaining the original credit of 4 as our profit. On the other hand, if the stock should decline to 40, at the puts' expiration here is what would happen. The 40 put, which we own, will be worthless, but the 45 put, which we have sold, will be worth 5 points, and we will have to buy it back for 5. Now our cost of getting out will be 5, and since we took in a credit of 4 getting in, we have suffered a loss of 1 point. The result is the same no matter how far below 40 the stock falls.

If the stock is 43 at the puts' expiration, the 40 put we own is worthless, and the 45 put we're short is worth 2, so we buy it back for that. This gives us a profit of 2 points when subtracted from our original credit of 4. For every point that the stock is above 43 we make one more point up to our maximum profit, at 45, of 4, and for every point below 43 we make one less point, so that our break-even is 41. The table shows the actual number for each stock price.

A PUT BULL SPREAD

At Initiation			*Stock Price at Expiration*					
Stock	40			40	41	42	44	44	45
Sell 45 put	6	Buy 45 put	−5	−4	−3	−2	−1	0
Buy 40 put	−2	Sell 40 put	0	0	0	0	0	0
Credit	4	Debit	−5	−4	−3	−2	−1	0
Cost	1	Original						
(Margin)		Credit	4	4	4	4	4	4
		Profit or Loss	−1	0	1	2	3	4

At any stock price below 40 the loss continues to be 1, and at any price above 45 the profit will be 4.

The fact that a put bull spread results in a credit rather than a debit really doesn't make much difference to you. What does make a difference in deciding whether to use a put or a call bull spread is where you can get the greater leverage. And here is where you will just have to figure out what each spread can do for you. As a rule, put prices are less than call prices, and this is especially so for out-of-the-money options. Where here the stock is 40 and the 40 put is 2, the 40 call might be 3, and where the 45 put is 6, the 45 call might be 1½. This means that to do a bull spread would result in a debit of 1½, whereas the put spread can be done for a credit of 4, meaning that you are putting up just 1 point. A difference between a cost of 1 and 1½ means a 50% higher cost for doing the call spread. Hence the moral, that if puts are traded on the stock you are considering doing a bull spread on, be sure to find out the cost of doing a put spread.

There are two other factors you should take into consideration. The first is commissions. The call bull spread involves options costing 3 and 1½, whereas the put bull spread involves options costing 2 and 6, which would result in higher commission costs. More important, if you are correct and the stock goes up to 47, for instance, the put spread evaporates with absolutely no commission costs whereas the call spread requires commissions on calls costing $2 and $7.

Second, you must always keep in mind the hazards of being short in-the-money options. With the bull spread here there is very little danger, since your short option is out of the money, and by the time it gets into the money, where it could be exercised, your position will be quite profitable. With the put bull spread, you are by its very nature selling a put which is deep in the money, here that 45 put for 6. It could easily be exercised on you. Especially the day after the stock goes ex-dividend.

Put bear spreads

The put bear spread is like the call bear spread in that in both cases you are selling the lower strike price option and buying the higher strike price option.

This table shows how a typical put bear spread works. Since it is done as a debit spread, it makes money when the spread increases.

A PUT BEAR SPREAD

At Initiation			*Stock Price at Expiration*					
			45	44	43	42	41	40
Stock	44							
Buy 45 put	−2	Sell 45 put	0	1	2	3	4	5
Sell 40 put	1	Buy 40 put	0	0	0	0	0	0
Cost	1	Credit	0	1	2	3	4	5
		Less original cost	1	1	1	1	1	1
		Profit or Loss	−1	0	1	2	3	4

At stock prices below 40 the profit remains 4 and at stock prices above 45 the loss will be 1.

A call bear spread creates a credit, while a put bear spread results in a debit. But, as we noted before, this really doesn't make very much difference to you. What does make a difference is the leverage you can get from the spreads, and here a put spread should be preferable to a call spread. The main reason is that most call bear spreads have to be done at least partly in the money to make them profitable, because you have to take in a lot of money for the lower strike option which you sell. Since you are selling the in-the-money option, you are normally selling an option with low future time value. You are buying an option which is either out of the money or not so deep in the money as the one you are selling, and this means that it is going to have a greater future time value. This in turn means tht you are losing out on this buy and sell, which is to say that if the stock stayed still until expiration, you would be losing money. But with a put bear spread just the opposite is true. Here you are selling the lower strike price put, which is the one with the greater future time value, while you are buying the higher strike price put, which has the lower future time value. This means that you are getting more than you are receiving as far as future time value on options goes, and therefore you should be able to make money if the stock stays still.

All this is simply a way of explaining that if you will compare the cost of doing a bear spread with calls and puts, you will probably find that it is better for you to use puts. In addition to the better cost-to-potential-profit ratio which puts give you, you also avoid the serious problem in call bear spreads of being short a deep-in-the-money option. Remember, when this option is exercised against you prematurely, you're in bad shape. You must now buy in 100 shares of stock for every call that was exercised, paying commissions on that purchase, and when you were exercised you were charged commissions on the sale of 100 shares of stock for every option that was exercised. After you have done that you are left dangling with the options you are long, which you will probably sell out, generating more commissions. And all this without the probability of making any money. So the absence of being short an expensive in-the-money option is a significant plus feature.

Put calendar spreads

Put calendar spreads follow exactly the same principles as call calendar spreads. Since put prices tend to be somewhat lower than call prices, you should be able to do put calendar spreads for a lower debit. But this is not the advantage you might think it is, because when it comes time to close out the calendar put spread, it will not be worth as much as a call calendar spread. So your percentage profit on a put calendar spread is not likely to be much higher than a call calendar spread. One word of caution is that as your put calendar spread gets into the money (the stock moves down to below the strike price) the chance of your short option being exercised starts to grow. Since put premiums tend to be less than call premiums, the chances of being exercised on the short in-the-money put are that much greater.

Any one of the complex spreads that were discussed for calls can also be done for puts, including butterfly spreads, ratio spreads, and domino spreads. In some cases there will be advantages in using puts, but since most traders will continue to use calls because of their greater availability, there really is no point in discussing in detail the use of puts in each complex spread. But if you are mathematically inclined, you might consider whether you could improve on the butterfly spread by using calls to do the bull spread on the bottom, and then using puts to do the bear spread on the top. Have fun with your calculations.

COMBINING PUTS AND CALLS: STRADDLES AND COMBINATION

So far we have discussed spreads using calls, and spreads using puts. Some of the most interesting things one can do with options is to combine puts and calls in the same transaction. Basically these fall into two categories, buying combinations and writing them. Generally you buy a combination of puts and calls when you expect a stock to move by a large amount in either direction, and this is called a volatility spread. Or you can sell combinations of calls and puts, which generally work out to be nonvolatility spreads, making money when the stock ends up near the strike price. When you buy or sell a combination of a put and a call with the same expiration date and the same strike price it is called a *straddle*. When you use a combination which has different strike prices or expiration dates it is called a *combination*.

The easiest of these to discuss is buying a straddle. The big advantage in buying a straddle is that you can make money whether the stock moves up or down. Either direction is equally profitable provided only that it moves far enough. For example, when a stock is 70 you might buy a January 70 call for 4 and a January 70 put for 3⅜ when each has about six months to go. The cost of buying this straddle would be 7⅜, and your initial cost is the most you can possibly lose. If your strategy is to buy the straddle and hold it until expiration, the stock must move by 7⅜ in either direction for you to reach your break-even point. If the stock goes up by that much to 77⅜, then your call will be worth enough to cover your costs. If the stock moves down that much to 62⅝, then your put will be worth your original total cost. Thus it is rather easy to decide whether or not you want to do a straddle. What do you think that the chances are that it will be either over 77⅜ or below 62⅝ six months from now?

Trading with a straddle. Buying and holding is not the only strategy open to a straddle buyer, and perhaps it is not the best one. Supposing that the stock were to move to 75 within four weeks. Probably the call would move up to 7 and the put would still have a value of perhaps 2, so that you could get out of the spread for 9 at a modest profit. One point that must be emphasized is the difference in trading strategy which I believe should be used with a straddle as opposed to buying a call or a put outright. The difference is that when you buy a straddle you should, by its very nature, be expecting to make a more modest profit than when you simply buy an option. Since you are paying approximately twice as much for the straddle as you would to buy just one side of it, and since under normal circumstances only one side of the straddle is going to make money for you, it follows that you have twice the cost with the potential for no more profit than you would have made had you purchased the call or the put alone. Hence, it is unreasonable to expect that you will make the same percentage profit. In fact, your percentage return may be about half as much as on purchasing one option alone.

But to counteract this smaller anticipated profit is the basic fact that you can make money whether the stock goes up or down. You are therefore literally doubling the chances you have of making money. And it should not be surprising that in exchange for this larger number of instances in which you will make money, you must give up a portion of the percentage return that you can make from any price move. To summarize this comment, while the straddle is speculative because it can be worth nothing if the stock hangs in at the strike price, it is more conservative than buying an option, because this is the only circumstance under which your cost will entirely dissipate. Whereas, when you buy a put or a call, if the stock goes in the wrong direction, which it has a 50% chance of doing, you are out every penny you paid.

Thus, the cost of a straddle may be twice as high as buying an option, but the chances of losing all your money are much less than half as much as with an option—perhaps they are only 10% as much as with one option. Furthermore, the chance that you will lose less than half your money with a straddle is quite good: as in our example here, the stock has to move less than 4 points in either direction. Get out some stock chart books and see how often any stock has been at exactly the same place it was six months earlier. Not very often, you can be sure. Now we have established that the odds of losing all your money on a straddle are far less than with buying an option, the corollary should also be clear: that you will be satisfied with and will expect less spectacular profits.

Your trading strategies should also be adjusted to this conclusion, so that instead of closing out half your position when your option has doubled, as was suggested when you bought an option, perhaps you should close out half your position when it has increased by 50%, and then close out the other half when it has doubled. But whatever you decide, use the one guideline which has been the theme throughout this book: Decide in advance what you are going to do and when you are going to do it. Holding a straddle intil the last day can be as disappointing as anything else you can do. If you have a profit on the call side of your straddle, and you don't close it out of greed, and you see the stock slipping back down to the strike price, you are losing money just like a call owner, and the fact that you also own a put at the same strike price doesn't do you one whit of good unless the stock moves all the way down to the strike price.

Closing out the other side of a straddle. One frequently asked question is whether there is any point in not closing out the other side of a straddle when you take a good profit from one of the sides. Thus, in our example, if the stock went up to 80, and you sold the call for 10½, making a nice profit, should you sell out the 70 put at the same time, when all you can get for it is a negligible ⅜ point? There is something adventurous about holding onto this near worthless item in the vague hope that perhaps the stock will plummet, and you will realize the option trader's equivalent of a hole in one. This is also called trading against a straddle. If the stock goes down, first you sell your put at a profit and hold the call. Then when it goes up you sell out your call at a profit too. You will make a big profit on both the call and on the put, thus astounding everyone and really getting your money's worth out of the straddle, instead of wasting a full half of your straddle, as one usually does. Yes, it certainly has a lot of romance, but to reach a rational decision, simply ask yourself this question: With the stock at 80, would you buy a 70 put for ⅜ when it had only a few months or weeks to go? I'm not going to answer the question for you, but if you would not be a buyer of that put, then you should sell it out when you close out the call side. It is not a free dividend which is left over after you have taken your profit out of the straddle. It is part of the profit you are entitled to and shold be treated as such.

Ratio straddles. Straddles don't have to be done on a one-for-one ratio, and I believe that ratio straddles are going to become more and more popular. Since most of us do have views on how the market is going to move in the next few months, it is natural that we will tend to favor the side we believe in. Of course, knowing that we are fallible, we may want to protect ourselves with a few options for the other side, but there is a big difference between a hedge and the main thrust of our anticipated profit making. Thus, if we are bullish on the stock in our example, we may decide to buy 10 calls and only 4 puts, reasoning that the stock will probably go up and our puts will expire worthless, so why throw away so much money on them? On the other hand, if for some reason we are wrong, and the stock plunges down to 60, it will be nice not to lose any money.

Using a 10 to 4 ratio, our cost for the straddle comes out to $4.97 for each share on which we own a call, versus the cost of a full straddle of $7.37, which is quite a significant reduction in cost. It means that our break-even point on the upside is reduced 32%, and our percentage profit will be twice as high at 70. On the downside it will be much harder to make a profit, but then we don't really expect to do that. All we are looking for is a "self-liquidating" feature to pay for the cost of the straddle. As it turns out, our break-even point on the downside now becomes 56.60, which is pretty low, but at 60, there would be a loss of only 1 point for each share on which we had a call, so the puts will have substantially accomplished their job of absorbing most of the cost of the straddle.

The combination. As has been pointed out, the cost of a regular straddle is substantial, and therefore the chance of a large profit is rather small, absent a really spectacular move in the price of the stock. One way of trying to overcome this is to use a combination, in which you buy a call with a strike price above the current price of the stock and a put with the strike price below the current stock price. For example, when Mesa Petroleum was 37⅝, the six-month 35 call was 5⅛, the 35 put was 1¼, and the 40 call was 2⅜. Thus, to do a regular straddle at the 35 level would have cost 6⅜, but to do a combination of the 35 put and 40 call cost only 3⅝, or just over one half as much.

The theory behind this type of combination is that you are going to make any real money on a straddle only if the stock moves by a large amount in either direction, so why not save money by cutting out the middle band of the straddle in exchange for a greatly reduced cost? In this type of combination if the stock moves much above 40 or much below 35 you will still make a profit, and since your total cost was so much lower than with a regular straddle, you can soon make a much larger percentage profit. With a volatile stock, with high prices for on-the-money options, this might make good sense.

The obvious disadvantage is that you are now losing a key feature of straddles, i.e., that the only way you can lose all your money is if the stock ends up exactly at the strike price. You now have a range of anywhere from 35 to 40 in which you will lose your entire cost of the combination if that is where the stock is at expiration.

Another popular type of combination is to buy calls of one duration and puts of another, depending upon which way you believe the stock is likely to move. Thus, if you believe that a stock is going to go up, you might decide to buy the nine-month calls and also some three-month puts just in case the stock falls down in the near term. Your strategy might be to get out of the calls in three months if the stock goes down, in which case the puts will cut your loss or actually turn it into a profit, and if the stock goes up as you expect, then you can ride it for a long-duration gain.

Selling straddles and combinations

The easiest way to use straddles and combination is to buy them, but there are also advantages to be gained from selling them, although selling straddles will probably not appeal to the same type of person. Let's make it clear at the outset that the effects of selling straddles are completely different from buying them. The straddle buyer wants the stock to move in a large amount either up or down and limits his cost and maximum loss at the outset. The straddle seller, not surprisingly, wants the stock to stay just about where it is. But this is the least of the differences in terms of investment philosophy. The biggest one is that unlike the buyer, the seller is faced with an unlimited potential loss. This is not surprising because the straddle seller is actually a naked call seller, and in addition he is also a naked put seller with all the possible liability that naked puts bring. Thus the straddle writer faces an almost unlimited loss if the stock goes either up or down too far! It is definitely not for the investor with limited resources because of this possible unlimited loss. Second the straddle seller has to put up margin, and just as in the case of the naked option seller, the amount of margin can increase from day to day at an alarming rate. Finally, while the straddle buyer can always dream of striking it rich, the straddle seller can never make more than he originally took in on the day that he sold the straddle. And he will take in this much profit only if he is exceptionally lucky, i.e., the stock is just exactly at the strike price when the straddle expires.

Higher income than from naked calls. Straddle writing does appeal to the person who may have considered writing naked calls but is a little afraid that he isn't getting enough premium to cover his risks. In selling a straddle, the writer may get up to twice as much money coming in as he could for selling a naked call, since he has the money from both the put and the call. And the beauty of selling a straddle is that although you take in up to twice as much money at the start, you should not lose any more if things go wrong than if you had sold only a naked call. That sentence must be read very carefully. It does not say that you have no more chance of losing money than if you had sold only a call, it says that you should lose no more than if you had sold only a call. The reason is that by following the basic rule of strategy for selling naked options, you will close out the position at a predetermined stock price or option price for a predetermined loss. When the stock goes up, you will close out the position when it reaches your price, and the loss on the call will be no greater than it would have been had you sold the call alone. But you will then be able to buy in the put at what should be a good profit, since the put will now be way out of the money. Thus, you lost no more on the call than you would have selling a naked call alone, but you made a large profit on the put, which in some cases could actually wipe out your loss and even result in a net profit. So the straddle can be a big advantage over simply writing naked calls.

If this is so wonderful, then why does anyone still write naked calls alone? The answer is that while the amount of your loss may be no greater than with calls alone, the chances of having a loss with a straddle are about twice as great as they are with calls alone, for the obvious reason that with the naked put, you now have the chance of losing money if the stock goes down. You must also select a price for the stock or the option on the downside at which you will close out the position and take your loss on the put. At the same time you should be able to close out your call position for a good profit.

Straddle writing strategy. The strategy in selling straddles involves first a careful consideration of whether you should sell a particular straddle at all. In order to do this you will want to know the percentage return on your margin. The amount of margin required for writing a straddle is determined by computing the margin for the naked call, then the margin for the naked put, and taking the greater of the two. To determine the amount of margin needed to write the straddle, you can subtract both the premiums you receive. So, actually, the margin rules for the sale of straddles are quite a break for the writer. He is getting up to twice as much premium income from the same amount of margin as he would have if he sold just a put or just a call. This should be an important factor influencing call sellers toward writing straddles where available. So, the first consideration is to determine the maximum profitability based upon the stock staying at the strike price.

The second consideration is to decide what you can realistically expect to make on the deal. When a person writes naked calls, especially if they are out of the money, he can reasonably hope that he will retain the entire premium as his profit. But with a straddle this is somewhat fanciful, since the only way this could happen is if the stock is right at the strike price upon expiration, and even then, since you have to close out the position by 3:00 P.M. Eastern time, one hour before the stock exchanges close, you would probably have to buy in your position just to protect yourself from a move in the final hour of trading. So you must expect that the stock is going to move to some extent from the strike price, and you should come up with a reasonable figure. Now, subtract that amount from the total premiums you are going to take in from selling the straddle, and you will have some idea of what a reasonable profit would be.

The third step is to decide where your stop-loss positions are going to be if the stock moves strongly up or down. You do this in the same way you do for the sale of naked options, except that you might be able to stand larger moves against you because you have the profit on the other option to help you pay for your losses. In any event, once you have picked this price, you should then estimate what your loss on the entire position would be.

Having done these three things you are now in a position to make a reasonable determination of what you should do. You know what percentage profit you can make, how much you can reasonably expect to make, and how much you can expect to lose if you are wrong. Of course, you will now consider the volatility of the stock to try to come up with a probability factor of how likely it is that the stock will move either up or down to your close-out points. If this sounds a bit complicated, it is, but not beyond the scope of any competent options trader. And who ever said that it was easy to make money? As everyone familiar with Wall Street knows, it is always very easy to lose money, but not so easy to make it.

As we have seen, one of the biggest drawbacks to selling straddles is that some cost of buying back one of the options at expiration is almost inevitable. And the loss could be fairly substantial. Wouldn't it be nice if there were a way of writing a straddle in which we had a good chance of getting away scot clear with a full profit on both the put and the call? There is such a way and it is called writing a combination, in which we sell the call with the strike price above the current price of the stock and we sell the put with the strike price below the current price of the stock. For example, if a stock is 37, we would sell the 40 call and the 35 put. This has a lot to recommend it, because it is really the closest analogy to selling out-of-the-money naked call options, and out-of-the-money naked puts.

Margin for combinations. To determine the margin required for this type of combination, we calculate the margin required for the put and then for the call, and use the greater of the two. Again we get a bargain, two for the price of one. Before deciding whether to set up one of these combinations we should go through the three steps recommended for the straddle, but we may not have to do anything about the second step of buying in the options if we can realistically expect that the stock will stay between the two strike prices until the options expire. It seems to me that the sale of a combination is preferable to the sale of either naked calls or naked puts under most circumstances. The only exceptions would be where one has a strong viewpoint on which way the stock is going to move, or where the premiums for the two options are out of line. For example, a stock could have a very generously priced out-of-the-money call option which just begs to be sold naked, but because the public is so bullish on the stock, the put premium might be meager and therefore not worth writing. But generally, put and call premiums are approximately in line, and a good call-writing opportunity should also be a good put-writing opportunity. And with no additional margin required to take in perhaps twice as much money, why not do it?

If one does have views on which way a stock is going to move, an alternative to a combination is to do a ratio combination. For example, if you thought that a stock now selling at 42 were overpriced and you wanted to write the 45 calls without writing the 40 puts, you might consider writing two or three puts for every ten calls just to give you some additional income in case you are wrong.

To summarize the writing of straddles and combinations, they are definitely not for everyone. In the first place, you must be approved for naked option writing. In the second place, you must have the emotional temperament to be able to withstand the potential losses of naked option writing. Finally, you must be willing to accept a limited maximum profit with the knowledge that there is the possibility of an unlimited loss, because even with the best stop-loss plans, if a stock stops trading on news of a take-over for example, and opens up 10 points higher, there is no way in the world that you can prevent what might be a catastrophic loss. But if you can accept all those caveats, then writing straddles and combinations can yield a relatively high return on your capital in good markets and bad. If a stock takes long enough to make a move, you will be a winner whether it goes up or down. It is only the sharp, sudden moves that will produce the large losses.

WRITING CALLS ON CONVERTIBLE BONDS

7

Since the danger in covered writing is that the price of the stock will go down by more than the amount received from selling the option, investors interested in covered writing would love to discover a method of doing it which would decrease the danger on the downside. One possible solution to this problem is to write options against convertible bonds. A convertible bond is similar to a regular bond issued by a corporation with one special feature: At the request of the bondholder it can be converted into a predetermined number of shares of the common stock of that company. For example, if you buy a convertible bond with a conversion factor of 22.8, you can at any time tender your bond to the company and receive 22.8 shares of common stock in return for the bond. The effect of this conversion factor is that as the price of the stock rises, the price of the bond will also rise. Thus it can be used for covered writing in place of common stock.

Most convertible bonds pay interest rates which are greater than the dividend rate of the common stock. This means that when the price of the stock falls, the price of the bond will not be likely to fall as much. In addition, there is little danger that the interest rate will be cut, since legally the company must pay the interest on a convertible bond, whereas the payment of dividends is at the discretion of the board of directors. But there is another feature of convertible bonds that helps to keep up their price. This is that all bonds mature at some set future date, and when that time comes, the issuing corporation must redeem them at par, which is normally $1,000. Since the corporation must eventually redeem them for $1,000, assuming only that the corporation stays solvent, there is a natural limit on how low the current price of the bond can fall.

There you have the basic reasons why some sophisticated investors prefer to do their covered writing against convertible bonds rather than against common stock. When the stock goes up, the convertible bond can go up also because of the conversion feature. When the price of the stock goes down, the bond may not fall as far because of the two features that distinguish it from the stock: (1) it usually pays a greater rate of return, and (2) at its expiration date it will be redeemed for par, which is usually $1,000. Let us now examine in more detail just how convertible bonds fluctuate in price, and then take a really close look at some of the disadvantages. Because here, as elsewhere, alas alack, an advantage gained is often accompanied by a benefit lost. And yet, to those who know stocks and bonds intimately, there is little doubt that in many instances writing options against convertible bonds makes much more sense then using common stock.

Description of convertible bonds

Convertible bonds are issued by corporations in the same manner as regular bonds. Corporations like to issue convertible bonds because if investors know that they can make a great deal of money on the bond if the stock goes up, they will be willing to buy a bond which pays less interest than a straight bond, and the corporation thus saves money in interest payments. Eventually, if the bond is converted by the bondholders into common stock, the corporation has managed to decrease its debt by the amount of the bonds and has increased its equity without all the fuss and worries of a new public stock underwriting. Because of the advantages to corporations in issuing convertible bonds, they are quite popular, and there are now over 75 companies with listed options that have convertible bonds. (See Appendix C for the list and description of the bonds.) Unfortunately, as we shall see, only a small fraction of these are really appropriate at any given time for use in a covered writing program.

First let us say just a word about bonds in general. Most of them are traded on the New York Stock Exchange, but unlike stocks, there is a rule which permits trades of ten bonds or more to be made off the floor of the exchange, directly between dealers. This means, in effect, that most trades are not made on the exchange. Therefore, the figures you see published in the financial section on NYSE bond transactions give only a very incomplete story of prices and absolutely no indication of volume.

The price of bonds is always given as if it were a $100 bond, but in fact bonds are generally $1,000 bonds. This is done just to make things more confusing. For example, if your broker tells you that a bond is 83, what he is saying is that the bond is really $830, and if you buy ten bonds at 83, you will be paying $8,300.

Every bond has a stated coupon interest rate, such as 4.25%. This rate is always stated as the rate of interest payable on the face amount of the bond, i.e., in almost all cases $1,000. For example, if you buy a 5.5% bond for $83, you will *not* be receiving interest of 5.5% times $830. You will receive interest of 5.5% times the face value of the bond, assume $1,000, or $55 per year. This means that if you paid $83 for the bond (actually $830) you are really receiving a higher interest rate on your investment than the stated rate. To compute your actual rate of interest, which is called the current yield, divide the stated rate of 5.5% by the price you paid, which is $830, and move the decimal point three places, giving 6.63%. If you have to pay more than par for the bond, your current yield will be less than the stated rate.

. Another way in which bonds differ from stocks is the way in which the return is built into the price of the underlying security. As you may know, when you buy a stock, you pay the agreed-upon price, and that is all. If it is about to go ex-dividend the day after you buy it, then you get that full dividend. If it went ex-dividended the day before you bought the stock, you then have to wait almost three months before you get your first dividend. Not so with bonds.

Accrued interest. Bonds are more sophisticated. Instead of having the all-or-nothing situation which prevails in stocks, the price of a bond is adjusted for the amount of the accrued interest. Thus, if you buy a bond for $83, and the last interest payment was made three months ago, you will pay $830 plus the amount of accrued annual interest prorated to the three months which have elapsed since it was last paid, since bond interest is usually paid every six months. This means that you are paying a bit more for the bond, but you will receive that interest back when six months' interest is paid to you. Thus, bonds don't go down in price after there has been an interest payment, and every bondholder gets the amount of interest he has earned for the exact number of days he has held the bond.

Convertibles enable the bondholder to convert the bonds into a predetermined number of shares of the stock. This conversion number is the most important feature of the bonds, as far as we are concerned. For it is the conversion number which tells how many shares of stock one is able to obtain by converting one bond. In other words, the conversion number tells you the equivalent number of shares for each bond you own. Thus, if we find that the conversion ratio of a bond is 39.409, and you own 5 bonds, you have the right to convert them into 5 times 39.409, or approximately 197 shares of the common stock.

You might be wondering at this point, what price am I going to pay for the stock? The answer is that you simply hand in your bond and receive the stock. When you buy the bond, it is an easy matter to determine what price you are paying for each share of stock, if you ever decide to convert. For example, if you buy a bond for $97 (remember, this means you actually pay $970 for the bond) and it has a conversion ratio of 30, you can convert that bond into 30 shares, giving you a cost per share of $32.33.

If the price of the stock later goes down, the price of the bond will go down, although, as we noted earlier, the fact that it will eventually be redeemed for $1,000 and the current interest rate it pays will help to keep up its value. If, on the other hand, the price of the stock goes up, then the bond will have to go up. It is a truism that the price of a convertible bond can never be appreciably less than the current price of the stock multiplied by the conversion ratio of the bond. Thus, if the stock involved in this example rose to $37 a share, your bond would have to be worth at least $37 times 30, or $1,110.

Now you may begin to appreciate why convertible bonds can be used to write covered options. Because when the price of the stock goes up, they must go up, at least to the extent that the price of the bond is equal to or greater than the price of the stock multiplied by the conversion ratio, whereas if the price of the stock goes down, the bond may well not fall as rapidly.

An almost valueless conversion feature. Some convertible bonds were issued when the price of the corporation's stock was selling for a far higher price than the stock is now. In such cases, the conversion feature of the bond may be almost meaningless. For example, the Xerox 6% of 1995 has a conversion ratio of 10.870. This means that if the bond were to sell at the conversion ratio based upon a price of the stock of 50½, it would be selling for 10.870 times 50½ or $548.93. But because the bond has a 6% interest rate and is going to be redeemed for $1,000 in 1995, it was not selling at its conversion price when the common was $50½. Instead, the bond was actually selling for $94 ($940). That is, the bond was selling pretty much at the price of a nonconvertible bond bearing interest of 6% and a maturity of 1995. Another way of looking at this is to say that with a conversion ratio of 10.870 and a bond price of $94, by dividing the one into the other we find that the stock would have to go up to $86½ before it would pay to convert the bond. Since Xerox was selling at such a great distance from that price, it is clear that the bond was selling almost entirely on its value as a bond, and not on its conversion price. It was therefore not appropriate to use for covered writing, as we shall see later.

Other bonds may be selling at a price that reflects just the opposite situation, that is, they are selling at a price greatly in excess of what an ordinary bond of that interest rate and maturity would be selling for, and they have such a high price solely because the stock is selling at a price high enough to bring up the price of the bond. Thus, on the same day that the Xerox bond was selling at nearly the price of a regular bond, the Occidental Petroleum convertible bonds paying 7.5% interest and maturing in 1996 were selling for 124 ⅜, while the stock was 25⅛. What was the reason for the high price of the bond? You can figure it out yourself, when I tell you that the conversion ratio of the bond was 50.0. Multiply the price of the stock, 25⅛, by 50 and you get 1,256.25.

As we said earlier, since the holder of a bond has the right at any time to turn his bond in to the issuing company in exchange for the number of shares indicated by the conversion ratio of the bond, it is impossible for the bond ever to sell for appreciably less than the price of the stock times the conversion ratio.

Thus, the bond must sell at or close to $1,256, and it sold at a slight discount. Here, then, is a bond which is selling solely based upon the price of the stock and not upon the intrinsic qualities of the bond, such as interest and maturity.

Small premium over conversion value. Then in between these two extremes are bonds which are priced higher than a regular nonconvertible bond would be, but not so high that the price reflects only the price of the stock times the conversion ratio. These bonds are said to be selling at a small premium over conversion value. An example would be the Owens-Illinois 4½% convertible bonds of 1992, which were selling at $96 when the common stock was 54¾. The bonds have a conversion ratio of 16.949, which means that if the bond was selling at merely its current conversion price, it would be at 54¾ times 16.949, or $927.95. The extra 32.05 per bond was the premium at which the bonds were selling. This extra price was due to the higher interest on the bond than the stock, and the fact that the bonds would definitely be redeemed for $1,000 in 1992, barring only a default by Owens-Illinois.

Selecting the convertible bond for option writing

In order to make money by writing options against convertible bonds, it is essential to have the one factor that is also needed to make money writing options against stock: There must be a worthwhile premium in the option. If there are no options around which carry any significant future time value, then you simply will not be able to set up a very profitable option-writing program. So you won't have to look for any convertible bond. The only advantages of a convertible bond over a stock are that if you make the right selection, the bond may not fall as fast as the stock and you may pick up some increase in interest. But if you can't get a decent price for the option, then this possible improvement is not going to transform a poor writing option into a good one.

In writing against stock, there is no difficulty in foreseeing what will happen at expiration for different prices of the stock. You know that the option will have zero future time value and will be selling for just about its cash value. It is a simple matter to figure out in what price range you will have made or lost money. With convertible bonds, we bring in an entirely new dimension, which makes predicting the results both more difficult and more challenging. This new dimension is simply that we cannot always be certain what the convertible bond will be selling for at any stock price. You can imagine the problems this can cause.

Let us suppose that your stock goes up 10 points, and you therefore lose 7 points on each option. No problem with stock. But what if the convertible bond you are using does not go up by 10 points for each equivalent share?

What if it goes up by only 7 points per share? Then obviously you are not making any money at all, and if the bond goes up by only 6 points for each equivalent share, then you are actually losing money.

Clearly, then, the most important criterion in selecting a convertible bond to use in covered writing is to have a very good estimate of how much the bond is going to go up for every point increase in the price of the common stock. It is not fatal if it does not go up point for point, because you can compensate for that by not writing one option for each 100 shares equivalent in the bond, but no matter how much the bond goes up, you must have a good estimate before you begin.

The easiest situation is a bond that is already selling at its par value with the current price of the stock. Since, as we pointed out, the bond can never sell for significantly less than its conversion value, if the price of the stock goes up, then the price of the bond must move up with it. In the example mentioned above the Occidental Petroleum 7½% of 1996 was selling for 125, being the equivalent to 50 shares, when the stock was selling for 25. Since 50 times 25 gives exactly 1,250, these bonds were selling at par with the stock.

Thus, when the price of the stock goes up one point, the price of the bond must go up by 50 times one. In other words, if you bought two bonds, you could write one option against them and be certain that as the stock goes up, and you lose money on the option you have written, you will be making it up point for point by an increase in the price of the bond.

For a look at the opposite extreme, let's examine the Xerox 6% of 1995 we mentioned above, which was selling at a great premium over the conversion value. Suppose that you decided to buy ten bonds, and write one option. The conversion ratio of 10.870 means that mathematically you are more than covered, since you actually have the equivalent of 108 shares of stock. Let's say that the Xerox common is selling at 50, and you decide to write the 50 option with about seven months to go which is selling at 4. That sounds like a pretty good premium. You decide that you should make about 8 percent, and with the greater downside protection that a convertible offers, you expect to come out with a good profit without taking a large risk.

The problem of a large premium. But let's see what could happen. Suppose that Xerox stock has a good move up and at the end of the option's duration is now selling for 60. You now buy back your options for 10, which, since you sold them for 4, produces a loss of $600. That's okay, you think, because since the stock has gone up 10 points, while you have a loss of only 6 points in the option, you should have a good profit.

You check the paper to see where your bonds are now selling, expecting that they will each be approximately $100 above your cost of $940 or about $1,040 (expressed as $104), and are amazed to find that they are selling at almost exactly the same price they were at seven months ago when the stock was 10 points lower. Horrors! You suddenly realize that instead of making money on this arrangement, you are going to lose about $600. The reason for this is that the bond was selling almost entirely on its value as a bond without any consideration for the conversion value. The conversion value of the bond was 54, but it was selling at 95. So it is clear that the price of the stock had almost nothing to do with the price of the bond. Therefore, when the price of the stock goes up to 60, giving a conversion value to the bond of 62.20, the bond will still be selling at its approximate value as a straight bond without any consideration to its conversion value. The moral of this story is simple: If a convertible bond is selling with a very large premium value over its conversion value, it is not a good candidate for use in an option-writing program. In the case of Xerox, the example is extreme. But even in other cases, where the price of the bond may move up somewhat for a move up in the price of the stock, if there is a large premium in the bond, then the bond may not move up enough to offset the loss in the options. Instead of going up in price, the amount of the premium will simply decrease.

Estimating price moves of convertible bonds. What you must do before you can write options against a convertible bond is to estimate how much it is going to move for each point rise in the price of the stock. Of course, if the bond is selling at close to its conversion value, you don't have to use any method. The bond will move up with the stock. For other bonds there are at least two methods of computing the price change. One is to use someone else's estimates, the other is to figure them out yourself using historical data.

The easiest, but perhaps not the most accurate way is to use someone else's estimates. A number of options services give what is called the hedge ratio for convertible bonds. This ratio is exactly what we are looking for, i.e., the amount that the bond will move up for a one-point move up in the price of the stock. A word of caution is in order. These hedge ratios are accurate only for small moves. For instance, they may be accurate for moves of 5 points, but for moves more than that the stock may have a higher hedge ratio. Obviously, as the price of the stock moves up, the premium in the bond tends to shrink, and the further it shrinks, the more closely the bond will move up point for point with the stock.

The second method is to construct your own chart of what prices the bond will be for various prices of the stock. To do this you should start with a chart of the stock's price action over a number of years, and then go to a library which has on file newspapers which have quotes for the convertible bond you are following. Then you simply look on your chart and find the highs and lows, get out the newspapers for those dates and make note of the price of the bond and the price of the stock on those days. After you have made enough notations, perhaps as few as five, you will begin to discern a pattern of how the bond moves in relation to the stock.

In general, you will find that the lower the stock goes, the less the bond moves per point. When the stock is low the bond is selling at a price well above its conversion price, which means that it has a high premium, and it is selling at a price close to its price as a straight bond. On the other hand, when the stock is at the high end of its range, the premium on the bond will be slight, it will be selling at close to its conversion price, and it will tend to move almost one point for every point move in the stock.

What you are trying to estimate is how far the bond will move up or down for certain percentage moves in the stock. For example, the Value Line Convertible and Option Survey estimates what percentage move the bond will make if the stock goes up by 25% and 50% and if it goes down by an equal percentage. If you can come up with estimates like that you will have a good idea of how the convertible will perform in relation to the stock.

Once you know this, then you can determine the ratio of options you want to sell for each bond. For example, if you found that when the stock went up 6 points, the bond, which has a conversion of 41 shares, went up $164, you would figure out how many options you would write as follows. The bond went up $164, but what we want to know is how much it went up on a per-share basis. To determine this we simply divide $164 by the number of shares into which the bond is convertible, here 41. 164 divided by 41 is 4. This means that for a 6-point move in the common stock, the bond has gone up by an amount equivalent to only 4 points a share. Therefore, if you want to be protected on the upside, you can only sell four-sixths or 66% of an option for each share equivalent. Here 66% of 41 gives 27 shares per bond, or .27 options per bond.

The fact that you cannot write on a one-for-one basis will result in a lower potential profit on the transaction and in less downside protection than if you had been able to write one for one. You must decide whether these disadvantages are offset by the greater downside resistance of the convertible compared with the common. If there is not an offset, then you are probably better off forgetting about the convertible and using the common stock.

An example of writing against a convertible. Now let's look at an example of a typical convertible write which was actually executed. On November 1, 1977, ITT common stock was at 30, the ITT 8 ⅞% convertible bond of the year 2000 was selling at 120, and the April 30 option was 1½. Before we can do anything, we must know the facts about the bond. The crucial fact is that it is convertible into 39.409 shares of common. We must now divide the price of the bond, $1,200, by the number of shares, 39.409, to determine what each share costs when we buy the bond. The result is a price of $30.44. This means that we are paying a premium when we buy the bond of 44¢ per share.

The first step in analyzing a convertible write is to decide how the bond will move when the price of the stock goes up. Here that is relatively easy, because, as we mentioned earlier, a bond will never sell for appreciably less than its conversion price. Since we are buying the bond at only 44¢ a share above conversion price, this means that no matter how high the price of the stock goes, the bond will go up point for point, with the exception that the 44¢ premium will shrink as the bond moves up and will completely disappear if the stock gets up high enough. Since, however, we are getting 1½ points for the option, we would be making a one-point profit even if the entire 44¢ premium disappeared. The worst that could happen is that the profit on 10 options would be reduced by $440, but this would happen only if the stock increased very substantially. Therefore, we do not have to worry about losing money on the upside and can safely write on a full one-for-one ratio, thus giving ourselves the maximum profit and downside protection. So for every bond we buy we would write .39409 options.

Profit if stock price stays still. Having determined what our strategy for the upside is, we now must analyze the situation if the stock stays still, to determine what our potential profit is. Let's assume that we decide to buy 26 bonds and to sell 10 options, which retains fairly closely the ratio of 39.409 to 100 on a smaller scale. The computation on a cash basis would be:

Buy 26 bonds at 120	$31,200
Commission of $7.50 per bond	195
Net cost of bonds	$31,395
Sell 10 ITT 4/30 at 1½	1,500
Less commission	−91.50
Net option proceeds	1,408,50

Subtract option proceeds from bond cost to derive cost of transaction:

Bond cost	$31,395
Option proceeds	1,408.50
Cost of transaction	$29,986.50

Potential Gross Profit if Stock Stays at Same Price

Option proceeds	1,408.50
Interest on bond	
$26,000 \times 8.625\% \frac{175}{365}$ (number of days) =	1,075.17
Profit	$2,483.67

As a percentage of initial investment of $29,986.50: 8.3%

As an annualized percentage $(83 \times \frac{365}{175})$ 17.3%

These figures assume that the position will be continued by selling other 30 options. If, however, the position is closed out, there will be closing costs:

Commission on Selling Bonds	$195
Loss by selling bonds at bid price which may be $10 less per bond than last sale price	260
	$455
Subtracting this from our original profit	2,483.67
	−455.00
Profit	2,028.67

Percent on Investment   6.76%
Annualized Profit   14.1%

Now let's compare that with the return we would get if we just bought 1,000 shares of common and wrote options against that. Using the method outlined in Appendix J for computing the actual profit potential in a covered writing position, and assuming we would receive two dividends of 44¢ a share, we find that the return on a cash investment would be 7.8% without the costs of closing out the position, which is therefore slightly less than the 8.1% we would get with the convertibles. The net return, including the costs of commissions if the stock is allowed to be called away, is 6.5%, which is also just below the 6.6% from the convertibles. So the conclusion of the second step is that if the stock stays still we will be slightly better off by using the convertible rather than the common stock.

The results are the same if one does this transaction on margin. Using an interest rate on the debit of 7½%, the return, including costs of closing out the transaction, is 9.9% for the 175-day period using the convertibles, and it is 9.7% for the period using common stock. These returns annualize to 20.6% and 20.2% respectively, which many would consider a very attractive return on a high-yielding, low price/earnings ratio stock like ITT.

The third step is to determine what our loss is going to be if the stock goes down. The Value Line Options & Convertibles Service estimated that for a 25% decrease in the price of the stock there would be a 15% decrease in the price of the bond. This means that our profit of $1,981.92 would be reduced by 15% of $31,200, or $4,680, giving a loss of $2,698.08. This is certainly not desirable, but it must now be compared to the loss which would be incurred if we had written options against the stock. If we had purchased 1,000 shares of ITT stock for $30 each, a loss of 25% would have meant a loss of $7,500, which would have been $2,820 greater than the loss projected by using the convertibles.

Having gone through these three steps we can now conclude that use of the convertible does indeed accomplish our objectives of giving meaningfully greater downside protection while giving even a slightly higher return if the stock stays at the same price or goes up.

No let's review the main pros and cons of using convertibles which we can learn from this example.

Summing up the benefits. 1. Less loss on the downside. This is the principal reason for using convertibles. In this example it was estimated that a 25% decline in the price of the common would reduce the price of the convertible by only 15%, resulting in $2,820 less loss than if we used the common.

2. Lower commissions. If we had purchased 1,000 shares of the common at $30, the commission would have been $400. Instead, the commission on 26 bonds was only $195, which means a saving of $205 in buying the securities. On the way out, if the position is closed out, there would be a similar saving of $205.

3. Higher yield. The ITT common stock was paying a dividend of $1.76 a year for a yield of 5.86%. The bond was an 8.625% coupon bond priced at 120, giving a current yield of 7.18%. This higher yield is usually the case for convertible bonds, and in this example it contributed an additional profit of $148.42. ITT happens to be a relatively high yielding stock, but in many cases the difference in yield between the common and the convertible will be far more dramatic.

Summing up the disadvantages. 1. Loss of premium. Perhaps the biggest disadvantage is the loss of premium the convertible bond will suffer if the stock price goes up. In this case we were paying a premium of only 44¢ a share so it was not crucial. But it is important to note even here that if the stock price goes up, that 44¢ premium will shrink or even disappear and we would have substantially less profit than when the price of the stock stays the same. If the stock went up high enough, we can assume that the premium would disappear entirely. This would decrease our profits by 44¢ times 1,000, or $440. This means that our profit of $1,981.92, including closing costs, is reduced to $1,541.92, which brings the percentage profit from 6.6% to 5.1%. But this is the worst that could happen, no matter how high the stock price goes, and must be compared to the very large savings if the price of the stock declines.

2. Higher closing costs. One of the beautiful aspects of a successful covered write against common is that it concludes automatically and at precisely the price one originally computed, i.e., the option's strike price. You

know in advance that if the stock is above the strike price you will sell the stock at exactly 30. Not 30 minus ⅛ or minus ¼ or maybe not at all because there are no bidders for the stock at the price you want to get, but precisely at 30. Contrast this with the process of selling the covertible. There is nothing automatic about it. Even if the stock is exactly 30, you must now sell the bond. You may find that although the bond should be selling at $120, that is the offering price and the bid is 117. But even worse than this is that your broker may tell you that the bid is for only 5 bonds, and since you may be trying to sell all your 26 bonds, this is not very helpful. Your broker will then probably try to sell the bonds off the exchange floor, and the price might be even lower than 117.

3. Danger of unwelcome exercise. When one writes options against common stock, it really doesn't matter if the stock is called away earlier than expected. It may mean that one doesn't get an expected dividend, but on the other hand it will mean that the position is being closed out more quickly than planned, which will increase the annualized return. The situation with a convertible bond is different. As soon as there is an unwelcome exercise it means that you have sold the common stock and have paid a commission on the sale.

You are now short the common and long the bond. What do you do? If there is no longer any premium in the convertible, you have no problem. Simply convert the bond into the common. But if there is a premium on the bond, you will lose the entire premium by converting. So you will try to sell the bonds, incurring another commission. Thus, you will have two commissions instead of one.

To summarize the use of convertible bonds as an option-writing vehicle, they can produce higher yield with much less downside risk than the common. On the other hand, they do have the three disadvantages mentioned above and they are complicated. They should be used only by investors who thoroughly understand convertible bonds, including the conversion features and the possible loss of premium on the upside.

OPTION MARGIN REQUIREMENTS

8

Getting the most leverage

This chapter concerns principally those who wish to sell naked or covered options. Those who wish to purchase either puts or calls must pay the full cash price for the options. There is, however, one important difference between buying stocks for cash and buying listed options. The date on which stock must be paid for, called the settlement date, is five business days after the date of the trade. Because options are so highly volatile in comparison to stock, the settlement date is the very next business day after the transaction. This rule applies whether you are paying cash for listed options, delivering shares as margin for writing covered options, or depositing cash as margin for writing naked options. Since it is unlikely that our postal service will deliver a letter the next business day, you should not be surprised or offended if your broker requests the cash or securities before he makes your trade. He is simply doing what he must to protect himself from being out of compliance with the option exchange rules.

The only margin that is required for those who wish to sell calls on stock that they own, i.e., write covered calls, is to deliver to their broker the underlying shares. The shares can either be owned fully by the investor, or they can be owned on margin. If it is inconvenient to actually deliver the shares, a certificate of escrow signed by the bank or the institution having their possession can be substituted for the shares themselves. In either case, the shares are the only margin that the option broker is likely to request. The reason is simply that if the price of the stock rises, producing a loss from the sale of the call, the gain on the price of the stock will produce a profit that will exactly cancel out the loss on the call. Thus, there is always a perfect match because the broker always has the shares to deliver if the call is exercised.

MARGIN AND COVERED CALLS

If the underlying shares themselves are bought on margin, the margin requirements are the regular Federal Reserve requirements in effect at the time for anyone who purchases stock without writing a call. When this book was written, that requirement was 50% of the price of the stock. Therefore, if a person wanted to sell a covered call on a stock costing $60, he would only have to put up $30 in cash, less the amount of the premium received from the call. If he was selling a call for $6, the net cash requirement would be $24. (Remember that when computing your percentage profit on the sale of a covered call, while $6 is only a 10% return on $60, it is a much bigger 25% return on your actual cash outlay.) Of course you must pay interest on the margin you use to acquire the underlying stock, but the dividends on the stock may cover this interest. If the interest your broker charges you is 9%, payable on the 50% that you bought on margin, and the stock is paying a 4.5% dividend, that dividend will cover the entire interest cost for you.

One further word must be said about buying stocks on margin and writing options. This is that if you are writing deep-in-the-money options, you might run into another requirement of margin which could partially reduce the leverage you get. In addition to paying for 50% of the price of the stock, there is a maintenance requirement which must be met after the position has been put on. At most firms this maintenance requirement prohibits the brokerage firm from lending you more than 65% of the current market value of the stock. Thus, when you buy a stock you must put up 50% of the value, and the brokerage lends you the other 50%, but if the brokerage firm were to never lend you more than 50% of the *current* price of the stock, they would be requesting more money from their margin customers every time the stock went down by one dollar. To prevent this, they provide that while they will lend you 50% of the price of a stock to purchase it, they will not ask you for more money until their original loan amounts to 65% of the current market value of the stock. So, for example, if you bought a stock for $12 and your brokerage firm loaned you $6, if the stock declined in value to $9 you would still owe the firm $6. But $6 is 66% of 9, which is above the limit of 65% which the loan can have in relation to the current value of your stock. You would therefore be asked to send in some more money to cover your margin, so that your loan would be reduced down to 65% of the current price of the stock. Another way of stating this is that your equity (the price of your securities minus your loan from the brokerage firm) must never be less than 35% of the total value of your securities.

Maintenance margin requirement. A problem can arise in covered option writing from the fact that after you have sold an option on a stock, the margin department is required to value the stock not at its current market value, but at the price of the strike price of the option you have sold. So, in this case, as soon as you have bought the stock for $12, and sold the 10 option on it, the margin department must value the stock at $10. Fortunately, the $6 which the firm loaned you is just 60% of $10, and so you will not have to send in any more money to meet a margin maintenance call. If, however, you had sold an option with a strike price of $9, then the $6 they loaned you would be 66% of the price at which they must value the stock, and so you would be over the 65% limit and would have to pay more money. In general, this maintenance margin rule does not come into play unless you are writing a deep-in-the-money option which is more than 33% below the current price of the stock.

Even if this maintenance requirement does not make you send in more money immediately following the trade, it can still have a bothersome effect on your account. The reason for this is that unless the amount which you have borrowed from the brokerage firm is less than 50% of the current value of your account, your account is called "restricted." This means that you are below the 50% requirement, and if you sell a stock, you cannot withdraw 50% of the proceeds from the sale. You are allowed to withdraw only 33.3%. So if you own stocks on margin in your account, and then you begin a deep-in-the-money option-writing program against stock you are purchasing for that purpose, do not be surprised if your account suddenly becomes restricted even though all your stocks have gone up. This is simply one of the disadvantages of in-the-money covered writing on margin which one must learn to live with.

There is one exception to the rule which permits you to keep only 33.3% of the proceeds of a sale when your account is below 50% equity. This exception is the "same day substitution" rule which permits you to reinvest all the proceeds of a sale, provided that the reinvestment of the proceeds is made on the same day as the sale. In other words, if you sell $10,000 worth of stock on March 18, and your equity in the account is only 40% of the total value of the account, you will be ordinarily allowed to withdraw only $3,333. But if you purchase stock on March 18, you will be able to purchase stock worth $10,000 on margin, that is, you will have $5,000 worth of cash available for reinvestment on that day. If you cannot find a good investment on that day, the next day you will have only $3,333 available, which means that you will be able to buy only $6,666 worth of stock. So by waiting one day you lose 33% of your buying power. For those who are in a continuing option-writing program using margin, this can be a very crucial distinction. The lesson is very clear. If your equity (the net value you have in your account after deducting what you owe your brokerage firm) is less than 50% of the total value of the account, and you know that you are going to be assigned some options which are expiring, check with your broker and make sure that he is prepared to reinvest that money on the same day if it is at all possible to do so.

SELLING NAKED CALLS

The seller of a naked call is in an unusual position. When he begins his transaction, he receives money. If there were no margin requirement, anyone could telephone an option broker and ask to sell as many calls as he wished, without having to pay any money, unless he eventually sustained a loss. Thus there is obviously a need for some margin simply to restrain people from excessive call writing. But what should the amount of the margin be? If a person wishes to sell stock that he doesn't own, that is, to sell the stock short, his broker must borrow the shares from someone before they can be sold. So the broker insists that the investor pay either the price of the shares or a certain percentage of their price. At the present time, the amount required for selling shares short on the New York Stock Exchange is 50% of their price. The minimum percent for selling naked calls on the other hand is 30%, although many brokerage firms require 35%, 40% or even 50%.

The 30% requirement is just the first part of the margin requirement for most calls. The second part is that one take into consideration the difference between the current price of the stock and the strike price of the call. This makes good sense, because obviously the risk that a call seller is going to have to come up with money to cover his position is much greater in the case of a call whose stock is selling above the strike price than one that is well below the strike price. The rule takes this into consideration by requiring that one dollar be added to the margin for every dollar that the stock is selling above the strike price, and by permitting one dollar to be subtracted from the margin for every dollar that the stock is selling below the call's strike price.

This requirement of adjusting the required margin to the difference between the price of the stock and the strike price can produce some very interesting and surprising results. If you wish to write a call with a strike price of 100 when the stock is at 77 you would first take the current market price of the stock, 77, and multiply that figure by 30%, getting $23.10. Now you compute the difference between the strike price and the current price of the stock. The strike price is $100, and the stock is now selling for $77, giving you a difference of $23. If you subtract this from $23.10 you will get just 10¢.

The regulations have already considered this possibility. There is a minimum margin requirement on each call of $2.50. So the margin required here would be $2.50 per share. On the other hand, if one wanted to write a call with an 80 strike price on a stock when it was 105, your margin requirement would be the price of the stock multiplied by 30%, giving $31.50, and to this add the difference between the stock price and the strike price (105 minus 80) which is $25. Thus your total margin requirement would be $56.50.

In each case, however, one is permitted to deduct the amount of the premium received to determine the amount of cash needed to sell the call initially. Thus, if you received 75¢ per share in our first example, you would deduct this from the $2.50 requirement, meaning that only $1.75 per share would be needed from you to write the option.

Marking to the market

All option margin requirements must be "marked to the market" every day. This means that each day your broker will recompute your margin requirement, and if your account requires more money you must supply it immediately. This can have very rapid effects upon your margin requirements under the above rules, because for every point that the stock moves up, you may have to put up $1.30 more for margin. This can be absolutely catastrophic where the amount of margin originally required was low because the stock was selling for a price far below the strike price. Suppose that when a stock was selling for 71 you decided to write a call with a strike price of 90; 30% of 71 is $21.30. The difference between the strike price and the price of the stock is 19, which when subtracted from $21.30 gives $2.30, so your margin is the $2.50 minimum.

Well, you put up the minimum margin of $2.50 and sit back and relax. After all, you figure that unless that stock suddenly shoots up by over 19 points to the 90 strike price you are going to collect that premium as pure profit. Right—but perhaps only if you have a big pile of money to back you up. Let's say the stock goes up four points to 75. The margin required is now 30% of that, $22.50, minus 15 (90 less 75), giving a margin requirement of $7.50. Since you already put up $2.50, you are now required to immediately deposit another $5.00. Not an earth-shaking amount, you say, but it is an increase of over 100% in the amount of margin you must put up. And if you wrote enough calls so that you had to deposit $10,000 it might take a bit of scurrying around to dig up that extra $10,000. But, wait. The stock just barely moved. Let's suppose that it went up a bit more, to 84. There is still probably nothing to worry about as far as your ever having to make good on the option; 84 is a long way from 90, and by the time the stock got up to 84, the call might be almost at the expiration date. So you can still relax. But there is that little detail of the margin requirement.

With the stock at 84, your margin is 30% of that, which is $25.20, minus the difference between 90 and 84, which is 6. This gives you a margin requirement of $19.20. $19.20? Yes, $19.20. That means that if you started out with ten contracts requiring a margin of $2,500, you now have to have margin of $19,200. Quite an increase, isn't it? And remember that all this margin is required merely to let you continue to have a chance to make a tiny premium per call. If the premium was 75¢ and if it takes $19,200 in cash to enable you to perhaps make a profit of $750, you can figure that your percentage return on investment will be pretty small. Needless to say, the story only gets worse as the price of the stock goes up.

Now, of course, if the margin requirement ever gets too steep for you to handle you can always close out your account. But this might not be what you would like to do, because the premium of the call may very well have increased and you will take a substantial loss. If you had been able to hold onto it, you might well have realized your profit goal of 75¢ per call.

So the moral of the story is, don't be fooled by the low initial margin requirements for calls that have strike prices far above the current price of the stock. That's like finding a great bargain on an umbrella only to find out when you need it during the next rainstorm that it has a large hole in it. If you write naked calls using the theories of this book you will want to hang onto them either until they expire and you keep the premium as profit, or until they go over the strike price and you are closed out at a loss or you decide to close out your position because you have made a quick profit due to their price decline. If you are writing a call and the required margin is very low because the price of the stock is down way below the strike price of your call, take warning! When the stock moves up, you may be forced to close out your position against your wishes. And that means that you may well take a loss that, had you been able to stick in there, would have been totally unnecessary.

OPTION COMMISSIONS

9

Small commissions can swallow your profits

It is often said (particularly by brokers) that the commission for buying or selling options on the exchanges is very reasonable, because the commission to purchase one option on 100 shares of a stock is so much less than the commission to purchase 100 shares of the stock itself. That statement, while true on its facts, is quite meaningless and, in my opinion, very misleading. It is about as informative as saying that the outboard motors on a ship's lifeboats are much more efficient than the ship's diesel engines, because they will propel the lifeboat 15 miles on one gallon, while the ship's engines take 20 gallons to move the ship one mile.

In fact, the commissions on stock options are often extremely high for the average-priced call. This did not come about through a diabolical plot on the part of brokers but rather from the side effects of the fact that options, by their very nature, are priced at only a fraction of the underlying stocks. When the option exchanges were seeking a model for their rate structure, they looked at the stock exchange rates and copied them.

Prior to May 1, 1975, each stock and option exchange was allowed to set minimum commission rates, and to strictly enforce these rates upon all its member firms. All commissions discussed in this book are based on the pre-May 1, 1975, rates. Today, most firms use rates which are not too different. See Appendixes G & H for complete commission rates on stocks and options of a typical brokerage firm. Your firm may vary somewhat from these rates. The New York Stock Exchange charged as part of its commission $4 or $6 per 100 shares, which is reasonable enough for shares typically priced at $20-$100. But when this same charge is applied to options that typically sell for anywhere from ⅛ point to a few dollars, the result is a commission that can become a very high percentage of the price of the option, especially of the lower-priced ones.

It is important to understand exactly how the commissions are determined, because from the investor's point of view they are extremely important and can influence one's investment decisions. Or let us say, that because of their nature, they *ought* to influence one's decisions.

On the New York Stock Exchange, the commission on a round lot of stock (100 shares) is usually less than 2% of the selling price of the shares. For example, if the shares cost $10 each, for a total of $1,000, the commission is only $21.40, or just 2.1%, and if the shares cost $50 each the total commission on a round lot is $79.60, which is only 1.6%. For higher-priced stocks and for order involving more shares the commission is even lower.

OPTIONS COMMISSION RULES

Now, what is the "bargain" commission for stock options? Would you be surprised to learn that it can amount to 50% of the price of the option at some brokerage firms, and that the average commission on the normal-size order of an individual can amount to just about 5% of the price of the options? That's why some of the commissions seem overpriced. But before we editorialize further, let's explain just how these commissions are computed. For orders totaling under $100 (which would be, for example, one option selling for less than $1) and for orders totaling over $30,000, there were no minimum commissions. So in the event that your order is outside these limits, check with your own broker for his rates, since firms differ widely here. The commission for selling a single option at $1/16$ ($6.25) ranges from 53¢ or less at some firms to $3 at others. Quite a difference, when one considers that this is a range of from 8.4% to 48% of the price of the calls.

On all orders totaling between $100 and $30,000 the minimum commission that the exchanges used to permit their member firms to charge was comprised of three parts. The first part was a fixed amount depending upon the total dollar amount of the transaction:

Amount involved in the order	Fixed amount of commission
$100–$2,499	$12
2,500–19,999	22
20,000–29,999	82

The second part was a percentage commission that was also a function of the total amount of money involved in the transaction:

Amount involved in the order	Percentage Commission
$100–$2,499	1.3%
2,500–19,999	0.9%
20,000–29,999	0.6%

The third part and the part that could really hurt, was a fixed amount for each option traded. For the first to tenth option covered by an order, this amount was $6 per option. For the eleventh option and over covered by the order the rate was $4 per option. Finally, in some cases a surcharge of 10% was added to arrive at the total commission.

The above rates were for orders covering more than one option. If the order should be for only one option, the rates were identical except that the third part of the commission was not charged, and the rates were slightly different for orders over $4,777. It is very unusual for an option to be selling for $47, and in practice they will be quite infrequent, so that the distinction in commission rates needn't concern us.

In addition there was a minimum fee of $25 for any order, whether it was for one option contract or any number, provided of course that the total order was over $100. The commission for a single option contract was not more than $65.

A single-contract commission

Let's take the following as an example of the commission for a single option. If you sell or buy an option for $1,200, i.e., at $12 a share, you will pay a commission of $12 for the first part, plus the $15.60 (1.3% times $1,200) for the second part, for a total of $27.60 plus the 10% surcharge $2.76, giving a total commission of $30.36. If the amount of the option was less, so that the commission calculation yielded less than $25, the commission would still be at the minimum of $25.

Multiple-contract commissions

Now let's take an example of a trade involving a number of contracts. Let's assume that you want to buy a call on Bethlehem Steel that is currently trading at 1½, and you decide that you will buy 20 options. The amount of your order is obviously the premium per contract of 100 calls, $150 × 20, or $3,000. Therefore, the first part of the commission is $22. The second part of the commission is 0.9% of $3,000, for $27. The third part; which is the fixed amount per option, is 10 × $6, or $60 for the first 10 options, plus 10 × $4, making $40 for the second 10 options. This comes to a grand total of $149. If 10% ($14.90) is added that makes $163.90. Note that this is a commission of 5.4% of the total price, which is fairly steep. Compare it to the commission of $30.36 on the $1,200 call purchase described previously, which amounted to 2.5% of the total amount involved. The reason for this difference is that the premium for each call was so much smaller in the second transaction.

As a general rule, the smaller the premium, the higher a percentage commission you will have to pay on a trade of a given total amount of dollars. The defense of this practice given by brokers is that it takes them just as much time, effort, and paperwork to process an order for a call whether the call sells for 12½¢ or $24. And of course there is some merit in this statement.

EXPIRING OPTIONS

The one time when the option trader must know the effect of commissions is when he is either the owner of, or the writer of, a call that is in the money and just about to expire. If the call is in the money it has an intrinsic value and will be exercised, if it is still in existence on the expiration date. However, both the option holder and its writer have a choice. The option holder can either exercise the option on the final day or he can sell his call on the last trading day of the call. Similarly the option writer can either buy back an identical call on the last day on which the call is traded or he can let the call be exercised against him and deliver the underlying stock. In each of these decisions the amount of commission is of great importance.

Let us take the case of the call holder first. If the successful call holder wishes to make a cash profit on his call by exercising it, as distinct from continuing to own the underlying stock that he has obtained for the strike price, he must pay two commissions on the underlying stock at the regular rates. First he pays a commission when he acquires the stock through the exercise of his option, and then he pays a commission when he sells the stock on the open market. On the other hand, if he decides to sell his call, he pays only one commission on the sale of the call.

Stock vs. options commissions

Thus a comparison of the commission for one option trade with the old minimum NYSE rate for two trades is necessary. The option commission rates were discussed earlier in this chapter. The NYSE rates are set out in the table below. On single round-lot orders (an order of 100 shares):

Amount involved in the order	*Minimum commission*		
$100–$800	2.0% of money involved		+ $ 6.40
$800–$2,500	1.3% " "		+ $12.00
$2,500 and above	0.9% " "		+ $22.00

On multiple round-lot orders:

Amount involved in the order	*Minimum commission*		
$100–$2,499	1.3% of money involved	+ $ 12.00
$2,500–$19,999	0.9% " "	+ $ 22.00
$20,000–$29,999	0.6% " "	+ $ 82.00
$30,000–$500,000	0.4% " "	+ $142.00

Plus, for each round lot:

First to tenth round lot, $6 for each round lot.

Eleventh round lot and above, $4 per round lot.

Finally, there is added a 10% surcharge on orders totaling $5,000 or less and a 15% surcharge on orders over $5,000.

You will immediately realize that the structure of the commission schedule is similar to that for options. To give an example of how the commissions work, let us assume that you own five call contracts on a stock that is now selling for $55 and your calls with a strike price of 50 are worth $5. First, you could sell your call, with the commission as follows:

Fixed commisssion of $12, plus $26 (1.3% of $2,000) plus $30 ($6 per contract × 5) a total of $68 plus 10% = $74.80. This is your total commission to transform your contract rights into cash.

Now let us compute the commission if you decide to exercise the call by buying the stock and then selling it. The commission on buying 500 shares at $50 a share is: $82 plus $150 (0.6% of $25,000) plus $30 ($6 per round lot × 5), totaling $262 plus 10% = $288.20. The commission to sell 500 shares at $55 comes to $304.70 for a total round trip commission of $592.90. Since the amount of money that you would realize from each method in this example is exactly the same, $2,000 profit, you would save yourself the difference between $592.90 and $74.80, or $518.10, by selling your call rather than exercising it.

In actual practice you might find that the difference between the two methods is closer than this, because the price of the call will be just a bit lower than the difference between the price of the stock and the strike price, in order to compensate for the amount of the commission.

CHOOSING A BROKER

Recently advertisements have been appearing in the financial press for "bargain rate brokers," and many of these brokers state that they will execute trades for options listed on exchanges. Just how much of a bargain are they for the options trader, and are they recommended?

First, one must understand how these brokers operate. They have low overhead and keep expenses down by not engaging in market research or giving market advice for their clients. In short, they are simply order takers and executioners. They will not follow a stock for you, which, as we discussed before, can be so important when you are selling uncovered options and you want to take some action when the stock gets to your stop-loss position.

As for the question of whether options investors and traders should use discount brokers, I am afraid that since I am now a broker myself, whatever I write would be considered self-serving by many readers. Therefore, I am going to quote from the first edition of this book, which was written when I was not a broker but a corporate lawyer and strictly a customer when it came to investments. Here is what I wrote then when I was paying commissions myself:

> In any event, my advice is that the newcomer, or even a fairly knowledgable new options trader, should definitely avoid the "bargain brokers." The savings on the commission is not going to be very meaningful in relation to the total amounts involved. And to most option traders the advice and expert execution that an experienced options broker can give are far more valuable than any discount could be. Remember that buying and selling options is a tricky business, far more difficult than the stock market, because the price of options fluctuates so much more rapidly, and because the liquidity of the market is so much thinner. If you ever needed a good person on your side, it is when you want to trade in options. So, find someone with experience in options and if he earns your trust and confidence, stick with him. His counsel and expertise will be worth many times his commissions.

Reducing your commissions

Now that we've discussed the nature of commissions, let's get down to the important point for all investors and traders: How can commissions be reduced without affecting your performance in a detrimental way? Here are four specific, concrete rules which can help you reduce commissions, and often by surprisingly large amounts.

1. *Simplify your strategy.* The more you simplify, the more commissions you eliminate. That sounds very simple, but it isn't always so easy to look at what you are attempting to do objectively and come up with a simplified version. Fortunately the equivalency table in Appendix D can tell you in a moment if there is a simpler method of achieving your goal. If you find that you can do something with an option only, you will be far ahead in savings on commission as compared with doing something that requires a position in the underlying stock as well as an option position.

One of the most dramatic examples of this is a covered call write. Covered call writing has become so popular that many people and institutions go into it without fully considering the alternative, which is simply to sell an uncovered put of the same duration and strike price as the call option in the covered write. There may be many reasons why an account can not write naked puts, and if there are such reasons, then they must continue with their covered call writing. But for the many investors who can write puts, it is well to stop and reflect upon the fact that selling a naked put is the same as writing a covered call, and the commission cost is only a fraction of that required for covered calls. As an example, let's assume that the stock you are interested in is at 22, and you want to sell the 20 call option for 4, giving yourself a gross spread of 2 points. If you sell the 20 put for 2 you will have achieved exactly the same objective, i.e., you can make a gross profit of $2 if the stock is 20 or better upon the option's expiration, and you have the downside risk of a price decline in the price of the stock below 20 reduced, however, by the 2 of net future time value you took in with the original option sale. Some of the details will be different, such as collection of dividends if you own the stock, but on the other hand you may have to put up substantially more margin to do a covered call write. Of course, there may not be a put available for this stock, and if it is available, you may not be able to sell it for 2 points. So there may be many reasons why you would prefer the covered call write, but you should at least be aware of the dramatic commission savings when it is possible.

Assuming you wish to buy 500 shares and write 5 calls, the commission on selling the 5 calls at $4 is $68. The commission on buying 500 shares of the stock at $22 is $187.50. If we assume that the stock stays at the same price of $22, the easiest way to get out of the covered write is to let the stock be called away. This results in a commission on selling 500 shares at $20 per share, which is $176.50. (If we had bought back the option and then sold the stock there would have been an additional commission on the purchase of the call.) These commissions total $432.00.

Now let's see what the commissions are on selling a naked put for $2. The commission on selling 5 puts at $2 is $55. If we assume, as we did above, that the stock remains at 22, then the put will expire worthless, and so there is no commission on closing it out. The comparison: Commissions of $432 to do the covered call write as against commissions of just $55 to do the equivalent transaction with a naked put. That's a saving of 87%. Enough said.

2. *Try to do your transactions in large quantities.* Commissions are computed partly on the amount of money involved, but also largely on the amount of work that is required of the brokerage firm. To a large extent it costs the firm the same amount to execute an order whether it is for one option or for 100 options. The result is that the commission per unit of stock or option goes down markedly as the quantity goes up. For example, the commission on 2

options at $3 is $31.80 or $15.90 per option. For 5 options, it is $12.30 per option, for 10 options it is reduced to $10.90, and for 20 options it is just $8.80, a reduction of 44%.

The same reductions occur with stock, as a quick look at the stock commission chart in Appendix H will show. For example, by buying 500 shares of a $20 stock instead of just 100 shares, one reduces the commission cost per share by 22%. And if one can afford to buy 2,000 shares of the stock at $20, the commission is reduced another 29% from that level. Thus the 2,000 share buyer is getting a savings of 44% over the 100 share buyer, based upon the standard rates.

And you don't even have to be a big spender to realize savings by buying in quantity. Two options at $1 have a commission of $13.30 each, but if you get 5 of them for $500 your commission is just $9.70 apiece.

So the second rule for reducing commissions is to take fewer positions and take a greater quantity of each position.

3. *Concentrate on the higher-priced options.* Because of the nature of the formula for computing option commissions, the percentage commission you pay is much less for the higher-priced options. Thus, if you spend $1,000 to buy 10 options at $1, your commission is $85. But if you spend $1,000 to buy one option at $10, your commission is only $25. That's a savings of 70.5%. Better than a discount store having its annual clearance sale. So if you want to save on commissions, take a look at the expensive options on the high-priced stocks. The biggest bargains in town, speaking strictly from the commission viewpoint, are the IBM options. Don't be scared of their bigger numbers, just buy fewer of them. By concentrating on options of the expensive stocks and leaving the cheap options on the low-priced stocks to someone else, you can realize substantial commissions savings.

4. *Never trade one option.* The reason for this rule is that almost every brokerage firm has a minimum commission of $25 for all options priced at $1 or more. (See the Options Commission Chart in Appendix G.) If you buy one option at $1 the commission is $25, which is an outrageous 25%. But if you buy two option at $1, the commission is increased only by a token amount of $1.60. Thus, the commission on two options is practically the same as for one, showing that you have grossly overpaid for the commission on one option. But in no case when you buy *two* options will you have to pay more than you should because of this $25 minimum. So that is why most options brokers will always buy at least 200 shares to write calls on and will try to do everything else in a minimum of twos. It is hard enough to make money in options without taking on the unfair burden of overpaying for commissions.

Every rule must have its exceptions, and the one which applies here is that the $25 minimum simply does not have any applicability to any option priced at over $10 because the regular commission is over $25. But remember, even if you initially trade an option at $10, you might close out your position for much less, and then you would be stuck with the $25 minimum if you have used only one option. Note also that the $25 minimum does not apply to options under $1, but many brokerage firms charge very high rates for these trades, in some cases as high as 50% of the amount of the trade.

To summarize our rules for saving commissions, they are:

1. Simplify. Before you enter into any transaction requiring stock and options, check the equivalency table in Appendix D to see whether there is an alternative that can be done with options only. Don't buy stock and write a call if you can sell a naked put. Don't buy stock and protect yourself by purchasing a put when you can get the same result by buying a call. The simplification will make it easier for you to get in and out of the positions and will save you up to 87% on your dollar commission costs!

2. Trade larger quantities. Remember, the commission rates are based upon the fact that it takes a brokerage firm about as much work to execute an order for one option as for 100. This doesn't mean that you risk more money, just use fewer positions.

3. Stick to higher-priced options. The same reasoning applies as for rule two above. Big savings result if you follow this.

4. Avoid single options. The $25 minimum commission is just lurking in the wings ready to snare you with an excessively high commission.

How your net profit is affected

The cry in every well-run corporation these days is, "What will it do to the bottom line?" What this means is that it is all very well to discuss a project that sounds good, but the acid-test question for every business idea is, "What will it do for the company's net profits?" It is on a company's net profits that it is really judged—not on its sales, not on its gross profits, not on its pre-tax profits. Similarly, the important question for the individual investor is "What will puts and calls do to my 'bottom line'—my net after-tax income?" There are so many complexities in dealing with stock options that it would be wonderful if one could just write a simple statement describing the tax consequences of all transactions involving stock options. Then after the investor had read that statement, he could go on about his business of trying to maximize his profits without altering his desired course of conduct because of the tax consequences.

Unfortunately this is not the case. Cynics have probably already said that it's impossible to name one case in which something involving taxes is simple. In the case of stock options the tax consequences are far from simple, in fact, they are very complicated. Even worse, they are also very important. So, this may be one of the most important chapters in this book. For while the rest of this book is concerned with earning money, this chapter is concerned with the equally vital function of keeping for yourself as much as possible of the money you do earn.

First a brief introduction to certain tax concepts is necessary. For tax purposes income is divided into two basic types.

ORDINARY INCOME VS. CAPITAL GAINS

The money that you get paid from your job, earn in your business, or receive in dividends or interest is called ordinary income. It is normally taxed at the highest rates. If you lost money in your business, this would be an ordinary loss, and that loss could be deducted from any ordinary income you had, to determine your net ordinary income.

The other basic type of income is the profit that is made from the "sale or exchange" of a capital asset and this type of income is called a capital gain. If the "sale or exchange" results in a loss, it is called a capital loss. A capital asset is difficult to define, but it is sufficient for our purposes to say that it includes stock and stock options. Capital gains and losses may be further divided into two types—short-term and long term. Those that occur within one year, that is, where the date of the acquisition of the asset and the date of the sale or exchange of the asset are not more than twelve months apart, are called short-term capital gains or losses. A short-term capital gain is taxed at the same rate as ordinary income, which is the highest rate.

On the other hand, a short-term capital loss can reduce these highly taxed short-term capital gains and can also reduce long-term capital gains. Strangely, and importantly, although short-term capital gains are taxed at the same rate as ordinary income, neither short-term nor long-term capital losses can be used to offset ordinary income except to the extent of $3,000 a year. (It was only $2,000 for 1977.) Watch out. The result may be that although you may have lost money from options, you will not be able to get a tax loss in the current year for it, because the capital losses cannot be deducted in full from ordinary income. This seems highly unfair, but the Internal Revenue Code was never noted for its evenness of application.

If the time elapsed between the purchase of the capital asset and its sale or exchange is more than twelve months, then the gain or loss is called a long-term capital gain or loss. Long-term capital gains (after subtracting capital losses) are taxed at greatly preferential rates, which are exactly one half of the rate of ordinary income up to a maximum tax rate of 25% on the first $50,000 of net long-term capital gain, with a somewhat higher rate on the excess. Because you do not pay the full tax on a long-term capital gain, you also do not get the full benefit when you have a loss. It takes $2 of long-term capital gain to offset $1 of ordinary income.

Now that we have these fundamentals out of the way, we can begin to analyze the tax consequences to you when you engage in various option transactions.

TAX CONSEQUENCES TO CALL BUYERS

If you buy a call, it is considered a capital asset, unless you are a dealer in options. Assuming that you are not, the question that should first spring to your mind is whether you are going to have a long-term or short-term gain or loss.

For capital assets which were sold prior to January 1, 1976, the assets had to be held for more than six months to qualify for long-term capital gain treatment. Assets sold in the calendar year 1977 had to be held for at least nine months to qualify for long-term, and now all assets sold after January 1, 1978, have to be held for over one year in order to qualify for long-term capital gains treatment. Since the longest option available is for nine months, it is obvious that it is now impossible to ever hold an option long enough for it to become long-term. Thus, traders in options must resign themselves to having short-term assets and paying the short-term tax rate on any profits, unless they take advantage of the procedure described below. If you make money on your purchase by selling the option for more money than you paid for it, then the profit you have made is a capital gain, determined quite simply by subtracting your cost, including all commissions, from the net amount that you received, that is, the amount after deducting all commissions and fees and transfer taxes, if any.

If you lose money by selling the call for less than you paid for it, you have a capital loss.

If you lose money because your call has become worthless at its expiration date and you simply let it expire while you own it, then your loss is still considered to be a capital loss because in the eyes of the tax law you are considered to have sold or exchanged the option on the expiration day, presumably for a price of $0.00. You thus have a capital loss equal to your net purchase price.

If, instead of selling your option, you exercise it and purchase the underlying stock at the strike price, then the premium that you paid for the option is added onto the price that you paid for the stock, and this total becomes your basis or cost for determining the profit or loss that you will make when you sell the stock.

CALL BUYER'S TAX STRATEGY

Let's illustrate that with an example. Suppose that on May 15 you pay $5 to buy a January call and that the strike price of the call is 50. The end of January finally comes around, and lo and behold the price of the stock has moved up to $65 and your call is now worth $15. At this point you have the choice of selling your call or exercising it and buying the 100 shares of stock for $50 a share. As we already noted, if you sell your call, the profit of $10 per call is capital gain, and since you bought the call less than twelve months before you sold it, you will have a short-term capital gain. This is the expensive kind—the kind that costs you maximum tax dollars.

If, on the other hand, you decide to take your alternate route, and exercise your option, you are purchasing the stock for $50. The $5 that you paid for the call is added on to your basis for the stock, which means that for tax purposes your cost of the stock will be deemed to be $55 a share. In other words, when an option holder exercises his option, the cost of the option is added to the strike price to determine the tax cost of the stock. Now when you later sell the stock, you will subtract $55 from your net sales price to determine your profit, and that profit is treated as a capital gain. Thus, the capital gain of $10 that you could have made by selling the call is carried over onto the stock. One advantage of this is that the profit of $10 that you made from your call is not taxed when you exercise the call. Rather, the tax is postponed until you sell the stock later. And of course you control the timing of selling that stock. If you happen to be a high tax bracket in the year when the option expires, it would be to your advantage, taxwise, to exercise the option and hold the stock until the next year, when you can sell it and be taxed when you are in a lower bracket, since short-term capital gains are taxed at your regular tax rate.

Achieving long-term capital gain

But an even bigger advantage than postponement of paying the short-term capital gains tax is that by exercising the option you have the opportunity to convert your short-term gain into a long-term gain. As we noted above, it is no longer possible to obtain a long-term capital gain from an option. But when you exercise the option to purchase stock, the gain from the option is transferred to the stock, and you can easily hold the stock for one year and a day, thus achieving long-term capital gain treatment on the stock and enabling you to have your profit from the option taxed as long-term capital gain.

Let's follow up on our example. You originally bought a January 50 option for $5 in May. January comes around and you exercise your option when the stock is $65. Your cost basis for tax purposes is the $50 you paid for the stock on the exercise plus the $5 you paid for the option, making a tax cost of $55. Your purchase date of the stock for tax purposes is the day of exercise in January.

Note that the date of purchase of the option is irrelevant. The IRS says that although purchase of the option gave you the right to buy the stock, and although you might feel as if you owned the stock since the value of your January 50 call was going up and down with the price of the stock, you did not actually own the stock until you exercised the call. Therefore, for purposes of determining whether you have held the stock long enough to qualify for long-term capital gains you are not allowed to add on the time during which you owned the option. The *price* you paid for the option may be added onto your purchase cost, but the *time* cannot be added onto the holding period of the stock.

You now own the stock with a cost of $55 and a purchase date of January. You hold the stock for one year and a day after you purchase and sell the stock. If we assume that the stock is still at $65 then you will be taxed on your profit at the preferential long-term rates. Your profit will be your tax cost of $55 subtracted from your sale price of $65 or $10 of long-term capital gains. By exercising your option and holding the stock you acquired for one year and a day, you have converted a short-term gain into a long-term gain.

Disadvantages of exercising and holding

There are, however, two disadvantages to this which should be discussed. The first is that you are tying up your capital for an entire year without necessarily expecting to increase your profit during that year. You would undoubtedly prefer to take that money out of the stock and put it into other options where it could be giving you higher leverage. Unfortunately the very essence of long-term capital gains is that you hold the asset for over a year.

The second disadvantage, and one which is more important than freezing your capital, is that you now face the risk of a decline in the stock for an entire year. You may have thought that the stock would go up to $65, but now that it's there you may be properly afraid that it will go down, and you don't want to end up a loser. Fortunately there is a partial solution to both these problems.

The answer is to write in-the-money calls on the stock. The deeper in the money you write, the more downside protection you get. The less deep in the money, the more profit you will take in from writing the calls. Writing calls does not give you complete freedom from downside risk, but it does give you protection to the extent of the premium you take in, and in normal times that should be enough to protect you from typical market fluctuations in the price of the stock. So here is a way to give yourself some downside protection, and to make a profit on the money you have tied up.

Writing even deep-in-the-money covered calls does not affect your holding period, which will continue to run from the day you acquired the stock. Try to roll over the calls whenever you see that they are getting down to their cash values, because you do not want to be exercised. If you are accidentaly exercised, you should buy in new shares to deliver, retaining your old shares so that when you do sell them you will get long-term tax treatment.

Thus, exercising a profitable call can have two distinct advantages to an option holder. First, he defers paying the capital gains tax and second, he can convert a short-term gain into a long-term gain. Here's another tip: The earlier you exercise the sooner your one-year holding period on the stock will be over. So once you have decided that you definitely are going to exercise, you might just as well do it early and not bother to wait for the expiration date. This is true even if the option sells at a premium above its cash value. Since you are going to lose that excess anyway by waiting, you might just as well do it now and start the clock ticking on your one-year holding period.

TAX CONSEQUENCES TO CALL WRITERS

Now let's go through a typical call-writing transaction and see how it is taxed. You sell an October 50 call on June 15 for $5. First of all, it is comforting to note that the $5 that you receive for the option is not taxed to you at the time of sale. This can be important where you sell an option in the final months of the year, and the call does not expire or you do not buy it back until the next year. So, initially, the money you receive is not considered income to you and you pay no taxes on it.

Let us assume that the price of the stock was below 50 when you sold the call, and never goes above 50, with the result that the option expires unexercised. At that date, for tax purposes, you have received a short-term capital gain of $5.

If you decided not to wait for the option to expire and decided to close out your position by purchasing an October 50 call in September for $1, you would have a short-term capital gain of $4 on that date.

That's relatively straightforward, and it does give the call writer the chance to do a little tax planning by deciding when he wants to take his profit. For example, if you are short some January calls that have depreciated greatly, giving you a good profit, you should consider whether you would like to have the profit in December of this year or wait to take it in January and be taxed next year. The decision involves weighing the advantage of postponing the tax for one year against whether you think that your tax bracket will be higher or lower next year. If you had big losses this year, then it might be prudent to offset them with your profit.

Historical treatment of option writers

As a matter of purely historical interest, it should be pointed out that this was not always the case for written options. All options written before September 2, 1976, produced ordinary income when they were closed out by other than an exercise. This produced some highly strange results, and in a rising market it meant that a person who was a covered writer could realize long-term capital gains on stock and ordinary losses from his options. This was highly favorable, especially to taxpayers who had excess capital losses.

But it also meant that in a down market covered writers and spreaders alike could get caught in a vicious whipsaw in which they made no money but were forced to pay taxes on large amounts of ordinary income, while they stood by helplessly accumulating ever greater amounts of totally useless capital losses. So let us not weep for the demise of the old law. The present law is far simpler to apply and more just in its effect. And what more can one ask of a tax revision than that it make taxes both more simple and more fair. Would that other sections of the tax code could be given similar revisions.

Tax choices

If you have not made a profit in your option writing, and the option has gone up in value, you have a choice of actions. You can close out your position by purchasing the identical call. In this case the difference between your original selling price and your purchase price is a short-term loss, tax deductible at the time you closed out your position.

Or you can acquire the underlying stock (or use stock you already own) and deliver it when your call is exercised. When you deliver the shares, the premium that you originally received from writing the call is added on to the exercise price of the call to determine your gain or loss. The gain or loss on the stock is long-term or short-term depending upon how long you owned the stock. Thus the length of time you were short the option is irrelevant to this determination.

Let's follow this through with an actual case. You sell an April 60 call for $9. The stock goes up to $65 by the end of April and you decide to deliver the stock, rather than to buy a call and close out your position. If you are a covered-call writer you may have purchased the stock over a year ago at $80. When you deliver the stock you receive the strike price of $60. Your tax position is: Your cost basis is $80. The amount you received for the stock is the $60 you got upon delivery plus the $9 premium, which makes a total of $69. Subtracting this from your $80 cost results in a tax loss of $11. This is a capital loss and it is long-term because you had held the underlying stock for over a year.

If, on the other hand, you had purchased the shares for just $45 a share, you would have a profit of $15 per share when the call was assigned to you at the strike price of $60, plus the $9 you receive for the call, making a total profit of $24. This entire profit would be taxed as capital gain, and if you had held the stock for more than one year when the call was exercised the entire gain would be taxed as long-term capital gain.

Note that you would qualify for long-term capital gain on the entire transaction even though you had sold the call less than one year before the exercise date. The legal theory behind this result is that the $9 you received when you sold the call is simply added on to the exercise price, giving you a sale price of $69. The cost of $45 when subtracted from your sale price of $69 gives you your tax profit of $24. And since you bought the shares of stock more than one year ago, the gain is taxed as long-term capital gain.

It is fairly easy to remember these rules because they are similar to the rules we discussed above which apply to option holders. In the case of both the option holder and the option writer, the original price of the option is added to the exercise price to determine the tax gain or loss on the underlying stock. In both cases there is no tax on the gain or loss in the option itself. And in both cases the length of time you held or were short the option is irrelevant in determining whether you have long-term or short-term capitals gains. In both cases the only determining fact is how long you held the stock.

It is possible to make money on a call and still be in the position where it may be exercised against you. If you sell a call that is deep in the money, and then the stock goes down but is still above the strike price, the call will be exercised and you will make a profit nevertheless. For example, if you sold an IBM 250 call for $20 when the stock was $258, the stock could stay at that figure, and the call would be exercised against you for a profit to you of $12. Whether you buy back the call or deliver the shares your profit is capital gain. Note, however, that the type of capital gain—long-term or short-term— depends not on how long you have been short the call, but on how long you have owned the stock.

TAX CONSEQUENCES OF PUTS

Put holder

A put is classified as a capital asset and therefore the purchase and sale of a put creates a capital gain or loss. Since the longest put is for nine months, and a capital asset must now be held for one year in order to qualify for long-term capital gains treatment, it is obvious that all purchases and sales of puts result in short-term gain or loss. As with calls, if a put expires worthless, it is deemed to have been sold for zero on the expiration date.

The more complicated question arises when the put holder decides to exercise his put and sell the underlying stock at the exercise price. The rule is that the amount of money which the put owner originally paid for his put is subtracted from the exercise price to determine his sale price for tax purposes. As an example, suppose an investor owns 100 shares of XYZ which he purchased for $47 and he is worried that the market may tumble and carry his XYZ down with it. To protect himself he buys a July 45 put which being out of the money is reasonably priced at 1. Sure enough, by the time the July expiration date rolls around XYZ is down to $41 and our investor decides to exercise his put and get rid of the stock for $45 a share. What are the tax consequences?

First let's see what really happened. He bought the stock for $47 and sold it for $45 for a loss of $2, and in addition he paid $1 for the put, so he actually had a loss of $3. The correct tax analysis of the transactions is that he bought the stock for $47; then he sold it for $45 minus the $1 paid for the put for a sale price of $44. A cost of $47 minus a sale price of $44 gives a loss of $3, so the tax effect squares with what actually happened.

The big question now is whether the loss, or gain as the case might be, is long-term or short-term. And here things are not as simple as they were for calls, because there is a rule which states that if you own stock which has not yet attained long-term status, i.e., you have not yet owned it for an entire year, then the moment you purchase a put in that stock you immediately cancel your entire holding period in that stock, and your holding period is frozen at zero until you no longer own the put. Your holding period then starts at day one. Thus if the XYZ had been owned for a year when the put was acquired, the loss is long term, otherwise it is short term. To explain this more fully let's look at another example.

Assume you buy 100 shares of GM on January 15. On December 15, eleven months later, you have a very good profit on the stock and are afraid that the stock might start going back down. You decide to protect yourself by purchasing a January put with the intention of selling the stock on January 16, when it will be long-term. That is not going to work.

Killing your stock holding period. The minute you purchase that put, your holding period in the GM stock becomes zero days. And it stays at zero until you either sell the put or allow it to expire in January. The day after you no longer own the put your new holding period starts. So the moral of the story is don't ever buy a put to protect stock you have held for a number of months but which is not yet long-term gain. If you had already owned the GM stock for one year, there would be no problem. Then you can buy all the puts you want and you will not change the status of the GM stock back to short-term.

The reasoning behind this rule is that you are permitted to get favorable long-term capital gains rates only as a reward for being a capitalist and taking the risks thereof. When you buy a put you have acquired absolute insurance against any risk of loss in the stock (below the strike price of the put and minus whatever future time value you paid for the put). Since you are no longer taking the risks of being a capitalist, the tax law says that you are no longer entitled to the rewards.

The solution to this problem of protecting a gain in a stock before it goes long-term is very simple. Sell a deep-in-the-money call. No matter how deep in the money it is, the IRS will never argue that this freezes your holding period on the underlying stock. And by selling a call rather than buying a put you might even make some money instead of spending some.

The one exception. There is one exception to the rule that the holding period of stock does not run when you own a put on that stock. If you purchase a put on the same day that you buy stock and notify your broker that you intend to use the stock to satisfy an exercise of the put, you are then said to have "married" the stock to the put. Under these circumstances, the holding period of the stock starts to run on the day you acquired it. Of course, if the price of the stock declines and you sell the put but hold onto the stock, then its holding period for you would start on the day that you sold the put and not when you originally bought the stock. If, on the other hand, the price of the stock is up, then you do not recognize any loss on the lapsed "married" put, but simply add its cost onto the tax basis of the stock. In this case you get the benefit of this "married" put exception, because your holding period for the stock starts on the day you buy the stock and the put.

Put writer

A put writer realizes a short-term capital gain or loss on the sale and subsequent purchase of a put just like a call writer. His sale price is whatever he received for the put originally and his cost basis is what he pays to close out the position. If the put lapses his cost basis is zero.

When a put writer is assigned his option, he is purchasing 100 shares of stock per option at the strike price. He will have a capital gain or loss on that stock with the date of acquiring the stock being the date he will use to determine whether it should be long-term or short-term. The amount he originally received for the put is subtracted from the exercise price to determine his cost basis in the stock. Thus, if a person sold a September 40 put for $3, and was assigned on the put, acquiring 100 shares for $40 each, he would subtract the $3 from the $40, giving him a tax cost for the stock of $37.

Note that as with calls, the rule for determining the basis of the stock involved in put exercises is the same whether you are the writer of the put or the holder. In both cases, with puts you subtract the original price of the put from the exercise price to determine the tax basis of the stock.

TAX CONSEQUENCES OF SPREADS AND STRADDLES

The rule for determining the tax consequences on spreads is the epitome of simplicity: There is no such thing as a spread for tax purposes. Each component of a spread is taxed as if it existed all by itself. The same rule holds true for a straddle or combination. So to figure out the tax consequence of any of these, just look at each particular side of the spread and work out the tax consequences.

WASH SALE RULE ON STOCKS AND CALLS

Just as the purchase of a put when you owned the stock cancelled out the incompleted running of the long-term period because you no longer had the risk of loss from the stock, so a similar rule applies on the other side when you sell a stock and take a loss. Under normal circumstances the "wash sale" rule states that if you sell a stock and claim a capital loss on the sale, you cannot buy the same stock within thirty days of the sale. The question has arisen as to whether it would be possible to avoid this consequence by purchasing a call on the stock instead of the stock itself. Unfortunately, the IRS has already thought of this, and there is no doubt that the purchase of a call on a stock made within thirty days of the sale of the same stock will cancel out the ability to take a capital loss on the stock. The reasoning is quite correct, in that if you want to claim the loss, you must be willing to give up the chance of making a profit on the stock if it should go up immediately. This is more of a nuisance and a trap for the unwary than a real problem. Simply buy your call more than thirty days before you plan to sell the stock.

TAX STRATEGIES

There is wide opportunity to use options in conjunction with tax planning, especially in the area of timing. And when it comes to capital gains and losses timing can have an unusually significant impact. The reason is that the Internal Revenue Code provides a rather strange method of computing capital gains and losses.

To review basics for a minute, you recall that long-term capital gains are generally taxed at only one half the usual tax rate, whereas short-term gains are taxed at the regular rate. On the loss side, a short-term loss can be subtracted directly from ordinary income (up to the $3,000 limitation) whereas long-term losses reduce ordinary income only by 50¢ for each $1 of loss. Thus, you want to get long-term capital gains and short-term capital losses, and each of these is worth, for tax purposes, twice as much as short-term gains and long-term losses respectively.

They are obviously quite different animals and worth quite different amounts of taxes to you. But here is how the tax you pay is figured. First, combine all your short-term gains and losses. Second, combine all long-term gains and losses. So far so good. But then the law requires you to combine the net short-term gain or loss with the net long-term gain or loss. This is exactly like adding oranges and apples (which we all learned long ago that we could not do) and arriving at a total number of "fruits." But that is the way the law is.

Now if you were in the fruit business and "fruits" were selling for $2.00 a dozen, and it cost you 10¢ to buy an orange and 20¢ to buy an apple, you would be damn careful that the "fruit" you sold would be made up entirely of oranges. And when you bought a dozen apples at 20¢ you would be careful not to let them find their way into the "fruit" boxes, but you would carefully segregate them and sell them as apples at the much higher price they commanded on the market. So it should be with capital gains and losses.

Avoid long-term losses. The astute taxpayer will realize that he wants to end up with either long-term capital gains, on which he pays the 50% tax rate, or he wants to end up with short-term capital losses which give him a full deduction from ordinary income (subject to the $3,000 annual limit). What he does not want is for his valuable long-term capital gains to be swallowed up by short-term capital losses. You also do not want to end up with long-term capital losses, since they are worth only 50¢ against ordinary income, but if you have short-term capital gains in the same year, they are worth a full $1 in offsetting them. What you do want is for your short-term capital gains to be used up by your long-term losses. By doing this you are saving yourself income taxed at 100% and only using up a loss which would give you 50% if applied to ordinary income or to long-term gains.

Therefore, the objective ought to be to have one year in which you will have net long-term capital gains, and in that year you try to avoid realizing any short-term capital losses. In the next year you might decide to realize a large number of short-term capital losses, but not realize any long-term capital gains. It is in effectuating this type of strategy that options can provide a wide variety of assistance.

We have already discussed how the owner of a profitable option can defer gain by exercising, and how the writer of an option can do the same by being assigned an exercise notice. The holder or writer of January options can usually decide whether he wants to close out his positions in the end of December or wait until the next year, and certainly the holder of long-term stock can easily determine whether he wants to realize his gain or loss in this year or next year. With the protection that covered deep-in-the-money calls offer, there is no longer a compelling reason for selling this year if next year is better from the tax viewpoint.

Now that we understand the basic principles of taxation which apply to options, let's see some specific examples of strategies which can actually reduce your taxes.

How covered writers can increase their long-term gains

Since it is desirable to get the maximum gains as long-term capital gains and to realize losses as short-term losses, especially if you already have short-term gains, this tip could be useful to the covered writer who has seen his stock appreciate since he wrote his call. Suppose that you already have about $2,000 in short-term capital gains. You also have 1,000 shares of a stock which you bought for $18 a share on which you sold the 20 option for $2. The stock is now long-term and has risen to 24. Absent tax considerations, you would normally let the stock be called away, since this is the method of getting out of the position with the smallest commissions (just one stock commission at 20 instead of a stock commission at 24 and an option commission at 4) and you don't have to worry about paying an eighth more when you buy the option and getting an eighth less when you sell the stock.

But when you consider the tax ramifications, you might well decide to buy back your option and sell out the stock. Here's why. If you let the stock be called away, you have a tax basis of 18, and a selling price of 20 plus the $2 premium you originally received, making a tax selling price of $22, for a long-term capital gain of $4 a share or $4,000. If your are in the 50% tax bracket, your tax at long-term rates would be only 25%, or $1,000, and the tax on your $2,000 short-term gain would be at the 50% rate for another $1,000, making a total tax of $2,000.

If, however, you decide to close out the position before exercise, look at how you can reduce the taxes. You sell the stock for $24 a share, and this gives you a long-term gain of $6,000. You then buy back your option for $4, and since you originally sold it for $2, you have a loss of $2 a share. This is a short-term capital loss of $2,000, and wipes out the other short-term capital gain of $2,000, which you already had. The result is that you have a net long-term capital gain of $6,000, on which you are paying 25%, for a total tax bill of $1,500. By simply closing out the position in a slightly different manner you have reduced your taxes by $500, or 25%. Pretty good when you consider that a saving of $500 in taxes is equal to making an extra $1,000 in salary or short-term capital gains.

Deferring capital gains with spreads

Despite the best of planning there may be years in which you find yourself with an excess of realized short-term capital gains. If you already happen to be in a high tax bracket that year, it would be beneficial if you could somehow defer those gains into the next year. Prior to 1977 it was common for sophisticated investors to use commodity straddles to roll over capital gains, but on May 23, 1977, the IRS issued Revenue Ruling 77-185 which said that if a commodity spread had no economic risk and no reasonable expectation of profit, it would be declared void for tax purposes. Since the reason commodity straddles were so favored for tax roll-overs was the very fact that there was hardly any economic risk, this ruling has inhibited many investors from relying upon them.

This ruling on its face does not apply to stock options, and the ruling's reasoning does not apply to option spreads to the extent that there is a real economic risk in the spread and the chance of making a profit. Since one can lose one's entire investment in a calendar spread if the stock moves too far in either direction, and since calendar spreads are recognized in both the CBOE and the AMEX explanatory booklets as accepted methods of attempting to make a profit, it may be assumed that the IRS will not apply the reasoning of the commodity ruling to calendar spreads.

Now, just how does a calendar spread work to defer a capital gain? Before explaining how it does so we must note a limitation, and that is that options are not suitable for deferring long-term capital gains; they can defer only short-term gains. To defer short-term capital gains you pick a spread where the economic risk of the spread is small in relation to the volatility of the stock. The usual type of spread is a calendar spread, and generally it is done with deep-in-the-money options.

Although calendar spreads are the favorite for tax deferrals, any type of spread with a low debit or high credit will do. The second most popular is a deep-in-the-money bear spread or bull spread with calls. As opposed to calendar spreads, these are available only when the market has recently risen substantially. If it has not, then there will not be any deep-in-the-money options to use as the bottom of your bull or bear spread. And if the spread is not deep-in-the-money, then the debit will be too high to put on the spread, which will both reduce your leverage and increase the risk of a loss from a subsequent diminishing of the spread. The deep-in-the-money bear spread is the safest, because if the stock keeps on going up you will lose only a small amount, and if by some stroke of luck the stock plunges, you could make a lot of money. The big disadvantage of the bear spread is that the option which is the most deep in the money is the one you are short, and there is probably very little future time value left in it, which means that risk of an unwelcome exercise is very high.

The advantage of the bull spread is that you are long the really deep-in-the-money option and so don't have to worry about premature exercise. The disadvantage is that while you will make a little bit of money if the stock goes up, if by some chance it should plunge down, you stand to lose a huge amount of money, and it would be very large indeed in relation to the amount you put up to do the spread.

Which kind of spread. The controlling factor in your decision of which type of spread to use should be the factors of unwelcome exercise, the risk of losing economically from a decrease in the spread, and finally and most important, the amount of money you have to put up to do the spread.

In order to reduce the cost of commissions one usually takes high-priced options. For all these reasons, plus the fact that there is high liquidity in its options, the favorite stock for these roll-overs is IBM. Let us therefore study in more detail an IBM calendar spread.

If IBM is currently at 280, and it is now October 1, the January 260 might be 22 and the April 260 might be 25. This means that for a cost of only 3 points, plus transaction costs, you could put on this calendar spread. Let us now assume that the stock rises 10 points by mid-December and the January 260 is now 31. This means that you have a loss of $900 on each January option. Of course, this loss is offset by the fact that your April option has probably gone up by about 9 points. To defer a capital gain of $900, you would buy in your January option for 33 in late December, thus realizing a short-term capital loss of $900.

This, however, leaves you long the April 260 option and you are now at risk the full $3,400 value of the April option. Since you don't wish to take the risk, you must immediately hedge this position by shorting another IBM option. Generally the best one to use would be the April 280. Although this gives you only limited downside protection, you do not intend to hold onto the option very long. The point is that you have realized your capital loss in the present year, and by selling the April 280 you have continued with a hedged position.

As soon as next year comes, you close out your current position by selling the April 260 and buying in the April 280. Unless the stock has moved in the few days between when you closed out the January 260 option and when you closed out the position, you will have a short-term capital gain of about 9 points on your 260 option and no appreciable gain or loss on the 280. If the stock has moved up or down a few points it doesn't matter, because the additional tax gain on one is offset by the additional tax loss on the other. So you have created a short-term capital loss in the current year and a short-term gain in the following year. Thus, you have deferred or rolled over into the next year $900 of short-term capital gain.

If the stock goes down. We assumed above that the stock went up 10 points. What would happen if the stock went down 10 points instead? Fortunately, we will achieve the same result. If the stock declines to 270, we can assume that the January 260 would be about 13 and the April about 16. Toward the end of December you would sell out your April 260 option for 16 and since you had purchased it for 25, you would realize a short-term capital loss of $900 per option.

At that point you would be naked the January 260 option, which you had shorted, and in addition to being at risk if the stock went back up, you would be faced with a very large margin call if you did not immediately hedge it with another long option. The obvious answer is to buy the July 260, which will probably cost you a few dollars more than you received for the April. Your position is now short the January 260 and long the July 260, which is still a nicely hedged calendar spread.

Comes the first of the next year, you simply close out both sides of your new calendar spread. If the stock has not moved appreciably since closing out the April position, you will realize a short-term capital gain of about $900 on the January option and no appreciable gain or loss on the July. If the stock does move, the net tax result is still the same. So, once again, you have realized a capital loss in the current year but have had to realize a capital gain in the next year. Thus, you have deferred the capital gain into the next year.

Now we have seen how you can defer the gain if the stock goes up and how you can defer it if the stock goes down. But what happens if the stock just stays at about the same price? Alas, that is the one soft spot in this method. If the stock just stays where it is, you cannot accomplish a roll-over or deferral. For that reason it is important to select a number of stocks, since the chance of a number of stocks all staying at the same price is obviously much less than for just one stock.

Points to consider. Points to watch out for in using option spreads to defer capital gains are:

1. Commission costs can be quite high in proportion to what is being accomplished. Remember, in the above examples there were six commissions in each one! And each time there was a commission you were buying on the offering price and selling on the bid, losing an eighth or a quarter. All those little fractions add up when you multiply them by six.

2. The obvious danger that the stock doesn't move, in which case the tax deferral is not accomplished. The three ways to minimize this risk are to pick volatile stocks, pick a variety of stocks, and give yourself as much time as possible before the year end in which the stock can move.

3. The spread can narrow, thus losing your money. It is for this very reason that I do not believe the reasoning in the IRS's commodity straddle ruling applies to option spreads, but it is also a reason why this can be an expensive proposition. In the IBM examples above I have just assumed that the spread remained the same, but in real life it will tend to increase as the stock declines toward the strike price and to decrease as the stock goes up away from the strike price. When you are going into the spread for only three points, a decline to a

point and a half means that you are losing half your money on the spread decrease alone, before even considering the commissions.

4. Since we are using fairly deep-in-the-money options for the reason of keeping the spread low and thus increasing your leverage, there is always the risk of unwelcome exercise on the short option lurking in the background. After all, we are short a near-term, deep-in-the-money option, and these are the very ones which tend to be exercised before they mature. So that is something that should be given careful consideration before you put on your spread. Pay special attention to any ex-dividend dates which might occur before year end, since this is a natural time for surprise exercises.

Once you are exercised on the short option the net tax effect is as if you had closed out that position. Thus, if the stock has moved up sharply and you are exercised, all is well, since when you buy in stock to deliver against the exercise you are realizing the short-term loss you had been striving for. But if the option is exercised after the stock has fallen, then you're in trouble, because this produces a short-term capital gain, just the opposite of what you want! Fortunately, the option is most likely to lose its future time value, and therefore most likely to be exercised when the stock moves up, and not when it moves down.

How to reduce the costs. There may be a way of reducing the costs of deferring capital gains through the use of spreads if the stock happens to go down during the spread period. This method relies upon the tax principle that gain on an option for the holder of the option is realized in the year in which the trade settles, while losses are realized in the year of the trade date; whereas for writers of options it appears that the settlement date determines the year in which both gains and losses are realized. Accordingly, if the stock has fallen while you had the spread, you could close out the spread on the last trading day of the year. Since you would have a loss on the options you owned, when you sold these the loss would be realized on the trade date, which is the current year. You would have a profit on the short options, and since both profit and loss on short options is reported in the year in which the trade settles, that profit would be reported in the following year. Therefore, if the stock goes down, you have an even simpler method of deferring your short-term capital gains via option spreads, since no intermediate roll-over is required. Just close out both sides of the spread on the last trading day of the year, and you've got your deferral.

How to prevent a stock from becoming long-term

As we learned above, it is the most advantageous to take short-term losses in years in which you do not have long-term gains, but it is usually better to have short-term losses than long-term losses. What can you do if you have a stock which has been a sheer disaster and is just about to turn into a long-term loss, but you don't want to sell it this year because short-term losses will be much more valuable to you next year? Thanks to the application of tax laws to options, there is a very simple technique by which one can literally keep the loss on a stock as a short-term loss in perpetuity.

As we mentioned above in talking about getting long-term capital gains, one of the "dangers" there was that if you inadvertantly owned a put on a stock, your entire holding period disappeared. Now here's an opportunity to use that rule to your advantage. Just when your depressed stock is about to go long-term you purchase a put on the stock, which you can then sell a few days later. Presto, chango! On the day you acquired the put, your stock, which had a holding period of 363 days, now has a holding period of zero and you have another 365 days in which to realize a short-term capital loss! Marvelous. One only wishes that the same principle could be applied to human holding periods. I for one would be very happy to purchase a put on myself the day before my next birthday if that meant that the birthday would legitimately be postponed until the same date next year. Ponce de León, we have discovered your fountain of youth! (Well, at least for stocks.)

Incidentally, if there are no puts available on your stock, you can achieve the same tax consequences by shorting the stock and buying a call, in effect creating a synthetic put.

Reference Note for tax practitioners: The IRS has summerized the tax treatment of options in Rev. Rule 78–182, issued May 15, 1978.

RECORD KEEPING

11

A necessity for option traders

Record keeping is important to any investor, but it is of unique importance to the stock options investor. The reason is that a typical investor, such as a stock purchaser, invests in an asset with a duration of unlimited time. If the investor doesn't know just where he stands at any moment, it probably won't be fatal because the stocks he owns will presumably continue to have the potential to appreciate and to earn dividends. No crucial action is required on the part of the investor at any specific moment in time.

Calls are completely different. They are a highly perishable commodity, and often action must be taken if the investor is to protect himself from large losses or protect profits that otherwise could simply vaporize overnight. The call buyer will want to enter mental stop-loss orders as soon as he has a profit. The call seller may want to do the same and will certainly enter orders to take effect if he has a loss. Furthermore, a call seller must know where he stands at any moment with respect to his margin limitation so that he can know whether he is free to sell more options or, conversely, whether because of a rise in the price of the underlying stock of calls already written, more margin will be required. And the most important record of all is the one that tells the call buyer to exercise or sell his profitable calls before they expire.

REASONS FOR RECORDS

In short, good record keeping is a must in the option game. Here are five more very practical reasons:

1. Anyone trading in options should have greater diversity in his position than a person owning stock, and therefore the option trader who has invested the same dollar amount as a stock purchaser will have more to remember. Furthermore, there are more facts to remember about each option than there are about a stock, e.g., strike price and expiration date. And option trades are

typically short-term, so that over a period of time an option trader will have more transactions to remember than a stock owner. Therefore, unless you have an exceptional memory, you must have records so that you can know what you are doing and where you stand.

2. You must report each transaction on your income-tax return next April 15. This can be a real chore if you leave it all to the day before the deadline. That's why smart traders keep their records on a current basis. Then when it is time to prepare their tax returns, they simply have a copy made of the records that they have already prepared, and attach them to their tax return as an exhibit to the appropriate section. This eliminates 90% of the work normally involved in preparing the return. All you, or your tax preparer, have to do is to add up the totals. Just make sure that you keep short-term gains and losses on one column and long-term gains or losses on another.

3. You must be able to check that your brokerage firm has prepared correct records. Your customer man or representative may have told you that you bought 5 RCA July 15s for $2\frac{1}{2}$, but if you don't write this down when he tells you, you might not find anything wrong with the confirmation slip you receive days later saying that you purchased 5 July 15s for $3\frac{1}{2}$. Or worse yet, that you sold them for $2\frac{1}{2}$. Yell loud and clear when you discover a mistake. In my trading experience, for example, I have found a number of mistakes in computing commissions, and this can be rather serious, especially in low-priced calls. Once I bought 5 Avon October calls at $\frac{1}{16}$ to close out a transaction at a profit. I was surprised when the confirmation slip arrived stating that the purchase price had been $625 per contract, and that the total purchase cost was $3,125 instead of $31.25. I immediately had the amount changed, but if I had not been alert and discovered the mistake at once I might never have known why my next statement would have shown a profit of $3,000 less than my records showed.

Remember, while the customer representatives with whom you do your business are generally very competent and accurate men, they are working under great pressures, and they can make mistakes. And it is even more likely that their hastily scribbled notes can be misunderstood by the back-office workers. So it is important that you check over each confirmation slip and statement as carefully as you do your paycheck.

4. If you are an option writer you must know at all times where you stand with relation to your margin, and accurate current records are the only way to do this. To explain, you may deliver $10,000 to your broker for your margin account. You then sell calls that require a margin of $8,000. Two weeks later, you must know whether you are about to get a margin call because the margin requirements of the calls you are short have gone up to $11,000, or, on the contrary, if you have excess margin that you can use to write more calls, because the margin requirements of your calls have gone down to $4,000. Only

accurate records can tell you. And don't wait for your broker to call you up and tell you that you must send in additional margin. By then it may be a little late to cover a transaction that you could have arranged easily a few days earlier and spared yourself the dilemma of either having to put up more money or closing out a transaction, which might not be at all in your interest at just that time.

5. Finally, half the fun of option trading is to follow what is happening and to study your transactions in the long hours of the evening. If you don't have accurate records, how are you going to enjoy the game of trading in stock options? The fun is to speculate on what might happen to the money you have already committed, and then to plan into the future what you are going to do with the proceeds of your present commitments. It takes records to do this.

Your broker will send you a confirmation slip for every transaction you make. This slip will give you the name of the call sold (or bought), its strike price, expiration date, the price you paid or received for the call, the commission, the net amount that you must pay or that you received, the date of the transaction, and whether the transaction was an opening or closing one. When you phone in an order to your broker and he tells you it has been executed, it is important that you then keep accurate records of all the transactions so that you can compare your phone call records with the confirmation slip and report any discrepancies to your broker immediately. And errors do happen, as the author has learned from personal experiences.

RECORDING METHODS

The best way to keep records is to obtain a 12-column-wide accountant's pad from a stationery store (for example, National's "Eye-Ease" #18–812). There is so much information that is either necessary or helpful to an option trader that you will want to have a piece of paper this wide.

The necessary items that you should put down are: In the extreme left-hand column, a symbol "B" for buying a call and an "S" for selling one. In the next column (which is a very wide one on accountant's sheets) the number of calls bought or sold, the name of the stock, expiration date, and the strike price. In the next columns, the date of the opening transaction, i.e., if you are primarily a call buyer, the date when you first purchased the call; and in the next column, the net amount involved. If you are mainly a call writer, then the first two columns would be the date and net amount of the opening sales. In the next two columns insert the price of each call and the price of the stock when you made the transaction. These last two items are not actually necessary for your records, but they are of interest and will make it easier for you to consider closing out your transaction.

Then enter the pertinent data concerning the closing transaction. First

S=SOLD B=BOUGHT	SC=SOLD COVERED H=HEDGE	QUANTITY, NAME, EXPIRATION DATE AND STRIKE PRICE		SOLD			OPENING DATE STOCK PRICE
				DATE	TOTAL NET	PREMIUM PER OPTION	
1							
2	S	10 AVON	AP 60	2-15	17760	1875	51⅜
3							
4	S	5 KERR McGEE	AP 85	2-25	945	200	75
5							
6	B	10 FORD	OCT 45	3-15	809375	825	44¾
7							
8	SC	2 ITT	JLY 20	3-21	350 —	18750	16½
9							
10	B ⎤	5 POLAROID	JLY 20	7-26	304488	62500	
11	⎬H						22½
12	S ⎦	15 POLAROID	JLY 30	4-28	304431	21250	
13							
14	S	10 McDONALDS	JLY 30	6-18	116175	125	26½
15							

comes the date, then the total net amount involved (gross sale price less commissions), price per call, and price of the common stock. If you are an option writer and the option expired, simply write the date of the expiration and write a dash in the space for the purchase price. In the next column (# 9) you will want to put the profit or (loss) for the transaction. Your next column (# 10) might be the cumulative profit or (loss) from your transactions. The last two columns are devoted to margin and are filled in only for any naked call writing you may do. Column 11 will be the amount of margin required for each option transaction. The final column on the page is for the cumulative amount of margin required for all your open naked call options sold. Of course this amount can never exceed the cash or equivalent that you have on deposit with your broker. It will become necessary to change each of these last two columns from time to time. The cumulative column will have to be adjusted if you close out a naked option. Each individual line will also have to be adjusted depending upon the type of margin you have and the movement in the underlying stock price.

There is another column that you might want to keep if you are an option writer, but since it changes so much it is easier to keep it on a separate piece of paper so that you can throw it out when it gets too messy and start out again. This is the potential profit that you could make at any one time, which is the total amount of the premiums you have received for writing all the calls that

⑥	⑦	⑦	⑧	⑧	⑩	⑪
—BOUGHT———			PROFIT	CUMULATIVE	—MARGIN—	
TE	TOTAL NET	PREMIUM PER OPTION	OR⟨LOSS⟩	P or L	PER LINE	CUMULATIVE
-27	978650	1/450 5/46250 4/475	⟨300799⟩	⟨300799⟩	10000	10000
4-30	—	—	945		5000	15000
-06	424420	41250	389950	1786 60	424420	1924420
7-29	—	—	350	2133 60	—	—
-28	2959 70	575	85 18	2221 78	—	—
7-29	—	—	3044 31	526509	7500	7500
-20	222463	21250	⟨106288⟩	420221	5000	12500

are still open. This figure changes every time you sell another call and close out an account. It can just as well be kept separate because there is no need to have this as a permanent record.

If you are a naked option writer you will want to have a record of what price you decided upon as the close-out price that you gave to your broker. An appropriate place for this information is just after the Sold information, which in our example is the right half of column 4. In this column you would write either the price of the call at which you wanted to be closed out or the price of the underlying stock. You will now have a complete record of your investments.

Comparing records with quotations

By looking at this record, you can see at any time exactly which calls you either own or are short, how much premium you paid or received for them, and the price of the stock when you first entered into the transaction. By comparing this information with the daily newspaper quotations you will know exactly where you stand. This is absolutely vital, so that you can compute your current margin requirements. By comparing the cumulative margin figure with the amount you have deposited with your broker, you can tell whether you have free margin available for further investment. Also, by comparing your initial premium with the current one, you can decide whether the time has come to cover and take your profit. As soon as a transaction is closed out, you will enter the closing data and compute your profit or loss. All these figures are the net figures, after adding or subtracting the commission. If you don't want to bother figuring the commission, you will have to wait until you receive your confirmation slip before entering these figures. By keeping a cumulative total of your gains and losses, you will be able to tell at any given moment just where you stand. If you are an option buyer, you can add your cash gains or losses to your total purchase price of calls to know what your maximum loss can be. If you are an option writer, you can add the cash profit or loss to the amount you currently have short to determine your maximum total profit. A word of warning, don't expect that the potential total profit will be the actual realized profit. Usually at least one of your calls will manage to wend its way up to the strike price and thus trigger your stop-loss order.

Broker's statements

Your broker will send you, in addition to a confirmation slip for every transaction except for the expiration of options, a statement once a month. If you do not receive such a statement you should request it. The statement is important because it is the only record you will receive from your broker that will tie in your margin account with the actual transactions you have entered into. Your opening balance in the margin account will be stated, then every transaction will be listed in precise detail, giving the date of the transaction, a description of the option involved, and the price. Then the statement will conclude with the closing balance. It is then a relatively easy matter to compare this statement with your record and make sure that it is accurate.

Incidentally, if you are planning to do any amount of trading, I strongly recommend buying a pocket calculator, which sells for as little as $9.95. It is invaluable in figuring all the amounts on the confirmation slips and your records, and is a great time saver in computing commissions, and if you purchase it for help in making money or computing your taxes, it becomes tax deductible by depreciating its cost over expected useful life. Furthermore, while on the subject, don't forget that the cost of this book is also tax deductible to you.

APPENDIX A

Put-call equivalency table

This table shows positions which are theoretically identical, but because of the effects of cost of money to buy stock, margin requirements to be short options and stock, and the effect of dividends, these equivalencies will not necessarily produce identical prices. Nevertheless, they are valuable in determining if substantially the same objective can be accomplished in a more advantageous manner.

Long 1 call	= Long 1 put and long 100 shares of stock
Long 1 put	= Long 1 call and short 100 shares
Long 100 shares and short 1 call (covered writing position)	= Short 1 put
Short 100 shares and short 1 put	= Short 1 call
Long 1 put and long 1 call (long a straddle)	= Short 100 shares and long 2 calls or = Long 100 shares and long 2 puts
Short 1 call and short 1 put (short one straddle)	= Long 100 shares and short 2 calls or = Short 100 shares and short 2 puts
Long 1 straddle and short 100 shares	= Short 200 shares and long 2 calls or = Long 2 puts
Long 1 straddle and long 100 shares	= Long 2 calls or = Long 200 shares and long 2 puts

Short 1 straddle and short 100 shares	=	Short 2 calls
		or
	=	Short 200 shares and short 2 puts
Short 1 straddle and long 100 shares	=	Long 200 shares and short 2 calls
		or
	=	Short 2 puts

APPENDIX B

Option expiration dates through the year 2000, with quick reference numbers for determining days to expiration

To determine number of days to expiration, simply look at any calendar which gives the number of the day in the year, i.e., if it is now February 13, that is the 44th day of the year. If it is now February 13, 1987, and you want to know how many days there are until expiration of the October options, you look at October 1987 and see that the expiration date is October 17, 1987, and that the quick reference number is 290. Subtract 44 from 290 and you have found that there are 246 days until expiration.

Expiration Date	Quick Reference Number	Expiration Date	Quick Reference Number	Expiration Date	Quick Reference Number
		1987			
Jan 17	17	May 16	136	Sep 19	262
Feb 21	52	Jun 20	171	Oct 17	290
Mar 21	80	Jul 18	199	Nov 21	325
Apr 18	108	Aug 22	234	Dec 19	353
		1988			
Jan 16	16	May 21	142	Sep 17	261
Feb 20	51	Jun 18	170	Oct 22	296
Mar 19	79	Jul 16	198	Nov 19	324
Apr 16	107	Aug 20	233	Dec 17	352
		1989			
Jan 21	21	May 20	140	Sep 16	259
Feb 18	49	Jun 17	168	Oct 21	294
Mar 18	77	Jul 22	203	Nov 18	322
Apr 22	112	Aug 19	231	Dec 16	350

243

Expiration Date	Quick Reference Number	Expiration Date	Quick Reference Number	Expiration Date	Quick Reference Number
		1990			
Jan 20	20	May 19	139	Sep 22	265
Feb 17	48	Jun 16	167	Oct 20	293
Mar 17	76	Jul 21	202	Nov 17	321
Apr 21	111	Aug 18	230	Dec 22	356
		1991			
Jan 19	19	May 18	138	Sep 21	264
Feb 16	47	Jun 22	173	Oct 19	292
Mar 16	75	Jul 20	201	Nov 16	320
Apr 20	110	Aug 17	229	Dec 21	355
		1992			
Jan 18	18	May 16	137	Sep 19	263
Feb 22	53	Jun 20	172	Oct 17	291
Mar 21	81	Jul 18	200	Nov 21	326
Apr 18	109	Aug 22	235	Dec 19	354
		1993			
Jan 16	16	May 22	142	Sep 18	261
Feb 20	51	Jun 19	170	Oct 16	289
Mar 20	79	Jul 17	198	Nov 20	324
Apr 17	107	Aug 21	233	Dec 18	352
		1994			
Jan 22	22	May 21	141	Sep 17	260
Feb 19	50	Jun 18	169	Oct 22	295
Mar 19	78	Jul 16	197	Nov 19	323
Apr 16	106	Aug 20	232	Dec 17	351
		1995			
Jan 21	21	May 20	140	Sep 16	259
Feb 18	49	Jun 17	168	Oct 21	294
Mar 18	77	Jul 22	203	Nov 18	322
Apr 22	112	Aug 19	231	Dec 16	350
		1996			
Jan 20	20	May 18	139	Sep 21	265
Feb 17	48	Jun 22	174	Oct 19	293
Mar 16	76	Jul 20	202	Nov 16	321
Apr 20	111	Aug 17	230	Dec 21	356

Expiration Date	*Quick Reference Number*	Expiration Date	*Quick Reference Number*	Expiration Date	*Quick Reference Number*
		1997			
Jan 18	18	May 17	137	Sep 20	263
Feb 22	53	Jun 21	172	Oct 18	291
Mar 22	81	Jul 19	200	Nov 22	326
Apr 19	109	Aug 16	228	Dec 20	354
		1998			
Jan 17	17	May 16	136	Sep 19	262
Feb 21	52	Jun 20	171	Oct 17	290
Mar 21	80	Jul 18	199	Nov 21	325
Apr 18	108	Aug 22	234	Dec 19	353
		1999			
Jan 16	16	May 22	142	Sep 18	261
Feb 20	51	Jun 19	170	Oct 16	289
Mar 20	79	Jul 17	198	Nov 20	324
Apr 17	107	Aug 21	233	Dec 18	352
		2000			
Jan 22	22	May 20	141	Sep 16	260
Feb 19	50	Jun 17	169	Oct 21	295
Mar 18	78	Jul 22	204	Nov 18	323
Apr 22	113	Aug 19	232	Dec 16	351

Data prepared by Michael Bernstein and Associates, Inc.

APPENDIX C

Option symbols

If you are in a brokerage office and want to find out the price of an option from a quote machine, here is what you do. First find out from someone what special instructions there are for getting options quotes. Then (1) Give the symbol for the underlying stock, which is shown in Appendix A, (2) give the symbol for the month of expiration, shown below, and (3) give the symbol for the strike price, also shown below. Thus, a Ford July 50 call is FGJ, a GM Oct 60 put is GMVL.

Expiration Month Symbols

	Call	*Put*		*Call*	*Put*
January	A	M	July	G	S
February	B	N	August	H	T
March	C	O	September	I	U
April	D	P	October	J	V
May	E	Q	November	K	W
June	F	R	December	L	X

Strike Price Symbols

5	A	40	H	75	O
10, 110, 210	B	45	I	80	P
15	C	50	J	85	Q
20	D	55	K	90	R
25	E	60	L	95	S
30	F	65	M	100	T
35	G	70	N		

The symbols are repeated every 100 points so that 120 is D and 200 is T. The 55, 65, 75, 85, and 95 strike prices are not used on most stocks, with AT&T being a notable exception.

APPENDIX D

Stock commission schedule in cents per share

Based upon NYSE minimum commissions in effect April 30, 1975. Since then brokerage firms are permitted to set their own rates. In early 1978 many firms raised their rates approximately 7% above these.

Price	100	200	300	400	500	700	1000	1500	2000
$ 1	10.0	10.0	10.0	10.0	10.0	10.0	10.0	8.8	8.2
2	12.4	12.4	12.4	12.4	12.4	12.3	11.6	10.2	9.4
3	14.7	14.7	14.7	14.7	14.6	13.8	13.0	11.3	10.9
4	17.1	17.1	17.1	16.9	16.2	15.1	14.0	12.9	12.0
5	19.5	19.5	19.5	18.4	17.7	16.2	15.1	14.0	13.2
6	21.9	21.9	21.1	20.0	18.8	17.3	16.9	15.2	14.3
7	24.2	24.2	22.7	21.1	19.8	18.3	18.0	16.3	15.4
8	26.6	26.6	24.2	22.2	20.9	20.3	19.1	17.4	16.5
9	28.2	28.2	25.5	23.3	22.0	21.4	20.2	18.5	17.6
10	29.7	29.7	26.5	24.4	23.1	22.5	21.4	19.6	18.8
11	31.2	31.2	27.6	25.4	25.2	23.6	22.5	20.7	19.5
13	34.3	34.1	29.7	28.8	27.4	25.9	24.7	23.0	21.0
15	37.4	36.2	31.9	31.0	29.7	28.1	26.9	24.6	22.5
18	42.1	39.4	36.7	34.4	33.0	31.5	30.3	26.8	24.0
20	45.1	41.6	38.9	36.6	35.3	33.7	32.5	28.3	25.0
21	46.7	42.7	40.0	37.8	36.4	34.8	33.3	28.8	25.5
25	52.9	46.9	44.5	42.2	40.9	39.3	36.3	30.8	27.4
30	58.2	54.6	50.1	47.8	46.4	44.4	40.0	33.3	29.9
35	63.6	60.2	55.7	53.4	52.0	48.1	42.5	35.8	32.4
40	68.9	65.8	61.3	59.0	57.6	51.8	45.0	38.3	34.9
45	74.3	71.4	66.9	64.6	61.4	55.0	47.4	40.7	37.4
50	79.6	77.0	72.4	70.2	65.1	57.5	49.9	43.2	39.9
55	80.7	80.7	78.0	73.9	68.8	60.0	52.4	45.7	42.4
60	80.7	80.7	80.7	77.6	72.5	62.5	54.9	48.2	44.8
70	80.7	80.7	80.7	80.7	77.5	67.4	59.9	53.2	49.8

Price	100	200	300	400	500	700	1000	1500	2000
80	80.7	80.7	80.7	80.7	80.7	72.4	64.8	58.1	54.8
90	80.7	80.7	80.7	80.7	80.7	77.4	69.8	63.1	59.7
100	80.7	80.7	80.7	80.7	80.7	80.7	74.8	68.1	64.7
125	80.7	80.7	80.7	80.7	80.7	80.7	80.7	80.5	77.1
140	80.7	80.7	80.7	80.7	80.7	80.7	80.7	80.7	80.7

APPENDIX E

Worksheet for computing return on investment from covered option writing, on a cash basis and on a margin basis

I. Cash Required for Position

Cost of stock per share	$ _____	
Multiplied by number of shares	× _____	
Cost of stock	$ _____	
Plus commissions on stock purchase	+$ _____	
NET COST OF STOCK		①
If using margin, multiply by 50%	× .5	
CASH REQUIRED TO PURCHASE STOCK	$ _____	⑴ⓂM
Price of option sold	$ _____	
Multiplied by number of options	× _____	
Amount received from options	$ _____	
Subtract commissions on sale of options	−$ _____	
NET PROCEEDS FROM OPTIONS	$ _____	②
From ① or Ⓜ stock cash requirement	① or Ⓜ $ _____	
Subtract ② net proceeds from options	② −$ _____	
CASH REQUIREMENT FOR POSITION		③

II. Changes During Position

Indicated quarterly dividend per share $ _____

Multiply by number of shares × _____

To get total dividend per quarter $ _____

Multiply by number of dividends expected
during life of option × _____

    TOTAL DIVIDENDS EXPECTED $ _____ ④

If stock is purchased on margin, enter here

Ⓜ Cash required to purchase stock Ⓜ$ _____

(Use this only as long as the margin requirement
is 50%. If it is not, then multiply net cost
of stock by whatever percentage the brokerage
firm is lending to you.)

Multiply by current margin interest rate × _____ %

To get the annual interest charge on your debit $ _____

Divide by 365 ÷ 365

    To get daily interest cost $ _____

Multiply by number of days to option's expiration × _____

    To get total interest cost $ _____ ⑤

Enter ④, total dividends expected ④$ _____

Subtract ⑤, total interest cost ⑤−$ _____

  To get NET CHANGE IN POSITION DURING DURATION (+) or (−)$ _____ ④Ⓜ

III. Proceeds from Closing Out the Position

A. IF STOCK IS CALLED AWAY

Exercise price of option $ _____

Multiply by number of shares × _____

To get gross proceeds $ _____

Subtract commission on sale of stock at strike price −$ _____

To get NET PROCEEDS FROM POSITION $ _____ ⑥

If purchased on margin, subtract amount originally
borrowed from brokerage firm −$ _____

To get NET PROCEEDS FROM POSITION $ _____ ⑥M

B. IF WRITING OUT-OF-THE-MONEY OPTIONS, AND
YOU ASSUME THAT THE STOCK PRICE WILL REMAIN
UNCHANGED AND YOU WILL SELL THE STOCK
AT EXPIRATION.

Enter original cost of stock per share $ _____

Multiply by number of shares × _____

To get gross proceeds from sale $ _____

Subtract commissions on sale −$ _____

To get NET PROCEEDS FROM POSITION $ _____ ⑥

If stock was purchased on margin, subtract amount
originally borrowed from brokerage firm −$ _____

To get NET PROCEEDS FROM POSITION $ _____ ⑥M

IV. Computing Return on Investment

Enter ⑥ or ⑥M net proceeds from position ⑥ or ⑥M $ _____

Add or subtract ④ or ④M, net change ④ or ④M

in position during duration + or −$ _____

To get total revenue from position $ _____

Subtract ③, cash requirement for position −$ _____

To get PROFIT ON POSITION $ _____

Divide this by ③, cash requirement ÷$ _____

To get percentage return on investment _____ %

To annualize this, multiply by 365 × 365

And divide by number of days until expiration of option ÷ _____

To get ANNUALIZED RETURN ON INVESTMENT _____ %

APPENDIX F

The ten biggest options mistakes

So much intense thought and effort go into the planning and execution of option strategies that it is a tragedy that many of them are later ruined by ignoring a few very simple principles. To help you avoid these pitfalls I have decided to list ten of the most common mistakes.

Making one of these mistakes is like planning out a picnic down to the last detail including the Thermos bottle, anti-bug spray, napkins, charcoal lighter fluid, cooking equipment, the ketchup, pickles, and relish and then not getting to the picnic because you run out of gas when you are halfway there. These mistakes are just as easy to avoid, and unfortunately, they are just as expensive as situations which are far more difficult to avoid. Like running out of gas, once they have occurred, it is often too late to go back and do much about them. So that you can prevent them in advance, they are listed here:

1. **Putting on one side of a position now, and planning to do the other side later when the stock moves in the right direction.** Every day I hear investors say that a certain stock looks like a good covered writing candidate, but since there isn't just quite enough money in the option to make it worthwhile, they will buy the stock now, wait until it goes up a couple of points, and then when the option has increased substantially they will sell the option. The problem with this is that the only reason a person sells a covered option in the first place is to make a profit in case the stock does not go up. If you know that a stock is going to go up, then you don't need to write covered options at all. You can make a fortune by simply buying options on those stocks. If you buy the stock now without writing the option, what happens if the stock goes down? Then you have lost money on the stock without the offsetting profit from the option. In short, just when you need the protection of the option, you don't have it. If you want to buy stock without writing an option no one is going to stop you. But don't think that you are doing it as part of a covered option writing program. Unless you buy the stock and sell the

option simultaneously you are not engaged in covered writing, you are simply buying stock. And if the stock goes down, you get stuck with the loss.

2. **Failing to close out a time spread when the near-term option expires.** In a time spread one buys a long-term option and sells the short-term option on the same stock usually at the same strike price. The positions are put on simultaneously and should be taken off simultaneously. But so often when the near-term option expires the remaining longer-term option is not worth what the owner believes it should be. The temptation is very strong to wait just a little while in the hope that the option will go up in price. But what is really happening is that what started out as a hedged position, with some downside protection, has been transformed to a very speculative unhedged position with no downside protection at all. And it is worth noting that there is no more chance of the stock going up in the next few days than there was that it would go up in the previous weeks when the spread was in existence. Unless it was part of your original plan to continue owning the long option, have the discipline to take a small loss by closing out the long position when the near-term option expires. If your calendar spread did not work out, have the maturity to accept that. They don't all work, but it is better to take a small loss now than to watch the option remaining dwindle down to nothing, as thousands have done.

3. **Calculating your return from covered writing without including all the costs.** Like every other security transaction, writing covered calls against stock involves transaction costs, such as commissions, and perhaps margin interest costs. But unlike most other types of investments, the amount of profit which can be derived from covered writing is strictly limited from the beginning, and especially in the case of in-the-money covered writing, the potential profit is usually limited to a very small profit relative to the amount of money involved. For example, a stock may be purchased for $22 and the 20 strike price option written for $3. Since this gives a gross spread of $1, at a quick glance it would appear as if this gives a return of 5.2% when buying the stock for cash (22 minus 3 gives a net cost of 19. $1 divided by 19 = 5.2%) or 12.5% when buying the stock on margin ($22 times cash required of 50% = $11; minus $3, means a cash requirement of $8 to do the trade. Gross profit of $1 divided by $8 = 12.5%). If this option had four months to run before expiration, the annualized rates of return would appear to be 15.6% and 37.5%, which are certainly well worth while.

But look at what an enormous difference the "little" transaction expenses make. Let's assume that you are doing 200 shares against two options. The commission to buy 200 shares of stock at 22 is 43.7¢ a share, and the commission to sell two options at $3 is $15.90 per option. If we assume that the stock is called away when the option expires, we are saved the commission on buying back the option, but there is the commission on selling 200 shares at 20, which is 41.6¢ a share. Adding up these costs gives $1.01 per share. With a maximum gross profit of $1.00, we find that the actual profit is a guaranteed loss of one cent per share! For the margin transaction one must also subtract the anticipated interest charges on the margin debit, although we can add any anticipated dividends. The lesson should be clear: The "little" transaction expenses cannot be ignored! They are an integral part of the transaction and will always have a profound effect on your return. Don't try to estimate them. You are talking about your money and it is well worth a few minutes of your time to find out just how much you will actually be earning. See Appendix J for a complete worksheet showing how to calculate the return.

4. **Failing to establish profit goals on long options.** If we were in a perpetual bull market there would be no need to establish goals for options purchased. Every option would simply be held until expiration because it would become worth more and more every day. But in the real world in which we are now living stocks tend to go up and down and option prices with them. The only rational way to deal with this phenomenon is to set a goal, and when the option reaches this goal, to sell it. Some investors will haggle over $1/16$ of a point when they buy an option, but when it comes to selling it they can't decide whether to try for 4 points or 6. Decide in advance what you want to do and then stick to that. And you don't have to have an all-or-nothing approach. There is nothing wrong, for example, in deciding to sell half your position if the option doubles, thus getting back your entire initial investment, and then letting the rest run. But at least you have some plan, instead of just drifting aimlessly.

5. **Being too bullish on the market.** Probably it is natural that investors who are used to buying stocks in the expectation that they will go up have a bullish outlook on the market. But with the advent of listed puts and with all the possibilities for selling naked calls and putting on bear spreads with calls, and with the "synthetic" puts which many brokerage firms are willing to create for customers from listed calls, there is no reason why option traders should not take a more neutral view of the market.

No matter what one's fundamental view of the market, such long-term views are not likely to have very much effect on the very short time span encompassed by the usual option trade. Therefore, short-term trends are likely to be independent of long-term fundamentals, and unless you are a confirmed chartist or other technician, this means that over the short term the odds are almost as good that the market will go down or stay still as that it will go up. The conclusion to be drawn from this is that in addition to buying options, speculators should be careful to include some underpriced puts in their portfolios and give consideration to bear spreads. A trader who puts all his trading money into one side of the market is likely to have no trading money if he is wrong. With the enormous profit possible from trading in options, there is no reason why some of it shouldn't be put into the other side of the market.

6. **Using covered call writing without providing some absolute downside protection.** Covered call writing is an excellent method of making a relatively small amount of money with a large degree of assurance that you will make that money. Especially if one writes in-the-money options, one can make a profit even if the stock declines by a moderate amount, such as 10 percent. The only way in which one cannot make money is if the stock declines by more than that amount.

The inherent danger in call writing is that one makes a limited small profit no matter how good the stock performance is, but one can lose an almost unlimited amount of money if the stock goes down. When one considers this basic premise of how covered option writing works, it follows as the night the day that one really bad collapse in a position can more than wipe out all the profit in six other positions. I remember well a broker who was making a very good profit for his customers in many different covered writing positions, until he decided that National Semiconductor (then selling at 43) was an ideal addition to his customers' portfolios. As National Semiconductor went down from 43 to 30 and then to 20, his customers (many of whom had bought the stock on margin) found their entire equity in that position completely obliterated. The result was that years of profitable investments became a disaster. All because of one stock.

So when you can make only a relatively small profit from a position, but you have the potential to have a large loss, you are playing with unfair odds.

The successful option writer modifies these odds to his favor by changing the rules of the game. He creates a situation in which, since he can make only a limited profit, he can also lose only a limited amount. The way to accomplish this is to place a stop-loss order to sell out the stock when it has declined to a predetermined price. This order can be entered on a Good Till Cancelled basis at the time that the covered writing position is begun.

Once that order is in you do not have to worry. Your maximum loss is limited. If the order ever goes off, then you should immediately buy in your outstanding option at the market price. When you close out the position by other means, remember to cancel your GTC order to sell out the stock.

In summary, the Achilles heel in covered option writing is that you can sustain a very substantial loss when the stock you are writing against goes into a nose dive. With the limited profit potential inherent in covered writing, you simply cannot afford such a large loss. The covered option writer who wishfully hopes that his favorite stock will come back up to its original price so that he can recoup his "paper" loss is doomed to disappointment. You should not let yourself be one of the people making this mistake, when overcoming it is so easy.

7. **Expecting an unrealistic profit from options.** Probably nothing is so important in any aspect of life as knowing what to expect. If a recent college graduate expects that his first job will be as a senior executive with responsibility for a $7 million division and a salary of $50,000 a year, he is doomed to disappointment. But even more important is that he will be so misguided by his false expectations that he will decline excellent job opportunities which perhaps could lead to such a job in the future. Instead, he will languish among the unemployed complaining about the lack of job opportunities and his bad luck in getting passed over for jobs and finally he may become convinced that business is prejudiced against young people.

So it is in the option market. Options, it cannot be emphasized too often, are not magic. They cannot create instant wealth. True, used in certain ways, they can give greatly increased leverage, but as this book has been at pains to point out, every increase in leverage is gained at a cost of increased risk of loss. And of course one could be lucky and make a great deal of money if one were leveraged at just the time that a certain stock made a big move in the right direction. But it is vital to understand that such a success would be attributable purely to luck. If anyone thinks that such a great profit is due to his skill alone, we will wait patiently to see whether he can repeat his feat of skill the next time and the next.

The fact is that options enable one to invest or speculate in the stock market through the use of many different techniques. But it is still based upon the stock market, and in general the returns available to the options investor or speculator are roughly equal to the risks taken, perhaps offset by whatever the fancy of the public happens to be at that time. This means that if one approaches options with the idea of making a 100% profit every year, he will not only be disappointed with the results (unless he is extremely lucky) but because he believes that he "ought" to make such an outlandish profit he will deliberately turn his back on many opportunities to make a very good return.

And when he does, he risks not making any profit at all. For example, the person who buys options to see them double and triple without closing them out and realizing at least part of his profit is leaving himself wide open for a reversal in the price of the stock and a complete disappearance of all his profits, and even worse, of his entire starting capital.

What should be a reasonable goal? The answer is that if any professional investment manager could devise a method of making 20% a year, year in and year out regardless of market conditions, he would be a hero without equal on

Wall Street. If a member of the public is willing to take much greater chances he might set a goal of slightly more, say 25 to 30% in a good market. But that amount would, in my opinion, be the upper limit that one could even reasonably have as a goal for the average year.

The mark of the unsophisticated options trader is a false expectation of high profits. Such an expectation can be as dangerous as being completely wrong on which way the market is going to go, because it not only leads to disappointment, but it automatically locks one out from many profitable opportunities. The most famous saying on Wall Street is "Bulls can make money and Bears can make money. But pigs never make money." The same thing applies in options. You don't want to be the kind of animal that is fat and short, has a large snout and a short circular tail, and oinks. You know what happens to pigs. They end up providing the bacon for someone else.

8. **Unwillingness to use naked options.** The very phrase "naked options" has an unfortunate connotation. One sees himself naked, shivering on an icy lake, while the frigid winds from the north slowly chill one's bones to the marrow. So the average investor looks upon naked options as a good way to be stripped of all his money in case the stock goes in the wrong direction. Because of this poor imagery, I prefer the more neutral term "uncovered options" and this is what we will use in this section.

It is true that uncovered options can bring quick losses of a very large size and that there is no way to completely guard against such losses. But these arguments alone should not deter investors from giving careful consideration to the advantages of using them. If the odds in favor of using uncovered options are so favorable that they outweigh even the theoretically unlimited loss potential, then we should use them, just as in our daily lives we are willing to take enormous risks to obtain slight benefits if the odds against those risks are remote enough.

For example, many people routinely fly distances of 200 miles or less when they could take a train or bus. They are saving perhaps an hour or so, but are willing to accept the unlimited risk of death which, however remote, is always a part of flying and certainly present in much higher degree than when taking the train.

Although uncovered options may present special risks, there are risks inherent in any investment founded upon stock prices. And in some cases the risks of uncovered options are no greater than the risks in other types of option strategies which are generally assumed to be quite safe. The most striking example is that the most conservative use of options is considered to be writing calls against stock which one owns, or writing covered calls. This strategy is the exact equivalent of writing uncovered puts. Nevertheless, thousands of investors, including professional fund managers, gladly write covered calls all year long but would be absolutely aghast if anyone even suggested that they write a few naked puts. And yet uncovered puts have a number of advantages over covered call writing. First, the commissions are less. Even if you own the underlying stock and intend to keep it, unless you are writing out-of-the-money calls, you will incur a commission at the end of the transaction. Second, it requires more margin money to write the same amount of covered calls as uncovered puts, and third, in many cases by using Treasury Bills to provide the margin for the uncovered puts, you are getting a higher yield on your money than you are from the dividends on the stock.

When used in conjunction with other methods of covered options, selling extra options, or "ratio writing" as it is called, can substantially increase the return from a position while increasing risk only if the stock moves by a very great amount. For example, if a stock is 19 and you write the 20 option for 2, you are getting a return of 10% without deducting commissions. If you can also sell a 25 option for ⅝ you would increase your return to 13% and begin to lose money only if the stock went above 25, which is a 31% move. Unless the stock increases by more than that, you will have boosted your return by 30%, a very significant increase.

The moral of this section is not that everyone should write uncovered options. They are clearly not appropriate for everyone, and many types of investors are not even permitted to use them, for good reason. But if you are one of the ones who are permitted to use uncovered options, then you should give careful consideration to using them in two ways: (1) Substitute uncovered writing for covered writing to save commissions and decrease the amount of capital required to produce a given amount of options income; and (2) supplement your covered writing and spreads with uncovered options to increase return while risking loss only if the stock moves by an abnormally large amount.

9. Refusal to realize losses. The most difficult aspect of options is not devising the strategies or executing them. Or is it deciding when to close them out after they have made money. While these activities may be challenging, they are also fun. The toughest thing to do in options is to close out a position when it has become a loser. This is definitely not fun. It is difficult to do because in most cases there is always the possibility that if the position is left alone it will reverse itself and what is now only a paper loss will become a gain. Once you have closed out the position, you have cast the loss in concrete, never to be able to reverse. So the psychology is against you, because we are all optimistic by nature, and having thought that our idea would make money when we started out, we are more reluctant to admit that we were wrong when it is going to cost us hard dollars of real cash.

But the alternative to closing out loss positions is to risk even greater losses. And while there is plenty of money available in any options program to afford small losses, there is not enough money to be able to afford big losses. Thus, in order to make money over any sustained period of time, it is necessary to ensure that there are no big losses. The only way to be certain of this is to take a lot of little losses, which if not stopped have the potential of becoming big losses.

The clearest example is with uncovered options. Since the profit potential of each option is limited, while the loss potential is very great, it is clear that one huge loss could wipe out the gains from an entire year of successful trades. But the same reasoning applies to other areas of options, including covered call writing.

It is also true when you are buying in-the-money options. If you don't try to rescue some of the premium when the stock starts to slide down, you may wind up losing more than you could reasonably have expected to gain.

The conclusion is that the only way to avoid costly losses is to take care of them when they are minor. You must realize that taking a loss is not a defeat. It is preparing for the next victory. In options as in war, "He who fights and runs away, lives to fight another day." If you don't, you won't.

10. Not using a broker who is thoroughly familiar with options. In today's market, there are basically two types of stock brokerage firms. There are the discount firms, which give no assistance, and there are the "full service" firms, which do. While commission rates between full service firms may differ, they are probably more alike than they are different.

In short, once you decide to use a full service firm, you are paying about the same commission dollars no matter which firm you use and which broker within the firm you use. This means that if you are interested in options and you are dealing with a broker who is not well versed in options, you are paying for something that you are not getting.

It is a relatively easy matter to work with brokers who are thoroughly familiar with options. One way is that if your present broker is not familiar with them, ask him who the options coordinator is at his local office. You can ask your broker to talk with him and relay the ideas to you, or you could ask to have this coordinator work with you directly.

If your brokerage firm is part of a national or regional firm, then there probably is a national options director at the main office of the firm. Ask your broker to contact this director for ideas. If you do a meaningful amount of business with the firm, you could ask to talk to the national options director yourself. Don't be bashful. Brokerage firms are in keen competition with one another and will go to quite some lengths to keep a customer.

Finally. there is nothing wrong with opening an account at another firm for the specific purpose of doing options where you can get the advice and benefit of a broker who really understands options. Most large investors have more than one account, and unless you are very small, there is no reason why you can't as well. By having two accounts you will be able to compare ideas and services provided by the two different brokers and thus get a better idea of what the standard of service ought to be.

In summary, your commissions are paying a broker to help you in options and to give you options ideas that are useful to you. To the extent that you are using a broker who merely executes orders which you must conceive, you are not getting the help you are entitled to. Since, as this book has emphasized, making money in options is not easy, you ought to see that you get all the help you are entitled to. Especially when it costs no more.

APPENDIX G

29 Options strategies ranked from extreme bullishness to extreme bearishness

Very Optimistic

Buy call with strike price above market
Buy call with strike price at market
Buy call with strike price below market
Buy stock on margin
    In conjunction with any of the above, to make them more speculative:
    Sell put with strike price above market
    Sell put with strike price at market
    Sell put with strike price below market

Moderately Optimistic

Buy stock, sell put
Buy stock, sell call with strike price above market (covered call)
Buy stock, sell call with strike price at market (covered call)
Buy stock, sell call and put, both at market
Buy stock, sell call and put, both with strike prices away from market

Neutral

Buy stock, sell one call with strike price above market, one at market
Buy stock, sell two or more calls with strike price above market
Sell put and call both with strike prices at market (straddle)
Sell call with strike price at market, put with strike price below (combination)
Buy stock and one put with strike price at market (call)

Moderately Pessimistic

Buy stock and buy two puts
Sell call with strike price at market or lower, buy call at higher strike price (bear spread)
Sell naked call with strike price above market
Sell stock short, buy two calls
Sell stock short, buy one call at market (synthetic put)
Sell naked call with strike price at market
Buy one call and two puts, all with strike prices at market

Very Pessimistic

Buy put with strike price at market
Sell naked call with strike price below market
Sell stock short, buy call with strike price above market (partial put)
Buy put with strike price below market
Sell stock short

APPENDIX H

Glossary of terms

Asked. As used in the phrase "bid and asked," it is the price at which a potential seller is willing to sell; in other words this is his asking price for what he is selling.

Away from the market. A stock option for which the strike price is a substantial distance from the current price of the stock. *See also* In the money *and* Out of the money.

Adjusted strike price. The new strike price after a stock declares a stock dividend or stock split. The purpose of the adjustment is to keep the value of the new options the same as they were before the split. Also accompanied by an increase in the number of shares per option. If a stock is 100, and it splits 3 for 1, the old 100 strike price option will now be a 33⅜ strike price option, and each option will give the holder the right to buy 300 shares.

Bear. An investor who believes that stock prices will decline. His strategies are to buy puts, sell naked calls, and sell stock short.

Bear spread. A spread which makes money when the price of the stock goes down. A bear spread consists of selling the option with the lower strike price and buying the option with the higher strike price. A bear spread with calls is a credit spread, a bear spread with puts is a debit spread.

Beta. A figure that indicates the historical propensity of a stock price to move with the stock market as a whole. The lowest theoretical Beta is 0, which indicates no movement, and the highest is 2, indicating wild gyrations for small movements in the market.

Bid. The price at which a potential buyer is willing to buy; he is bidding that amount to purchase the security offered. As used in "bid and asked prices," the two prices give the current market for an option or stock.

Bull. An investor who believes that stock prices will rise. He buys calls, sells puts, and buys stocks on margin.

Bull spread. A spread which makes money when the price of the stock goes up. It consists of buying the lower strike price option and selling the higher strike price option. A bull spread with calls results in a debit, and with puts in a credit.

Butterfly spread. A spread consisting of being short two options, and being long one option of a higher strike price, and being long one option of a lower strike price, e.g., long a January 30 and a January 40 and short 2 January 35s. In theory it can never be worth less than zero and is most profitable when the stock is at the mid strike price on expiration.

Calendar spread. Buying a long-duration option and selling a shorter-duration option of the same strike price on the same stock. A calendar spread makes money by the expiration of future time value in the short option at a greater amount than the loss in value of the longer-duration option.

Call. An option giving the buyer the right to purchase 100 shares of the stock for a given price within a given period of time.

Cash value. The value which an option has if it were to be exercised now. It is the amount by which an option is in the money. If a stock is now 22, the 20 call has a cash value of 2. Also known as intrinsic value. Out-of-the-money options do not have any cash value. Compare Future Time Value.

CBOE. Chicago Board Options Exchange, which opened April 26, 1973, as the first exchange in the world for stock options. In order to have an exchange of options, the CBOE had to make two major modifications to options as they had previously existed: standardize the expiration dates and standardize the strike prices. By offering liquidity, the CBOE vastly increased the popularity of stock options.

Cemetery spread. What happens to a spread when the stock goes in the wrong direction. The spreader gets killed. An example of the humor (?) of Wall Street.

Closing transaction. The sale of an option by someone owning it or the purchase of an option by a person who previously sold it short. These transactions terminate the investor's position in the option.

Conversion. Converting puts is transforming them into calls. This can be done without risk by buying a put, selling a call, and buying the underlying stock. Conversions are made because the supply of puts normally exceeds the demand.

Covered call writer or seller. A call seller (writer) who owns the stock underlying the calls he sells. By owning the stock he is protected from any loss by an increase in the price of the stock during the duration of the call.

Cover. To close out one's position. A call writer who is short 2 RCA April 25s may decide that he has made a mistake and that he had better get out of the position. He will cover his position by purchasing those calls. Can also be done when most of the profit has been realized.

Credit spread. (1) A spread which produces money upon its execution, e.g., selling a 35 call for 4 and buying a 40 call for 1. A credit spread has a margin requirement and makes money when the credit increases. (2) The amount of the credit resulting from doing a credit spread. For example, when placing an order for the spread in (1) one could request that it be done at a credit spread of 3 points.

Debit spread. (1) A spread which produces a debit upon execution, e.g., buying a 30 call for 4 and selling a 35 call for 1. A debit spread makes money when the amount of the spread decreases. (2) The amount of the debit resulting from doing a spread. The above spread could have been executed with the request that it be done at a debit spread of no more than 3 points.

Deep in the money. An option which has a large cash or intrinsic value because the price of the stock has moved far beyond the option strike price. A call is deep in the money when the stock is much higher than the strike price, and a put is deep in the money when the stock is far below the strike price.

Diagonal spread. A spread in which a long-term option of one strike price is purchased and a shorter-term option of another strike price is sold. A common example is to purchase a long-term call at, say, a 40 strike price and sell the shorter-term 45 call. Basically a bullish spread.

Ex-dividend. The date on which a purchaser of a stock does not receive a dividend. For example, if a stock goes ex-dividend on the 15th, anyone purchasing the stock on the 14th will receive the dividend, but those purchasing on the 15th will not. Usually the opening price on the 15th will be reduced from the previous day's close by the amount of the dividend. A call owner who exercises the day before a stock goes ex-dividend is entitled to the stock and the dividend, notwithstanding that the call writer will learn of the assignment only after the stock has gone ex-dividend.

Exercise price. The price at which the buyer of a call can purchase the underlying stock during the life of the call, and the price at which the buyer of a put can sell the underlying stock during the life of the put. *Also called* strike price.

Exercise. To do what a stock option gives one the right to do, i.e., to purchase stock for the strike price in the case of a call and to sell stock for the strike price in the case of a put. Exercising an option requires paying a commission on the underlying stock. Options need not be exercised since they can always be sold for approximately the same profit that would be made by exercising them and immediately closing out the stock position.

Expiration date. The date on which the option becomes null and void, i.e., the final date on which it may be exercised. The expiration date is the Saturday following the third Friday of the month. Note that trading in the options ceases at 2:00 p.m. Central Time of the business day immediately prior to the expiration date.

Future time value. That part of the option price which does not represent cash value. Future time value is the excess which option buyers are willing to pay in order to obtain leverage and to limit exposure. It is the only part of the option price which produces a profit for the covered writer. In the case of out-of-the-money options, the entire option price is future time value.

GTC (Good Till Cancelled). An order to buy or sell an option that remains in effect until it is executed or is cancelled by its originator. For example, a GTC order would be to buy 5 Polaroid July 25 calls now trading at 4 when they are at 3. At the present time one is not permitted to enter a GTC stop-loss order on an option. Thus, one cannot enter a GTC order to buy a Polaroid July 25 call for 3 if it is now trading at 2.

Hedge. A transaction consisting of two or more separate transactions with the objective of providing a greater chance of making a profit, although perhaps a smaller one, than a single transaction. See Chapter 6 for a complete discussion.

Horizontal spread. A spread involving options with the same strike prices and different expirations. When connected in the daily newspaper report they make a horizontal line.

In the money. An option that is worth money because of the current market price of the stock. A call would be in the money if the current price of the stock is above the strike price of the call.

Intrinsic value. *See cash value.*

Legging, as in legging in a position. Executing one side of a position first, in the hope that the stock will then move in the right direction so that the other side of the position can be executed at a more favorable price. One can also leg out of a position with the same objective. Opposite of executing something as a spread, which means doing both sides simultaneously.

Long. To be long is to own something.

Margin. The amount of money that must be deposited with a broker in order to buy or sell a security. See Chapter 8 for the requirements.

The market. As applied to an options exchange, the market for a particular option is the current bid and offer prices on the floor of the exchange. This tells the potential customer the probable price if he wishes to buy or sell a call.

Mark to the market. The process of adjusting a margin account each day to the current prices of the underlying stocks.

Naked option writer or seller. One who sells (writes) a call without owning the underlying stock, in contrast to a covered call writer. The naked call writer may be able to make a higher return on his money, but he faces an unlimited liability if the stock rises. Also, one who sells a put without being long a put of equal or longer duration and of equal or lower strike price. See, however, the chapter on selling naked calls for ways in which this liability can be controlled.

Open interest. The number of calls that are outstanding at any time. Unlike shares of stock that are issued by corporations, usually via a formal registration statement, calls are issued any time that an investor decides to write one. Thus the open interest fluctuates daily.

Option. A legal right allowing the owner to buy or sell 100 shares of stock at a specific price during a specific period of time. A *call* is an option allowing its owner to buy stock at a specific price, and a *put* is an option allowing its owner to sell stock at a specific price.

Out of the money. An option that, because of the difference between the strike price and the market price of the underlying stock, will be worth nothing unless the stock moves in price. A call is out of the money when its strike price is above the current price of the stock.

OTC (Over the Counter). When applied to stock options, this means all options other than those traded on an exchange. Generally OTC options expire 90 days, or 6 months and 10 days from the date of purchase, and the strike price is usually the same as the price of the stock at the time the option was written, although the options may be for any duration and written at any strike price.

Parity. When the price of an option is equal to its cash value. Thus, if a stock is 22, the 20 strike price call is at parity if it is 2. Useful in executing orders on a volatile stock, when you can request a purchase at no more than parity plus a given amount, such as parity plus a half. Especially useful in closing out covered writing positions.

Point. One dollar.

Premium. The price that the buyer pays the writer for an option contract (the term is synonymous with the price of an option).

Put. An option giving the owner the right to sell 100 shares of the underlying stock for a specified price within a stated period of time. The purchaser of a put profits from a decline in the price of the stock.

Ratio writing. Writing more than one option against each long position. Involves the use of uncovered options with its margin requirements.

Restricted options. An option on which orders cannot be accepted, unless a closing transaction, or covered by stock or part of a spread in which the other side is worth more than the restricted option. An option becomes restricted when *both* the closing price of the option on the previous day was less than one half *and* the option was more than five points out of the money.

Short. To be short an option or a stock means to owe it to someone. Whereas the investor who is long buys a security and then sells it, hopefully for a higher price, the short seller sells the security first, and then buys it back later, hopefully for a lower price.

SIPC (The Securities Investor Protection Corporation). Established by Congress to protect customers of brokerage firms, it insures the customers' accounts of brokerage firms that belong to SIPC for loss if the firm goes bankrupt or otherwise cannot pay its customers' claims. Limits are $50,000 for each customer for losses of securities and $20,000 to the extent the loss is in cash that the firm was holding in the customer's name. All firms that are members of the NYSE, Amex, or CBOE are members of the SIPC.

Special puts and calls. Those OTC options that dealers have in their inventory. This is different from the normal method of trading OTC options, which is to find a seller in response to a particular request from a potential buyer.

Spread. A combination of long and short positions in options of the same underlying stock, which calls have different strike prices or different expiration dates.

Straddle. A position consisting of a put and a call on the same stock for the same strike price. Each option may be exercised separately but they are sold as a unit.

Strap. Two calls and a put on the same stock with the same strike price and expiration date.

Strike (or striking) price. The price at which the buyer of a call can purchase the stock during the life of the option, and the price at which the buyer of a put can sell the stock during the life of the option. *Also called* exercise price.

Strip. Two puts and a call on the same stock with the same strike price and expiration date.

Time spread. *See calendar spread.*

Uncovered. *See naked options.*

Vertical spread. Buying one option and selling an option on the same stock with a different strike price, usually with the same duration. Bull spreads and bear spreads are examples. When seen in the daily newspaper report they form a vertical line.

Writer. The grantor of an option contract. Also called the maker or the seller. Further divided, with respect to call writers, into covered writers, who own the underlying stock, and naked writers, who do not.

INDEX

Accrued interest. *See* Interest, accrued
Adjusted strike prices, 10–12
American Telephone and Telegraph
    Company, 25
Annualized rates of return, 85
  on buying calls, 45–47
  on covered calls, 58, 85, 87

*Barron's National Business and Financial
    Weekly*, 4
Baruch, Bernard, 97
Bear spread(s), 143, 153–159. *See also
    specific types*
  defined, 153
  profitability of, 154
  put, 179–180
  ratio, 169–170
  strategy for, 158–159
  types of, 155–159
Beta (measure of volatility), 48–51, 114
Bonds, convertible
  accrued interest of, 191
  common stocks vs., 189–192
  defined, 189
  description of, 190–193
  premiums and, 193, 194–195
  price movements of, 195–196
  selection of, 193–199
  writing calls on, 189–200
    benefits of, 193, 199
    disadvantages of, 199–200
Breaking even in buying calls, 27–28
Broker, choice of, 211–212
Broker's statements, 240
Bull spread, 142, 143–153. *See also specific
    types*
  buying option vs., 148

defined, 139
margin rule in, 144–148
profitability of, 147
puts, 177–179
strategy for, 153
two-on-one, 168–169
types of, 148–152
Butterfly spread(s), 140, 171–174
  disadvantages of, 172–174
  function of, 171–173

Calendar spread(s), 159–167. *See also
    specific types*
  advantages of, 163
  defined, 159
  profitability of, 160–162
  put, 180–181
  ratio, 169–170
  strategy for, 166–167
Call(s). *See also* Covered calls; Naked
    calls; Options; Put(s)
  annualized rates of return on, 45–47
  buying, 15, 17–55
    advantages and liabilities of, 5–8,
      16
    breaking even in, 27–28
    doubling investment in, 28–29
    tax consequences, 218–219
  on convertible bonds, 189–200
  dangers of speculation in, 15–33
  defined, 1
  elements of, 1–9
  exercising of, 2, 4, 8–9
  forecasting prices of, 24–26, 48
  limit of loss in buying, 6–7
  margin requirements for, 9, 15
  psychology of investor purchase of,
    24–25, 43